Praise for Bulletproof Problem Solving

"The Bulletproof Problem Solving approach acknowledges the reality many environmentalists face today: this is hard work. Conn and McLean's guide makes it a little bit easier."

-Mark R. Tercek, CEO of The Nature Conservancy and author of *Nature's Fortune*

"Conn and McLean have distilled their matchless experience in attacking challenges of every scale and level of complexity into this virtual war-room of a book, creating an indispensable resource for the 21st century problem-solvers upon whom our future depends. A must-read for all aspiring change agents!"

-Sally Osberg, retired CEO of the Skoll Foundation, co-author of *Getting Beyond Better: How Social Entrepreneurship Works*

"Navigating ambiguity and solving complex problems creatively is the truth test for humans to complement rather than substitute the artificial intelligence of computers. Without much better approaches to teach those skills, our schools risk preparing second class robots rather than first class humans. Rob McLean and Charles Conn show that this can be done and provide an intuitive roadmap for how to do this, with lots of real-world examples that make it fun."

-Andreas Schleicher, Director for the Directorate of Education and Skills, OECD

"Great strategic problem solving is an essential tool, one whose value is only going up. *Bulletproof* provides the secret sauce behind the McKinsey framework to help structure and guide the problem-solving process. I want to hire people who understand this approach."

-Barry Nalebuff, Milton Steinbach Professor, Yale School of Management and cofounder, Honest Tea

"The old paradigm of strategy departments and planning cycles has been overthrown by agile and rapid team-based problem solving, providing better solutions and better organization alignment to implement. This book, written by two of the smartest people I know, provides the needed blueprint for how build these world-beating problem solving teams."

-Mehrdad Baghai, Chair of Alchemy Growth and author of *As One*

"The world has never been in more need of extraordinary problem solvers-in business and every other walk of life. Rob McLean and Charles Conn powerfully demonstrate that problem solving is a structured process that can be learned and applied to the benefit of everybody. Their book is such an important contribution to the resolution of our biggest problem solving challenges."

-**Nick Lovegrove**, Professor of the Practice, Georgetown University and author of *The Mosaic Principle*

Bulletproof
Problem Solving

Bulletproof Problem Solving

Charles Conn and Robert McLean

WILEY

Library of Congress Cataloging-in-Publication Data is Available:

ISBN 9781119553021 (Paperback)
ISBN 9781119553045 (ePDF)
ISBN 9781119553038 (ePub)

Cover Design: Wiley
Cover Image: © Marish/Shutterstock

Printed in the United States of America
SKY10041678_012023

Contents

Foreword

Bulletproof. At McKinsey there is no greater compliment than to have your reputation as a problem solver described as "bullet-proof." While it takes many skills and types of intelligence to make a modern consulting firm work, the cornerstone capability is always creative problem solving.

The importance of great problem solving has only grown as the pace of economic and technological change has accelerated in recent years—and the scope and complexity of the problems we need to address increases alongside it. Today we are just as likely to be hired to help a country public health system prepare for the next Ebola outbreak as to develop a digital marketing strategy for a new consumer product. As ever more data becomes available, the bar on the quality of thinking rises. We need bulletproof problem solvers.

Whether you work in industry, the nonprofit sector, or government, there is no way to anticipate and plan for the new structures and operating rules that are unfolding. Nor is simply accelerating and adapting traditional, domain-oriented, training approaches suffi-cient. The only way to successfully navigate this level of change is to be a fluid and creative problem solver. That's why the World Economic Forum labeled complex problem solving its number one skill for the twenty-first century. Organizations everywhere are look-ing for this capability in their talent recruiting above all else.

What is perhaps surprising is that a disciplined, comprehensive approach to problem solving isn't taught in schools or universities. It is absent from most curricula even in many business schools. You can see elements in things like root-cause analysis or the current vogue for agile teams and design thinking, but they don't go far enough. This book introduces the systematic process for problem solving that has been missing, a version of the time-tested methodology we have used for many years in McKinsey.

The seven-step method Charles and Rob demonstrate here is transparent and straightforward. It doesn't require specialist skills or fancy mathematical talent—though the authors do show when more sophisticated analytic techniques can be valuable, and why they are often more accessible than you think. It is iterative and flexible; it can be applied quickly to get rough-cut answers, and more slowly to fine-tune nuanced answers. It shows how to fight the human biases in decision making that we have learned so much about in recent years. And it works on nearly any kind of problem, from personal life decisions, to business and nonprofit questions, to the biggest policy challenges facing society.

As a longtime runner, I was especially drawn to Rob's analysis of whether or not to have knee surgery. I was also impressed by the straightforward analysis that can help voters consider their response to complicated policy decisions in areas like fisheries and educational funding. I naturally enjoyed reading the cases covering business strategy or enhancing profitability. And while there are some genuinely intractable social and environmental problems, this methodology can still shine light on solution paths to even the trickiest challenges, including fighting climate change and obesity.

You couldn't ask for more qualified authors to write a book of this kind. Charles drafted the original internal McKinsey presentation on problem solving, *7 Easy Steps to Bulletproof Problem Solving*, one of our most requested professional development documents ever, when we were young consultants in Toronto. I have known Rob for more than 35 years, starting with a project we did together on how to leverage the time of the CEO of Australia's largest company.

During their time at McKinsey, Rob and Charles collaborated with other colleagues to develop the horizons approach to growth strategy that we still use today. After they left the firm, I enjoyed watching them both continue to apply their problem solving method as entrepreneurs and as change makers in the nonprofit sector. In recent years I have had a front-row seat as Charles brought this distinctive mindset to strategy development and transformation at the Rhodes Trust.

Problem solving is the core skill for the twenty-first century. Now, finally, we have a guide to doing it right that any of us can follow.

Dominic Barton

Managing Director (Retired),
McKinsey & Company

Introduction

Problem Solving for the Challenges of the Twenty-First Century

Great problem solving has never been more important for business and society. The problems facing humankind are larger, more complex, and moving faster than ever before. Previous approaches to training for careers are now outmoded as change in technologies and business models accelerates. Learning how to define a problem, creatively break it into manageable parts, and systematically work toward a solution has become *the* core skill for the twenty-first century workforce, the only way to keep up. But how problem solving is taught in our schools, universities, businesses, and organizations is coming up short. We need a new approach.

Let's start with a definition:

> *Problem solving* is decision making when there is **complexity and uncertainty** that rules out obvious answers, and where there are **consequences** that make the work to get good answers worth it.

We all know the consequences of poor problem solving can be costly to business and communities, human health, and the environment. This book introduces a long-tested and systematic approach that can be taught to anyone who wants to become a better problem solver, from corporate strategists to nonprofit workers. This powerful framework, *Bulletproof Problem Solving*, is an approach we learned and helped develop at McKinsey & Company, the global consulting firm. This seven-step process hasn't been shared widely outside McKinsey until now. It can be used by individuals, teams, executives, government policy makers, and social entrepreneurs—anyone with a complex and uncertain problem of consequence. This systematic approach to problem solving could help you get a great job, make you more effective in your work, make your role as a citizen more fulfilling, and even make your personal life work better. These are big claims, but we know it works.

Problem Solving Capability

This new era of focus on creative problem solving has been ushered in by massive disruption of the old order in business and society. New business models are rapidly emerging from revolutionary Internet, machine learning, and bioscience technologies that threaten the status quo in every field. New rules are being written for conducting business and dealing with social and environmental challenges. Succeeding requires complex problem solving skills as never before. If you're a product manager who faces disruptive competition, you need to have a game plan and command of resources to overcome competition. You will only get resources if you make a persuasive case based on hypotheses about a winning plan, accompanied by analysis to support the key propositions. If you're a nonprofit leader of a team dealing with communities facing generational disadvantage who has seen new initiatives come and go, you have to be able to articulate a theory of change that links issues with interventions and outcomes if you want support from the board of your organization.

As organizations seek to become clever and agile to address this new world, they take on the persona of problem solving organizations—a drive to be working on the right problems, addressing root causes, engaging teams around short duration work plans, and allocating responsibilities and timelines with accountability. Over the course of our careers, we have seen the focus of organizational capability aspirations shift through distinct eras: from *strategy* to *execution* to *complex problem solving*.

The 70s and 80s were characterized by intense interest in strategy development. That was displaced by an era from the 90s onward that focused on execution, including deep attention to getting things done, as exemplified by the book *Execution* by Ram Charan and Larry Bossidy, and a number of books on business process redesign.[1] However, a ruthless focus on execution assumes you have strategic direction right and can adapt to new competition, frequently from outside your industry. This can no longer be assumed.

MANAGERIAL SKILLS EVOLUTION

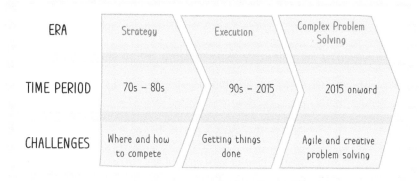

ERA	Strategy	Execution	Complex Problem Solving
TIME PERIOD	70s – 80s	90s – 2015	2015 onward
CHALLENGES	Where and how to compete	Getting things done	Agile and creative problem solving

As this new era of the problem solving organization takes hold, we expect it will trigger even more interest in how teams go about sharpening complex problem solving and critical thinking skills— what is called *mental muscle* by the authors of *The Mathematical Corporation.*[2] The other side of the equation is the increasing importance of machine learning and artificial intelligence in addressing fast-changing systems. Problem solving will increasingly utilize advances in machine learning to predict patterns in consumer behavior, disease, credit risk, and other complex phenomena, termed *machine muscle.*

To meet the challenges of the twenty-first century, mental muscle and machine muscle have to work together. Machine learning frees

---

[1] Larry Bossidy and Ram Charan, *Execution: The Discipline of Getting Things Done* (Random House, 2008).

[2] Josh Sullivan and Angela Zutavern, *The Mathematical Corporation: Where Machine Intelligence and Human Ingenuity Achieve the Impossible* (Public Affairs, 2017).

human problem solvers from computational drudgery and amplifies the pattern recognition required for faster organizational response to external challenges. For this partnership to work, twenty-first century organizations need staff who are quick on their feet, who learn new skills quickly, and who attack emerging problems with confidence. The World Economic Forum in its *Future of Jobs Report*[3] placed complex problem solving at #1 in its top 10 skills for jobs in 2020. Here is their list of important skills that employers are seeking:

TOP 10 SKILLS IN 2020

1. Complex Problem Solving
2. Critical Thinking
3. Creativity
4. People Management
5. Coordinating with Others
6. Emotional Intelligence
7. Judgment and Decision Making
8. Service Orientation
9. Negotiation
10. Cognitive Flexibility

It is becoming very clear that job growth is focused in areas where tasks are *nonroutine* and *cognitive*, versus *routine* and *manual*. The intersection of nonroutine tasks and cognitive ability is the heartland of complex problem solving. The authors of a recent *McKinsey Quarterly* article made the point that "more and more positions

---

[3] *Future of Jobs: Employment, Skills and Workforce Strategy for the Fourth Industrial Revolution* (World Economic Forum, 2016).

require employees with deeper expertise, more independent judgment, and better problem solving skills."[4] We are already seeing that many organizations place a premium on analytic skills and problem solving and make it the essential criterion to be hired. Commentator David Brooks of the *New York Times* takes this conclusion even further when he says, "It doesn't matter if you are working in the cafeteria or the inspection line of a plant, companies will only hire people who can see problems and organize responses."[5]

Education Gaps

If creative problem solving is the critical twenty-first century skill, what are schools and universities doing to develop these skills in students? Not enough. It remains early days in codifying and disseminating problem solving best practices in educational institutions. Andreas Schleicher, Director of Education and Skills and Special Advisor to the Secretary General of the OECD, explains the need for developing problem solving skills in students this way: "Put simply, the world no longer rewards people just for what they know—Google knows everything—but for what they can do with what they know. Problem solving is at the heart of this, the capacity of an individual to engage in cognitive processing to understand and resolve problem situations where a method of solution is not immediately obvious."[6]

The OECD Program for International Student Assessment (PISA) started testing individual problem solving skills in 2012 and added collaborative problem solving skills in the 2015 assessments. One of the interesting early findings is that to teach students to become better problem solvers involves other capabilities than simply teaching reading, mathematics, and science literacy well. Capabilities such as creativity, logic, and reasoning are essential contributors to students becoming better problem solvers. That is what this book is about.

---

[4] Boris Ewenstein, Bryan Hancock, and Asmus Komm, "Ahead of the Curve: The Future of Performance Management," *McKinsey Quarterly*, May 2016.

[5] David Brooks, "Everyone a Changemaker," *New York Times*, February 18, 2018.

[6] Beno Csapo and Joachim Funke (eds.), *The Nature of Problem Solving: Using Research to Inspire 21st Century Learning.* (OECD Publishing, 2017).

Universities and colleges are being challenged to demonstrate that their graduates have developed problem solving skills to prepare them for the demands of the workplace. One method of evaluating whether over a college degree there is improvement in critical thinking is the CLA+ test (Collegiate Learning Assessment plus) developed by the nonprofit Council for Aid to Education (CAE). The *Wall Street Journal* reported in 2017 that of the 200 colleges that apply the test "a majority of colleges that took the CLA+ made measurable progress in critical thinking"—although some well-respected colleges didn't show much difference between incoming freshmen scores and those of seniors.[7] Effective university approaches to develop critical thinking and problem solving range from analyzing classic poems like *Beowulf*, to teaching logic structures, and setting practical group projects that require demonstration of problem solving abilities. What we glean from the article and college practices generally is an awakening of interest in student problem solving, and expectations that problem solving will be enhanced over the course of a degree program. But we have not seen a common framework or process emerge yet.

The Seven-Steps Process

The heart of the book is a seven-step framework for creative problem solving, *Bulletproof Problem Solving*, starting with these critical questions:

1. How do you define a problem in a precise way to meet the decision maker's needs?

2. How do you disaggregate the issues and develop hypotheses to be explored?

3. How do you prioritize what to do and what not to do?

4. How do you develop a workplan and assign analytical tasks?

5. How do you decide on the fact gathering and analysis to resolve the issues, while avoiding cognitive biases?

[7] Douglas Belkin, "Exclusive Test Data: Many Colleges Fail to Improve Critical-Thinking Skills," *Wall Street Journal*, June 5, 2017.

6. How do you go about synthesizing the findings to highlight insights?

7. How do you communicate them in a compelling way?

In the book we take you through the seven steps in a way that builds understanding and mastery through examples. We highlight a variety of analytic tools available to aid this process, from clever heuristics, analytic short cuts, and back-of-the-envelope calculations, to sophisticated tools such as game theory, regression analysis, and machine learning. We also show how common cognitive biases can be addressed as part of the problem solving process.

The final two chapters explicitly deal with how you solve problems when uncertainty is high and interdependencies or systems effects are significant. We believe that even the so-called "wicked problems" of society can be tackled, such as obesity and environmental degradation. These are tough problems that have multiple causes, are affected by externalities, require human behavioral change, and have some solutions that may bring unintended consequences. These chapters are for people dealing with advanced problem solving situations, but the cases are fascinating reading for anyone interested in the major issues business and society needs to address.

High Stakes

Good problem solving has the potential to save lives and change the fortunes of companies, nonprofits, and governments. On the other hand, mistakes in problem solving are often very costly and sometimes can cause great harm, as we saw in the Space Shuttle *Challenger* disaster.

THE SPACE SHUTTLE *CHALLENGER*
A TRAGIC ERROR IN ANALYSIS

On January 28, 1986 the Space Shuttle *Challenger* exploded over Cape Canaveral, Florida 73 seconds after lift-off into its tenth mission. The consequences for the families of the astronauts watching below, the NASA aerospace engineers, mission control workers, and the American space program itself were tragic and catastrophic. For those of us who watched this tragedy unfold on televisions around the world, we could only imagine the horror and devastation. The *Challenger* exploded because of a failure of its O-rings — small rubber rings that prevent hot gases from leaking. These conclusions emerged from the Rogers Commission and the work of physicist Richard Feynman.

While the *Challenger* case has been studied over many years, it remains relevant to this book. That's because it wasn't just an O-ring failure, as most had come to accept, but a problem-solving failure, and that aspect of the case is little understood. The O-ring failure was brought on by Mother Nature herself, a very unusual drop in temperature in Florida the day of the launch — 21°F colder than the coldest previous launch at 53°F. At this dramatically colder temperature, the rubber in the O-rings failed to expand.

The error lay in an incomplete and flawed analysis linking failed O-rings and temperature at launch. It was only when the full data set of successful and unsuccessful launches is examined that the risks of failure at such a low temperature becomes clear. NASA put the chance of failure at 1 in 100,000, whereas Feynman argued it was more like 1 in 100. More recent re-analysis by Bayesian researchers put the probability of failure at the launch temperature close to certainty. We discuss the *Challenger* case in more detail in Chapter 6.

Pitfalls and Common Mistakes

When we listen to people describe their approach to problem solving, they invariably identify one step they feel they do well. Some will confidently describe their approach to problem definition as SMART (specific, measurable, actionable, relevant, and time frame); others will cite their knowledge of inductive and deductive logic; some will point to their workplans bringing accountability to team processes; many will point to their ability to do fact gathering and analysis; and a few will mention the way they use the pyramid principle to write a persuasive document with a governing thought. But we see very few who say they do all the above, coupled with a way to cleave problems and address bias. To do good problem solving, you have to do all the steps in concert. This is what is so powerful and distinctive about the seven-steps process.

Despite increasing focus on problem solving in schools and universities, businesses, and nonprofits, we find that there is confusion about what good problem solving entails, There are a number of pitfalls and common mistakes that many make. These include:

1. *Weak problem statements.* Too many problem statements lack specificity, clarity around decision-maker criteria and constraints, an indication of action that will occur if the problem is solved, or a time frame or required level of accuracy for solving the problem. Rushing into analysis with a vague problem statement is a clear formula for long hours and frustrated clients.

2. *Asserting the answer.* The assertion is often based on experience or analogy ("I've seen this before"), without testing to see if that solution is really a good fit for the problem at hand. Answers like this are corrupted by availability bias (drawing only on facts at hand), anchoring bias (selecting a numerical range you have seen already), or confirmation bias (seeing only data that aligns with your prejudices).

3. *Failure to disaggregate the problem.* We see few problems that can ever be solved without disaggregation into component parts. A team looking at the burden of asthma in Sydney got the critical insight into the problem only when they broke it down along the lines of incidence and severity. In Western Sydney the incidence of asthma was only 10% higher than Northern Sydney, but deaths and hospitalization were 54–65% greater. The team was familiar with research that linked asthma with socioeconomic status and tree cover. It turns out that socioeconomic status is significantly lower in Western Sydney, tree cover is about half Northern Sydney, and daily maximum particulate matter (PM 2.5) is 50% higher. By finding the right cleaving point to disaggregate the problem, the team was able to focus on the crux of the issue. This led to them proposing an innovative approach to address respiratory health through natural solutions, such as increasing tree cover to absorb particulate matter.

4. *Neglecting team structure and norms.* Our experiences in team problem solving in McKinsey and other organizations highlight the importance of a diversity of experience and divergent views in the group, having people who are open-minded, a group dynamic that can be either competitive or collaborative, and training and team processes to reduce the impact of biases. This has been underscored by recent work on forecasting.[8] Executives rank reducing decision bias as their number one aspiration for improving performance.[9] For example, a food products company Rob was serving was trying to exit a loss-making business. They could have drawn a line under the losses if they took an offer to exit when they had lost $125 million. But they would only accept offers to recover accounting book value (a measure of the original cost). Their loss aversion, a form of sunk-cost bias,

---

[8] Philip Tetlock and Dan Gardner, *Superforecasting: The Art and Science of Prediction* (Random House, 2015).

[9] Tobias Baer, Sven Hellistag, and Hamid Samandari, "The Business Logic in Debiasing," *McKinsey Latest Thinking*, May 2017.

meant that several years later they finally exited with losses in excess of $500 million! Groupthink amongst a team of managers with similar backgrounds and traditional hierarchy made it hard for them see the real alternatives clearly; this is a common problem in business.

5. *Incomplete analytic tool set.* Some issues can be resolved with back of the envelope calculations. Others demand time and sophisticated techniques. For example, sometimes no amount of regression analysis is a substitute for a well-designed, real-world experiment that allows variables to be controlled and a valid counterfactual examined. Other times analysis fails because teams don't have the right tools. We often see overbidding for assets where teams use past earnings multiples rather than the present value of future cash flows. We also see underbidding for assets where development options and abandonment options, concepts akin to financial options, are not explicitly valued. How BHP, an Australian resource company, addressed these issues is developed in Chapter 8.

6. *Failing to link conclusions with a storyline for action.* Analytically oriented teams often say, "We're done" when the analysis is complete, but without thinking about how to synthesize and communicate complex concepts to diverse audiences. For example, ecologists have pointed to the aspects of nature and urban green spaces that promote human well-being. The message has frequently been lost in the technical language of ecosystem services—that is, in describing the important role that bees play in pollination, that trees play in absorbing particulate matter, or water catchments play in providing drinking water. The story becomes so much more compelling when, in the case of air pollution, it has been linked to human respiratory health improvements in asthma and cardiovascular disease.[10] In this case, by completing the circle and finding a way to develop a compelling

---

[10] *Planting Healthy Air* (The Nature Conservancy, 2016).

storyline that links back to the "hook" of human health makes all the difference in capturing an audience and compelling action.

7. *Treating the problem solving process as one-off rather than an iterative one.* Rarely is a problem solved once and for all. Problems we will discuss often have a messiness about them that takes you back and forth between hypotheses, analysis, and conclusions, each time deepening your understanding. We provide examples to show it is okay and worthwhile to have second and third iterations of issue trees as your understanding of a problem changes.

What's in Store?

This is a how-to book. We work through 30 real-world examples, employing a highly visual logic-tree approach, with more than 90 graphics. These are drawn from our experience and honed over an intensive summer of research with a team of Rhodes Scholars in Oxford. They include problems as diverse as the supply of nurses in the San Francisco Bay Area, to capital investment decisions in an Australian mining company, to reduction of the spread of HIV in India, to air pollution and public health in London, to competitive dynamics in the hardware home-center industry, and even to approaches to address climate change. The insights in some cases are novel, in other cases counterintuitive. The real-world examples behind the cases have created value amounting to billions of dollars, saved hundreds of thousands of lives, and improved the future for endangered species like salmon.

If you want to become a better problem solver, we show how you can do so with only a modest amount of structure and numeric ability. Individuals make decisions that have lifetime consequences—such as career choice, where to live, their savings plan, or elective surgery—often without due consideration. These are among the examples we walk you through in the book to illustrate the value of a structured process to improve your prospects of better outcomes in your own life.

PROBLEM SOLVING CASES

INDIVIDUAL

- » Should I put solar panels on my roof?
- » Should I support the school bond?
- » Where to live
- » Is where I live affecting my health?
- » Should I have a knee arthroscopy?
- » How to judge contested characters in history
- » Will I outlive my savings?
- » What career should I choose?
- » Where to serve in tennis

ORGANIZATIONS

- » Pricing decision at Truckgear
- » Competitor analysis-Home Depot vs. Hechinger
- » Drones to the rescue/shark spotting with machine learning
- » Airport capacity
- » Growth strategy at J&J
- » Drone company staircase
- » Should we defend our IP in court?
- » Bias in mineral exploration
- » Predicting sleep apnea with machine learning
- » Bus routing with machine learning
- » Classifying heart attack risks in hospitals
- » Oil refinery strategy communication
- » Electronic Arts: A/B testing
- » Crowdsourcing problem solving in organizations
- » Supply of quality nurses in Bay Area
- » How to make long-term resource investments
- » Root cause of market share loss

CITIZEN / POLICY

- » Protecting salmon in the Pacific Northwest
- » HIV in India
- » How to tackle climate change
- » Can obesity be reduced?
- » *Challenger* Space Shuttle disaster
- » How to reduce overfishing

As citizens we have a desire to understand issues of the day more clearly and to be able to make a contribution to resolving them. There is a temptation to say, "That issue is way too complex or political for me to add a perspective." We hope to change your mind about that. There are few bigger problems on the planet than climate change, obesity, reducing the spread of infectious disease, and the protection of species, and we demonstrate how to tackle problems also at this societal scale.

For college students and graduates in analytical roles we hope this book will become an important resource for you—a comprehensive suite of tools and approaches that can make you a better problem solver, one you will return to again and again. For managers we set out how to evaluate your competitor's performance, decide where and how to compete, and develop a strategy in uncertain and complex settings.

Our aim is simple: to enable readers to become better problem solvers in all aspects of their lives. You don't need post-graduate training to be an effective problem solver. You do need to be prepared to work through a process and develop cases of your own where you can try-test-learn the framework. This quote from Nobel Laureate Herb Simon captures much of what we set out to do in the book: "Solving a problem simply means representing it so as to make the solution transparent."[11]

---

[11] Herbert Simon, *The Sciences of the Artificial* (MIT Press, 1968).

Bulletproof
Problem Solving

Chapter One

Learn the Bulletproof Problem Solving Approach

In the 1980s, when Charles was at business school, he wanted to understand the then-ascendant Japanese business practices better. He wrote to dozens of Japanese companies to see if they would host him for a summer internship. Most never replied, but just as he was thinking he might be unemployed for the summer, Charles received a letter from a Dr. Utsumi at Canon, the camera and printer company. Canon was prepared to hire Charles as its first western intern, and soon he was winging his way to Japan.

It sounds like a fun adventure, and it was, but it was also a huge shock. Charles was seconded to the production planning division in a distant Tokyo suburb, and assigned to a Canon men's dormitory, three train lines and 90 minutes away. He couldn't speak or read Japanese. He was assigned what seemed at first an impossible task: develop a model for how to site factories. He despaired—what did he know about where to put factories? It seemed like a specialist problem.

But, with the help of a translating colleague, he began to interview the team about their experiences in different factory location decisions around the world. Patterns began to emerge in his findings. He learned which variables were involved, from local authorities' incentives, to local taxation rates, wage levels, raw materials transportation cost, and so on, and eventually he figured out which were more or less important. Finally he built a logic tree that captured the variables, the direction or sign of impact, and the weight of the factors. He tested the model with data from past factory decisions and honed its accuracy with the senior team. In the end, this little model became the core tool used by the department to make complex factory siting decisions! The secret was that it was a single-page way of seeing complicated trade-offs that had previously been buried in dense reports. It made the logic of the criteria clear, and opened weighting of variables up to discussion.

It saved what might have been a disastrous internship, but more importantly, it convinced Charles of the decision-making power of relatively simple logical structures and processes in problem solving. That is the core focus of this book.

Problem solving means different things to different people. When Rob asked his seven-year-old granddaughter how school was going, she said to him, "Papa, I'm very good at problem solving." This of course was music to Rob's ears! Of course, she was really talking about doing math and logic problems in a school setting. Unfortunately, these essential problem solving building blocks are seldom taught as a systematic process and rarely in a way that addresses problems of everyday relevance and consequence. For us, problem solving means the process of making better decisions on the complicated challenges of personal life, our workplaces, and the policy sphere.

The magic of the *Bulletproof Problem Solving* approach we introduce here is in following the same systematic process to solve nearly every type of problem, from linear ones to problems with complex interdependencies. It sets out a simple but rigorous approach to defining problems, disaggregating them into manageable pieces, focusing good analytic tools on the most important parts, and then synthesizing findings to tell a powerful story. While the process has a beginning and end, we encourage you to think of problem solving as an iterative process rather than a linear one. At each stage we improve our understanding of the problem and use those greater insights to refine our early answers.

In this chapter we outline the overall *Bulletproof Problem Solving Process,* introducing you to the seven steps that later chapters will address in more detail. We demonstrate the use of logic trees to uncover the structure of problems and focus on solution paths. We provide several straightforward cases to get readers started. Later chapters will introduce advanced techniques for more complicated and uncertain problems.

The Bulletproof Problem Solving Cycle

The bulletproof problem solving process is both a complete process and an iterative cycle. This cycle can be completed over any timeframe with the information at hand. Once you reach a preliminary end point, you can repeat the process to draw out more insight for deeper understanding.

We often use the expression, "What's the one-day answer?" This means we ask our team to have a coherent summary of our best understanding of the problem and a solution path at any point in the project, not just at the end. This process of creating active hypotheses is at the heart of *Bulletproof Problem Solving*. It can even help you face the dreaded "elevator test." The elevator test is when you, as a junior team member, find yourself in an elevator with the most senior person in your organization and they ask, "How is your project going?" We have all had this happen. You panic, your mind goes blank, and you stammer out a nonsensical dog's breakfast of an answer. The bulletproof problem solving process in the following pages can help you beat this situation and turn the elevator test into an opportunity for promotion.

The kind of problem solving we describe can be done alone or in teams. If you're tackling a problem by yourself, we suggest building in review processes that you can use with family and colleagues to get the higher objectivity and other bias-fighting benefits of a team.

The seven steps are introduced in Exhibit 1.1.

EXHIBIT 1.1   The bulletproof problem solving cycle

STEP 1: DEFINE THE PROBLEM

When a problem's context and boundaries aren't fully described, there is a lot of room for error. The first step in our process is to arrive at a problem definition that is agreed upon by those involved in making a decision. We test the problem definition against several criteria: that it is specific, not general, that we can clearly measure success, that the definition is bounded both in time frame and by the values of the decision maker, and that it involves definitive action being taken. This step may appear constraining, but it leads to the clarity of purpose essential for good problem solving.

STEP 2: DISAGGREGATE THE ISSUES

Once the problem is defined, it must be disaggregated (or broken down) into component parts or issues. We employ logic trees of various types to elegantly disassemble problems into parts for analysis, driving from alternative hypotheses of the answer. There is both an art and science to 'cleaving' problems—revealing their fault lines—that drives better solutions. This is the stage at which theoretical frameworks from economics and science provide useful guides to better understanding the drivers of your problem solution. We usually try several different cuts at disaggregation to see which yields the most insight.

STEP 3: PRIORITIZE THE ISSUES, PRUNE THE TREE

The next step is to identify which branches of the logic tree have the biggest impact on the problem, including which you can most affect, and focus your initial attention on these. We employ a simple matrix of size of impact of each lever and ability to move the lever as a way to prune our logic trees. Prioritizing analyses helps us find the critical path to the answer efficiently, making the best use of team time and resources.

STEP 4: BUILD A WORKPLAN AND TIMETABLE

Once the component parts are defined and prioritized, you then have to link each part to a plan for fact gathering and analysis. This workplan and timetable assigns team members to analytic tasks with specific outputs and completion dates. We'll show you best practices in workplanning to move quickly and accurately to solutions. A good workplanning process also includes team norms around generating a diversity of views, use of experts, role-playing, and flattening team hierarchies to achieve better answers. Good team norms and process help us avoid common pitfalls and biases in decision making, including confirmation bias, sunk costs fallacies, and anchoring bias.

STEP 5: CONDUCT CRITICAL ANALYSES

Data gathering and analysis is often the longest step in the process. For speed and simplicity we start with simple heuristics—short cuts or rules of thumb—to get an order of magnitude understanding of each problem component, and to assess priorities quickly. This helps us understand where we need to do more work, and especially when and where to use more complex analytic techniques, including game theory, regression, Monte Carlo simulation, and machine learning. Don't worry Complex techniques are rarely needed, and when they are, new online analytical tools make them much more accessible than you think. To keep the team on the critical path we make frequent use of one-day answers that summarize our best understanding in the form of situation, observations, and initial conclusions—and team review sessions to pressure-test these hypotheses.

STEP 6: SYNTHESIZE FINDINGS FROM THE ANALYSIS

Problem solving doesn't stop at the point of reaching conclusions from individual analyses. Findings have to be assembled into a logical structure to test validity and then synthesized in a way that convinces others that you have a good solution. Great team processes are also important at this stage.

STEP 7: PREPARE A POWERFUL COMMUNICATION

The final step is to develop a storyline from the conclusions that links back to the problem statement and the issues that were defined. A powerful communication will use a governing thought or argument that derives from your refined situation-observation-conclusion logic from earlier stages. This will be supported with your synthesized findings and assembled into component arguments that may follow inductive or deductive logic. It will either lead with action steps, or pose a series of questions that motivate action, depending on audience receptivity.

Prepare for an Avalanche of Trees!

We use logic or issue trees to visualize and disaggregate problems. We employ several types, including hypothesis trees and decision trees, as you will see in the cases we present throughout this book. We learned the power of logic trees at McKinsey and continue to find them essential to good problem solving. Why? Because they do the following:

- Provide a clear visual representation of the problem so that everyone can understand the component parts.
- Done correctly, they are holistic in the sense that everything relevant is captured in the tree.
- Lead to clear hypotheses that can be tested with data and analysis.

Our logic trees are sometimes simple and sometimes highly complex. But they all started on a sketchpad or a whiteboard.

Let's Start with Some Case Studies

To illustrate the bulletproof problem solving process, we chose some case studies that represent classes of problems that many of our readers will face, and that exhibit the power and utility of the process described in detail over the next several chapters.

1. Is Sydney airport capacity adequate for the future?

2. Should I install solar panels on my roof now?

3. Where should I move?

4. Should a start-up raise its prices?

5. Should I support a K–12 school education levy in my town?

These relatively simple cases will outline each of the seven problem solving steps, but with a focus on the use of logic trees to help you represent the problem and break it into manageable parts. Later chapters will go into the fine points of the other steps in more detail and for more complicated problems.

Case 1: Does Sydney Airport Have Adequate Capacity?

When Rob was the lead partner in recruiting for the Australian and New Zealand practice of McKinsey, the consulting firm made the decision to look beyond traditional hires with MBAs to try to attract clever physicists, scientists, lawyers, engineers, and liberal arts graduates. Discussing business cases in interviews put many of the potential hires at a disadvantage. So his recruiting team came up with a non-business case that they called the Sydney Airport case. It is pretty simple, but it is a good way to show the seven-steps method.

All of the candidates had flown into Sydney Airport and were aware of discussions in the newspapers about whether another airport was needed at that time. Sydney Airport has two of the 10 busiest air routes in the world, so this is a real-world example. At the interviews the candidates were given a simple problem definition (step 1 problem definition): "Will Sydney Airport capacity be adequate in the future?" and asked how they would think about that question. The problem statement was bounded around passenger airport capacity, so the candidates didn't have to spend a lot of time on policy factors that might warrant a second airport, such as greater accessibility, safety, or environmental factors like noise, or even alternatives like a very fast train link between major cities. As we'll see later, the boundaries on problem definition are really important to agree on up front.

Candidates would often ask a clarifying question or two and then outline their approach to addressing the issue. So what was Rob's team looking for? They wanted to see if the candidates used a logical structure to help them solve the problem. It's much easier to show the parts of the problem in written form, so we encouraged candidates to use a whiteboard or pad of paper. It is usually a trial and error process to get the breakdown right to solve the problem. This is step 2, problem disaggregation, and Exhibit 1.2 shows a simple first cut.

SYDNEY AIRPORT
FIRST BREAKDOWN

Will airport capacity be adequate?

Supply

Demand

EXHIBIT 1.2

In this case, the simplest possible way to cleave the problem is to define airport capacity as supply (of landing slots) less demand. You could have a more complicated tree with competition from other ways to get to Sydney (and you might get extra credit for showing how those affect demand), but it probably isn't necessary in this relatively simple case.

A good candidate would dig a little deeper of course. Exhibit 1.3 shows one way of defining airport supply capacity (number of runways, capacity of each runway, and utilization) and demand (Sydney's share of regional demand). In the short term, the number of runways is fixed, and so is runway capacity (defined mostly by aircraft type).

SYDNEY AIRPORT
SECOND BREAKDOWN

- Will airport capacity be adequate?
  - Supply
    - Number of Runways
    - ×
    - Capacity / runway
    - ×
    - Runway utilization
  - —
  - Demand
    - Regional Market Demand
    - ×
    - Sydney Market Share

EXHIBIT 1.3

Candidates would typically explain their approach to modeling demand growth by making different assumptions about gross domestic product (GDP) growth, fuel costs, and relative location attractiveness of Sydney relative to other destinations (see Exhibit 1.4).

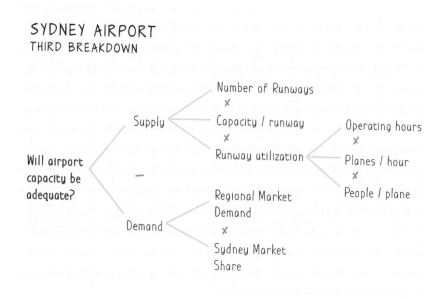

SYDNEY AIRPORT
THIRD BREAKDOWN

EXHIBIT 1.4

But the most productive approach to this problem is to go deeper into runway utilization, as it is one of the few variables that can be actively managed by transportation planners. Runway utilization is determined by hours of operation, spacing between aircraft movements, and the number of people per airplane. Hours of operation are limited by curfew periods, weather, and maintenance. Thinking about how you could vary these is the heart of steps 4 (workplanning) and 5 (analysis).

The answers Rob most liked were the ones where candidates would say something along these lines:

> Runway utilization is the key so I'd be looking at operating hours, planes per hour, and the people per plane. You probably can't do much with operating hours because there are curfew restrictions

between midnight and 6 a.m. because of the residents nearby. With planes per hour—a core variable for utilization—I'd want to see if they could safely reduce further the time between take-offs and landings. The third factor is the people per plane and that comes down to slot pricing favoring larger planes and policy about light aircraft use at peak hours (steps 6 and 7 synthesis and storytelling)

Good candidates might also propose to raise prices to curtail demand, a tool for airport capacity management, though one that could result in Sydney market share loss, which city economic planners might not embrace.

The branches on this kind of simple logic tree are joined together mathematically, so it is possible to model simple scenarios and show different alternatives by modifying the variables that planners could affect. A really outstanding candidate might show the impact of increasing utilization by 20% on passenger numbers, or employing larger planes.

What actually happened at Sydney Airport? Sydney got a third runway some years later and has managed the impact of significant traffic growth by working on the key variables identified in the case. Despite the current airport authority's opposition, Sydney is to get a second airport in the next decade.

Case 2: Should Rob Install Solar Panels on His Roof Now?

A few years ago Rob thought it might be time to install solar panels at their house in the Australian countryside. Rob and his wife Paula wanted to do something to offset their carbon footprint for some time, but were struggling to make a decision with reducing (and now eliminated) subsidies available from the power company, declining costs of installing solar PV, and questions over the future level of feed-in tariffs (the price at which the electricity company buys *from* you when you generate excess power at home). Was now the right time? He decided to approach it in the way he had learned at McKinsey and started with the hypothesis, "We should install solar PV now." He hadn't reached a conclusion by framing it this way, nor was he setting out to confirm it without regard to the facts. He was using the hypothesis to bring forth the arguments to either disprove it or support it.

Rob felt that the hypothesis would be supported if the following criteria could all be sustained:

- If the payback on the investment was attractive, something less than 10 years.
- If the decline in the cost of panels was slowing down such that he should not wait and make the investment later at substantially lower cost. Rob felt that if solar panel costs were going to continue to decline and be significantly cheaper in three years, he'd consider waiting.
- If the reduction in his CO_2 footprint was material, by which he meant 10% or more (other than air travel he is required to do and can offset independently).

Rob knows that constraining the scope of the problem with clear boundaries makes problem solving more accurate and speedy (step 1).

This kind of problem sounds quite complex at first, a jumble of unfamiliar terms like feed-in tariffs and avoided carbon. A logic tree helped Rob see the structure of his problem in one picture, and helped him break up the analyses into manageable chunks. He started by laying out the reasons and supporting facts that he would need to resolve the issue. You can also think of it this way—for Rob to answer the question affirmatively what would he have to be convinced of? What are the major reasons for going ahead and installing solar panels? Exhibit 1.5 is a first cut of Rob's logic tree (steps 2 and 4).

FIRST CUT: SOLAR PANEL LOGIC TREE

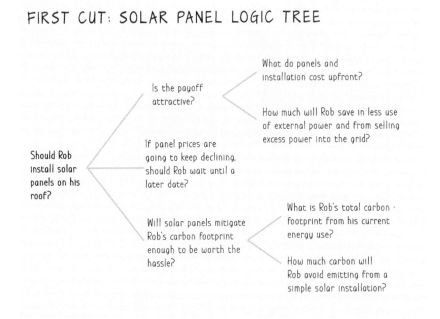

EXHIBIT 1.5

The first part he tackled was payback, because if the economics didn't work, the two other questions didn't need answering. Payback is pretty straightforward: the cost of the installed solar panels and inverter, divided by the annual electrical cost savings. The denominator in this analysis includes both estimating net savings from the installation from avoided electricity charges because he was using his own power, plus income from supplying electricity to the grid via feed-in tariffs. Most of this analysis can be done by online calculators that solar installers offer, once you know the size of the system, roof orientation, solar electric potential, and the efficiency in power generation. Rob simplified the analysis by leaving out battery storage options that add to cost but provide the opportunity to replace peak power charges. With an annual cost savings of around $1,500 and investment costs of just over $6,000, payback was attractive at about four years (step 5).

The next question was whether he should make the investment now, or wait, hoping for lower solar panel costs later. Rob was aware that the cost of a watt of PV had fallen almost 30% from 2012 to 2016, and almost 90% from the early days of solar PV. He wasn't sure whether this would continue in the future. With some simple Internet research, Rob learned that declining costs of equipment was still uncertain, but the cost per watt was unlikely to fall by more than 30% for at least the next three years. There is also uncertainty about future feed-in tariffs that have been set to encourage sales of solar PV. This has to be considered against rising retail prices for electricity customers.

At $1,500 per year, the cost savings lost by waiting would be $4,500 over three years, so the up-front cost of the solar PV installation would have to fall by 75% to make waiting worthwhile. Rob could have used a net present value analysis where the time value of money is considered rather than a simple payback. But in this case the simple method is fine: He felt comfortable with the four-year payback providing an implied rate of return of 25%. It was worth doing now.

Finally, he wanted to estimate how much of his CO_2 footprint he would reduce by going ahead. This depends on two things—one is what fuel source he is displacing (coal or gas in this case), and the second is the kilowatt hours (kWh) he is generating compared to his electricity use, which he knew from the first step. Rob simplified the analysis by looking at the carbon footprint of the average Australian citizen, and found that the avoided carbon from his little solar project could reduce his footprint by more than 20%. Since the payback as an investment is very solid in this case, Rob really could have pruned off this branch of the tree (step 3) and saved some time—but he and Paula had multiple objectives with this investment.

Whenever you do this kind of analysis, it is worth asking what could go wrong, what are the risks around each part of the thinking?

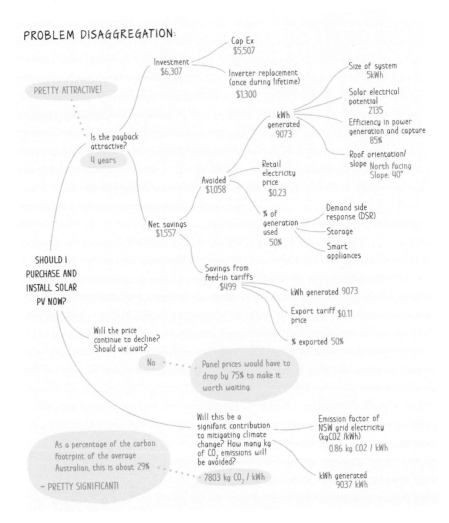

Exhibit 1.6
Assumptions: House type: detached bungalow, Roof orientation: north, Slope: 40°, Suitable roof area: 40m2, Installation size: 5kWh, Shading: none, Numbers for calculations are from 2017, Australia.

In this case there is a chance that the power company would reduce the subsidies for installing solar PV. This can be mitigated by acting quickly. The power company could also reduce the feed-in tariff rate at which it purchased any excess power produced by Rob—and in fact they did that later. But with a four-year payback the exposure is reasonably limited.

The result of Rob's analyses is shown in the more complicated tree shown in Exhibit 1.6.

With only a bit of online research, Rob was able to crack a relatively complicated problem. Rob should install solar panels now. The payback is attractive, and likely cost declines to install later are not enough to offset the savings he could earn now. As a bonus, Rob and Paula were able to reduce their carbon footprint by nearly 30% (steps 6 and 7).

The core of this good result was asking the right questions and disaggregating the problem into straightforward chunks.

Case 3: Where Should I Move?

In the early 2000s Charles was living in Los Angeles. Having recently sold the company he cofounded, his family wanted to move to a small-town environment where there would be more opportunities for recreation and really good schools. They liked the ski towns they had visited, and they had always enjoyed college towns. But how to choose? There are so many variables involved, and it is easy to get it wrong with only impressions from brief visits. Then Charles remembered the factory siting problem he worked on back at Canon in Japan and set up the decision-making effort in a similar way.

The whole family got involved in the problem solving brainstorming, kids included. They started by listing out what mattered to each of them, so their personal factors defined what it meant to be a good place to live. The family agreed on a weighting that favored the school system first, then the natural environment and recreation, and finally characteristics that made for

FAMILY BRAINSTORMING SESSION: WHERE TO LIVE?

ELEMENTS OF A GOOD LIFE	WHAT DOES THAT LOOK LIKE?
Really good schools for the kids	Great teachers Small class sizes Good taxpayer support for education School choices: public, charter, private Graduates get into good colleges
A clean environment and lots to do outside	Water and air quality high A four season climate Lots of sunny days, but sufficient rain Rivers to fish in Great hikes nearby Skiing and mountain biking
A cool, friendly town	A walkable town center Arts, theatre, libraries Not too much traffic Fun coffee shops and good restaurants Do any friends live there? Is it a university town? Is crime a problem?
Can you earn a living?	Cool, small companies Diverse local economy Not too far to West Coast work for Charles

EXHIBIT 1.7

a cool, in-town experience. Charles then added the elements of the ability to earn an income! These were agreed after lively debate with everyone involved (step 1). They planned to use the list to develop a set of towns to visit during family vacations (see Exhibit 1.7).

Charles began the analysis by breaking down the problem into the major elements the family said they valued, then identifying subelements, and finally measurable indicators or variables that captured each subfeature, such as sunny days or a comfort index (defined by temperature and humidity) for climate variables (step 4). It was a little work, but he discovered that most of the data was available online. With the family's input, he put a relative weight next to each variable, to reflect the importance of each element to their final decision.

He developed a tree of around 20 variables and gathered data for about a dozen towns (step 2). The tree he developed is shown in Exhibit 1.8, with the weightings shown in red.

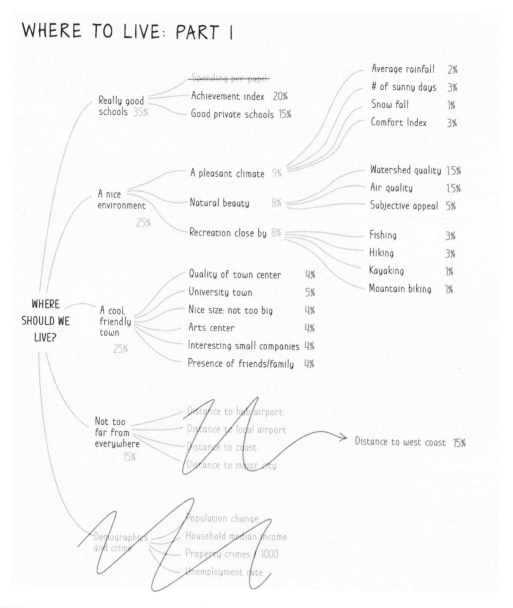

WHERE TO LIVE: PART I

WHERE SHOULD WE LIVE?

- Really good schools 35%
  - Spending per pupil
  - Achievement index 20%
  - Good private schools 15%
- A nice environment 25%
  - A pleasant climate 9%
    - Average rainfall 2%
    - # of sunny days 3%
    - Snow fall 1%
    - Comfort Index 3%
  - Natural beauty 8%
    - Watershed quality 1.5%
    - Air quality 1.5%
    - Subjective appeal 5%
  - Recreation close by 8%
    - Fishing 3%
    - Hiking 3%
    - Kayaking 1%
    - Mountain biking 1%
- A cool, friendly town 25%
  - Quality of town center 4%
  - University town 5%
  - Nice size: not too big 4%
  - Arts center 4%
  - Interesting small companies 4%
  - Presence of friends/family 4%
- Not too far from everywhere 15%
  - Distance to hub airport
  - Distance to local airport
  - Distance to coast
  - Distance to major city
  → Distance to west coast 15%
- Demographics and crime
  - Population change
  - Household median income
  - Property crimes / 1000
  - Unemployment rate

EXHIBIT 1.8

Once Charles gathered the data on a set of small college cities and mountain towns, it became clear that some of the variables were repetitive and others didn't really help distinguish between locations. He pruned his tree to make the analysis simpler and faster. It meant some locations didn't need to be visited. It also revealed that some factors he felt were important around airports and hubs could be encompassed in a single measure of commute time from each town to the West Coast, where most of Charles's work with young companies was located. A variable included early in the analysis was community safety or crime, but that turned out not to be a differentiating factor among the preferred communities, so it was also pruned (step 3).

He converted all the data for each factor to a common scale from 1 to 100, and then applied the weightings. There are various approaches to what is called normalizing data, but they are straightforward and can be found online. As you can see, some of the variables have a positive slope (for example, more days of sunshine is good), and some are negative (for example, longer commute times). So a 100 for Amherst, Massachusetts, on travel time is a negative weight in this case. If we were to get fancy, you could have more complex line shapes to the weighting for variables like rainfall, where you want some rain, but not too much! Exhibit 1.9 shows Charles's analysis (step 5).

In this case, the family was able to reach a conclusion to choose Ketchum, Idaho (steps 6 and 7). They all agreed on the choice because they had agreed on the factors that made for a good location and how to weigh or trade them off. There was a big trade-off in moving to Ketchum, Idaho that Charles was prepared to accept—the commute time to the West Coast for business was longer than other locations.

We sometimes hear a criticism with systematic problem solving like this example that you went through a phony process to prove what you had in mind from the beginning. In this case it isn't phony at all: Ketchum wasn't even on the list of the initial towns under consideration and was only added after a trip

AND THE BEST TOWN IS....

NORMALIZED TABLE	Weight	Healdsburg, CA	Fort Bragg, CA	Bend, OR	Victoria, BC	Boulder, CO	Amherst, MA	Steamboat, CO	Ketchum, ID
Avg rainfall per annum	2%	71	24	0	58	82	29	100	92
# of sunny days	3%	100	91	39	0	74	35	79	52
Snowfall (inches)	1%	0	0	4	4	36	36	100	62
Watershed quality (best=100)	2%	0	7	45	41	100	35	94	57
Air quality (best=100)	2%	0	33	36	33	38	73	82	100
Comfort index (best=100)	3%	30	46	40	46	100	0	86	80
Air time to West Coast (worst=100)	15%	0	17	33	17	33	100	50	58
Availability of private schools (index)	15%	100	0	17	67	83	83	17	83
Achievement index	20%	46	0	38	65	97	100	78	76
Presence of friends/family	4%	100	0	0	0	0	0	0	100
University/college town	5%	0	0	100	100	100	100	0	50
Arts center	4%	50	25	0	100	100	75	0	75
Quality of town center	4%	67	33	0	67	67	50	50	100
Physical beauty of area	5%	25	50	0	50	50	0	100	100
Interesting small companies	4%	60	0	40	60	100	80	0	20
Size	4%	51	100	90	21	0	94	98	100
Recreation	8%	50	40	60	50	70	20	60	90
	100%								
TOTAL WEIGHTED INDEXED SCORE		48	20	34	51	70	70	52	76

EXHIBIT 1.9

to visit friends. But it is worth pointing out some risks in this analysis too. Boulder and Amherst are really close in total score to Ketchum, and quite small changes in how Charles ranked factors such as recreation or quality of town center—which are subjective—could have a big impact on the numerical conclusion. In this case the family could mitigate the risk by visiting each town and testing their feelings about the quantitative variables firsthand.

The where-to-live case illustrates how you can start with a simple list of issues or elements that are related to your problem statement, disaggregate the elements further into indicator variables, then finally add concrete measures and weights. The rest is straightforward arithmetic based on a considered ranking of features. This type of tree and analysis approach has applicability to many choice problems. Charles and Rob have used it to assess what apartment to buy, what employer to join—and, of course, where to put your factory.

Case 4: Making Pricing Decisions in a Start-up Company

In the past few years, one of Charles's friends started a company that makes an accessory for pick-up trucks that has a unique and clever design. The company, which we'll call Truckgear, sells around 10,000 units a year, a number that is growing quickly. It is at break-even on a cash basis (cash basis means not taking into account the accounting charge for depreciating assets). Charles invested in the company and helps devise its strategy.

Start-up companies face big and complex problems early on in the process and, compared to larger companies, they have limited cash resources and team members to address them. Truckgear had to make decisions on whether it should own its own manufacturing plant, which market segments to compete in (there are new and used truck segments and several sales channels to each), whether it should have its own sales force, how much to spend on marketing, and most fundamentally, how fast to grow given limited cash? No wonder start-up teams hardly sleep!

Recently the company had a big decision to make: Should it raise its prices (step 1)? It had held its initial pricing of around $550 for three years. Materials and manufacturing costs had increased as the product features were improved, crimping its margins and lowering the cash generated per unit. Obviously in young companies cash is even more critical than in established ones, as the sources of external financing are significantly fewer. The dilemma Truckgear faced was this—if the marketplace reacts negatively to the price increase, Truckgear growth would slow and perhaps even drop in unit sales.

There is no perfect answer to this kind of question, but we employed a particular kind of logic structure to assess it, a profit lever tree (step 2). We wanted to hone in on the key factors around the decision, and this kind of tree is mathematically complete, so we could use it to model different assumptions.

Exhibit 1.10 is a simple version of this kind of tree.

TRUCKGEAR PROFIT LEVER TREE

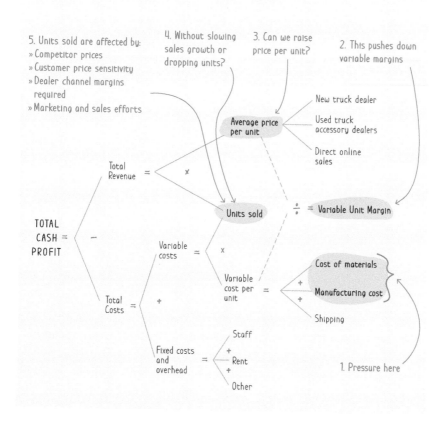

EXHIBIT 1.10

You can see how the tree makes Truckgear's problem visual: Pressure on costs pushes down variable margin per unit—can the company increase unit prices without slowing sales growth or even dropping volume?

Exhibit 1.11 displays the numbers for Truckgear.

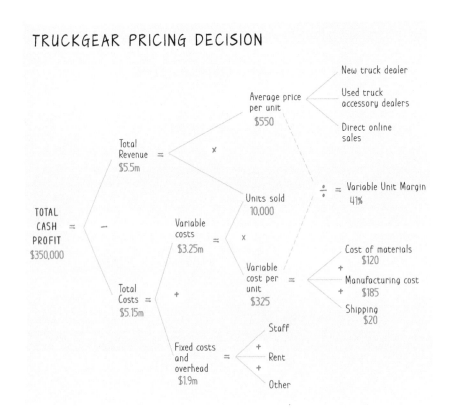

EXHIBIT 1.11

If the company could hold its current unit sales, a price increase of 7% would yield a $385,000 improvement in cash profitability, a substantial increase that could help fund additional marketing and sales programs. But you can also see that it would only take a drop in unit sales of 650 to neutralize the benefit of the price increase (step 5). What to do?

Whether a price increase leads to a loss in total cash profit (or, less seriously, slowing of growth) depends on competitor pricing, customer price sensitivity (which economists call price elasticity), whether the third-party dealer sales channels will absorb some of the price increase by accepting lower margins, as well as marketing and sales efforts. The company initiated a large phone survey of its recent customers and determined that:

- The largest volume customer segments were not sensitive to a modest cost-based increase.
- The competitor products were roughly comparable in price and quite different in functional characteristics.
- Dealers were not willing to reduce their margins to accommodate the price increase.

The company also evaluated whether it could achieve the same result by reducing its fixed overheads or taking manufacturing in-house. With few costs other than a lean staff and rent, the first was not an option. With limited current cash resources, investing in its own extremely expensive manufacturing presses and assembly also didn't make sense (step 3). On balance a small price increase to restore unit margins was worth the risk (step 6 and 7).

This kind of financial tree is particularly useful for solving problems that involve monetary trade-offs of alternative strategies. You can use it to track almost any kind of business problem. We'll show a number of more sophisticated versions in later chapters.

Case 5: Should Charles Support the Local School Levy?

In Charles's former hometown in Idaho, public education funding is supported principally by real estate taxes, which are levied as a percentage of property value each year, and by state sales taxes. When a local school board has bigger strategic investments to fund, it seeks approval through a vote by taxpayers for an additional levy to pay down a bond secured for that purpose. In the late 2000s the Blaine County School Board proposed a bond of more than $50 million to support a large set of investments across the county. With a population of only 20,000 people, depending on the size of your property, the levy could cost a homeowner thousands of additional dollars per year.

As taxpayers and citizens, people face this kind of decision all the time—a spending levy, a one-time referendum, or whether to support a candidate pitching a new state or national policy. The problems seem complex and are often swayed by partisan debate rather than informed by straightforward problem solving that any of us can do.

Charles was aware of press stories that K–12 education in the United States is lagging behind its peers globally, and so was in principle supportive of additional taxes on his house if it really improved local education. But he wanted to know whether voting for the school bond would really have an impact on closing the gap locally (Idaho ranked in the bottom half of US states in school-testing results).

Charles is no expert on education policy. He started by asking a simple question: What is the key problem with K–12 education in the US versus its peers, and does the proposed school levy address these issues (step one)? He knew the United States spends a lot per student in most jurisdictions, among the highest in the world, and he knew overall results were middle of the pack compared to peer countries. So he asked, is the problem:

- Per-student funding?
- IQ or demographics?
- Teachers and schools?

His research showed that the answer is mostly with *teachers and schools*. There was nothing in the data to suggest either that funding levels per student (higher in the United States than most countries) or student IQ levels (comparable to other countries) were the reason for poor student outcomes in the United States (step 3). Study after study shows that student outcomes on international test scores vary widely and are best explained by teacher characteristics and the school environment. Charles then proceeded to research which factors about teachers and schools had most impact on student outcomes and found four, ranked in approximate importance (step 4):

- Teacher numbers and classroom size
- Teacher quality (education, experience, training) and compensation
- School environment and facilities
- Technology

Next, he overlaid the extent to which the proposed bond would provide funding against these factors. It turned out that the funding was mainly directed at clean energy and school facilities, low-impact factors. There was little allocation of funding to the higher ranked factors, especially related to teacher recruitment, pay, and training (step 5). Charles decided not to support the bond on these grounds. Exhibit 1.12 shows what the analysis looks like in a decision tree format.

This analysis illustrates bulletproof problem solving for a societal-level policy problem: It takes a real issue, frames a question followed by a series of sub-questions, and guides research and analysis. Charles collected facts about education performance and the details of the school bond planned spending allocation. It took him only a few hours of framing and online research and helped move him from an emotional decision ("I support education and am concerned about local school performance,") to a reasoned one ("I can't support this levy, given how it is allocated.") (steps 6 and 7).

On the third attempted school levy a few years later, the measure contained funding for early childhood education and more teacher training—and the vote passed.

The next chapters will examine each of the seven steps to bulletproof problem solving in more detail, introducing more complex problems, and more sophisticated approaches to solving them.

K-12 EDUCATION LEVY IN IDAHO

K–12 education in the United States is lagging behind its peers (globally). Will voting in favor of the local school bond have an impact on closing the gap (locally)?

WHAT IS THE KEY PROBLEM WITH K-12 EDUCATION IN THE UNITED STATES?

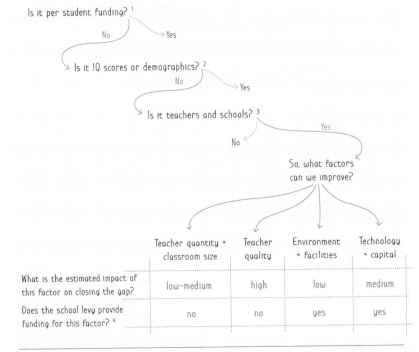

	Teacher quantity + classroom size	Teacher quality	Environment + facilities	Technology + capital
What is the estimated impact of this factor on closing the gap?	low–medium	high	low	medium
Does the school levy provide funding for this factor? [4]	no	no	yes	yes

[1] OECD PISA scores
[2] IQ Research
[3] How the World's Best Performing School Systems Come out on top, McKinsey and Co. Sept 2007
[4] School board approves October levy election, Terry Smith, 2009

EXHIBIT 1.12

Chapter 1 Takeaways

- Good problem solving is a process, not a quick mental calculation or a logical deduction. It applies to even highly complex problems, like where to put factories around the world, as Charles experienced as an intern at Canon.

- The problem solving process we outline in the book is a cycle of seven steps that you work through; each step is important and lots of mistakes result from skipping steps.

- The most important step is to disaggregate the problem in a logical way into component parts, so you can isolate the most important analyses; logic trees are our prime work tool—they make it easy to see the structure of the problem.

- Prioritizing analyses is essential so that you avoid working on parts of the problem that don't contribute much to your answer—we call this being on the critical path.

- A well-defined work plan is needed to allocate analysis to team members and time frames for completion (in this chapter not much work planning was required because the problems were simple).

- How you go about analysis, using simple tools or sophisticated ones, is important to problem solving success; we always start with simple estimates and heuristics or rules of thumb.

- Problem solving isn't over until you can synthesize the results of your analysis and tell a story that convinces someone to act.

- We use different types of logic trees for different problems; in this chapter we have shown mathematically complete deductive logic trees for business problems, weighted factor analysis for making decisions, and decision trees for walking through complex choices.

Problems to Try on Your Own

1. Individual: Show the logic tree for whether you should make a job change—try a decision tree or a factor-weight tree (like where to live, but with job characteristics that are important to you); or try it for a new house or apartment, with weighted characteristics you would look for, and compare them against listings near you.

2. Business: Lay out the profit tree for your business or social enterprise to the third breakdown.

3. Societal: Draw a logic tree for Britain's decision whether or not to leave the European Union (the Brexit decision).

Chapter Two

Define the Problem

Getting a crystal-clear definition of the problem you are solving is the critical starting point to bulletproof problem solving. And it should be relatively straightforward. But a surprising number of failures in problem solving originate in poor problem definition. Teams and individuals surge off into data gathering or expert interviews without being very clear about the boundaries of the problem, the criteria for success, the time frame, or level of accuracy required.

This is bound to lead to disappointment. A scattergun approach to data gathering and initial analysis always leads to far more effort than is necessary. And the answers often miss the mark with decision makers whose values and boundaries need to be taken explicitly into account in problem solving planning.

Charles saw this kind of mistake first-hand in the 1990s when he was running Citysearch, an Internet city guide company that sometimes collaborated with local newspapers and sometimes competed with them. Newspaper companies were the kings of local advertising then and had been for 100 years, despite the earlier advent of first radio and then television. Surely, the little Internet company entrants would be no different?

Charles met with many senior leaders in the newspaper trade during those years and witnessed a kind of arrogance rooted in inaccurate problem diagnosis. These managers believed that the problem statement around new competition was: "Do the new Internet entrants have better content (news and other writing) that would win over readers?" They concluded that their newspapers had editorial content that the entrants couldn't match and therefore they didn't need to worry too much. When Charles was invited to give a keynote presentation to the 1997 Newspaper Association of America annual meeting and suggested that the competitive attack would instead come *from behind*, from erosion of near monopoly positions in classified advertising in segments like autos, real estate, employment, and personals, the room was entirely silent. This upstart was telling them about *their* market in a way that made no sense to their worldview. At the end no one clapped—it was awkward!

Over the next few years it played out as predicted. New vertical players in online classified advertising sprang up and slowly cannibalized the long-held newspaper dominance in these categories. Consumers still wanted newspaper editorial content, but they began to find their jobs, cars, homes, and dates online, stripping away the key source of revenue for old-line media companies. Failure or consolidation of many great newspaper names followed. This turns out to be common in cases of disruptive technology or business model innovation. The existing players literally cannot see the threat from new entrants because their mindset, their problem boundary definition, makes them blind to it.[1] The takeaway point here is clear: Getting problem definition right, including boundaries, is essential to good problem solving and can be an essential competitive advantage.

Good problem statements have a number of characteristics. They are:

- Outcomes focused: A clear statement of the problem to be solved, expressed in outcomes, not activities or intermediate outputs.
- Specific and measurable wherever possible.
- Clearly time-bound.
- Designed to explicitly address decision-maker values and boundaries, including the accuracy needed and the scale of aspirations.
- Structured to allow sufficient scope for creativity and unexpected results—too narrowly scoped problems can artificially constrain solutions.
- Solved at the highest level possible, meaning for the organization as a whole, not just optimized for a part or a partial solution.

Teams we worked with sometimes used a mnemonic—SMART—to remember these characteristics: whether the problem statement was specific, measurable, action oriented, relevant, and timely. SMART covers most but not all of these factors—make sure to have an outcomes focus and work at the highest level.

Usually you can't fit all those characteristics into a single statement, so we like to use a problem statement worksheet that captures the whole context, as in Exhibit 2.1.

---

[1] See, for example: Clayton M. Christensen, *The Innovator's Dilemma: When New Technologies Cause Great Firms to Fail* (Harvard Business School Press, 1997).

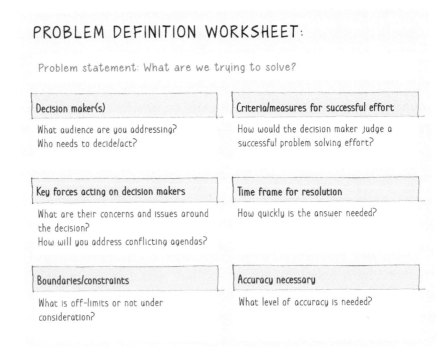

PROBLEM DEFINITION WORKSHEET:

Problem statement: What are we trying to solve?

Decision maker(s)	Criteria/measures for successful effort
What audience are you addressing? Who needs to decide/act?	How would the decision maker judge a successful problem solving effort?

Key forces acting on decision makers	Time frame for resolution
What are their concerns and issues around the decision? How will you address conflicting agendas?	How quickly is the answer needed?

Boundaries/constraints	Accuracy necessary
What is off-limits or not under consideration?	What level of accuracy is needed?

EXHIBIT 2.1

How a Problem Statement Is Refined: The Case of Pacific Salmon

Let's illustrate how this works with a specific example. Charles was asked by a newly formed charitable foundation, the Gordon & Betty Moore Foundation, to look into the question of how to preserve wild Pacific salmon, a hugely important species in the north Pacific rainforest ecosystem. The iconic salmon species in the Atlantic Ocean had seen huge declines from mismanagement that caused large-scale ecosystem harm and community economic losses, and the foundation's founder wanted to ensure that this didn't occur in the Pacific. As you can see, this is a much larger and more complicated problem than our more narrowly bounded problems of

Chapter 1. But you'll see the same principles apply in solving harder problems—you just need to put a bit more work into each of the seven steps.

Here is what the team knew: Pacific salmon are a critical element in northern rainforest ecosystems, sometimes called an apex species for the role they play in these systems. Nearly half a billion Pacific salmon are a substantial biomass in their own right, and have massive impact on both freshwater and marine ecosystems. They provide nutrition for many animal species, jobs for commercial fishers, food and cultural meaning for indigenous people, recreation for sport anglers, a huge boost to local economies, and are a conduit for marine nutrients to help forests thrive. It is hard to overestimate their importance in the environment, economy, culture, and food webs of this huge region. And they are in trouble, at least in many parts of their historic range, pressured by human development in land use and fisheries management approaches that affect both habitat and salmon numbers.

The team wanted to help reverse these declines, but frankly weren't sure where to start. The foundation was new, but it was already committed to a long-term model of philanthropy, whereby it would only focus on a few initiatives and would fund them for substantial periods. The founder is a world-famous engineer, and his personal values were core in developing the foundation's four filters for the work it agreed to take on, one of which was to only work on projects with *measurable outcomes*. The other three filters were *importance* (working on things that really mattered); only working on initiatives where the foundation could make a *difference* (working on things where the foundation's unique contribution mattered); and, working on initiatives that over time would contribute to a *portfolio effect*. This means that the grants it made would invest in capabilities and outcomes that would build off and support each other. Based on this, an initial problem worksheet looked something like Exhibit 2.2.

PACIFIC SALMON PROBLEM WORKSHEET

Problem statement: To substantially increase the number of Wild Pacific Salmon.

Decision maker(s)	Criteria/measures for successful effort
» Head of Foundation Environment Program » Foundation board of trustees » Other stakeholders: environmental organizations, other grant makers, government agencies, fisheries, and indigenous groups	» Four foundation filters: 1. Importance 2. The organization could make a difference and have enduring impact 3. Outcomes can be measured 4. Contributes to a portfolio effect » Could team demonstrate credibility of foundation initiative approach?

Key forces acting on decision makers	Time frame for resolution
» First initiative done by new foundation » Wanted to establish a good reputation » Wanted to prove a new model of philanthropy	» Up to 15 years but had to prove we could design a program and get traction » Annual reviews to test

Boundaries/constraints	Accuracy necessary
» Foundation did not favor direct political policy work or hard-edged advocacy (science over politics, pragmatism over movements) » Willing to spend $10–15m per year » Outcomes, not activities	» Need to demonstrate that the initiative could generate ecosystem scale outcomes over a single generation

EXHIBIT 2.2

The team found this sharply defined problem context extremely valuable. They knew they had up to 15 years to work on the problem and very substantial financial resources to invest if progress remained good. But the team had some real constraints it had to work within. It had to demonstrate that it was making traction on the problem quickly in frequent top-level reviews, and it had to develop strategies that would yield *measurable* ecosystem-level outcome improvements over time. It had to build portfolio effects of capabilities and connections that would benefit other foundation environment work. And, as the first team, it was important to show to the broader grant-making and conservation communities that the focused portfolio approach to environmental grant making would really work. These are high bars, but it is really useful to know what the threshold for success is in advance.

It is also critical to know what is *off limits* and to understand the implications of the boundaries to the solution set. In the salmon case, we knew that grassroots advocacy campaigns could not be a primary strategy, with a similar conclusion for large-scale direct policy efforts, given the foundation's lower level of comfort with these approaches.

Let's turn to the problem statement itself. One of the reasons the foundation selected saving Pacific salmon as one of its first granting programs was the apparent fit with the foundation's filter of measurability, a deeply held core value. After all, you can count fish, right? You can see this coming: It turns out it is a little harder than it looks.

There are five different Pacific salmon species spread around the Pacific Rim from California through British Columbia, Alaska, Russia's Kamchatka and Sakhalin regions, all the way to Japan. Some species are doing well in some places, many not so well. And overall numbers go up and down each year due to a number of factors. One of the biggest of these are ocean conditions that lead to more or less of the smaller creatures that salmon eat; these follow a rough temporal pattern related to ocean temperatures called the *Pacific Decadal Oscillation*. While that sounds like a fancy bit of climatology, in fact it meant that it was very difficult to separate and account for the causes of interannual variation in salmon numbers. In short, salmon aren't easy to count, and it isn't easy to determine in strict numerical terms what the positive or negative impact is of a new policy or fisheries management program, or a new bit of protected habitat. For the team, that meant measurement would have to be over longer periods of time, making estimates of the impact of uncontrollable factors like ocean productivity.

As the team understanding of the issues grew via early analysis and work with potential grantees, the problem statement evolved and improved. Most importantly, the team added more emphasis on maintaining salmon stock diversity and full functioning of all the elements of the ecosystem. Stock diversity means all the different ways smaller populations of the same kind of salmon use the rivers and oceans, eating different food and migrating at different times and on different routes. Diversity in the structure of the different sub-stocks helps the overall population weather environmental shocks better, and so contributes to long-run abundance. Exhibit 2.3 gives

SALMON PROBLEM STATEMENT EVOLUTION

	Statement	Positives	Critique
First cut	To substantially and sustainably increase the number of wild Pacific salmon	» Simple » Appears measurable	» Measurability is challenging » Ignores importance of species diversity » Doesn't link to full ecosystem health » Specific enough?
Second cut	To have a substantial and measurable impact on the long-term sustainability of the wild Pacific salmon, and ensure that the northern Pacific Rim watersheds that they inhabit remain diverse and well-functioning ecosystems	» Expressed in outcomes » Indicates importance » Aims for long term » You can count fish	» Ecosystem or species program? » Salmon numbers alone don't provide threshold: how much is enough? When are we done?
Third cut	Maintain a well-functioning salmon ecosystem at the scale of the North Pacific by preserving the potential for salmon populations to fully utilize the naturally fluctuating carrying capacity of the ocean	» Identifies specific natural mechanism for answering threshold question » Meets the other foundation criteria » Ties ecosystem and species survival together	» Carrying capacity is not scientifically understood yet » Can be overwhelmed by other factors

EXHIBIT 2.3

a flavor of that evolution and an assessment of the quality of these problem statements. As you can see, one of the ways of addressing the challenges of counting salmon is to introduce the notion of sufficient populations to make use of available ocean-carrying capacity, a measure driven by food availability and habitat. This sets a bar for healthy salmon numbers as the abundance and diversity of subspecies to utilize all of the available ocean capacity, and is a much more useful concept than plain numbers in any one year.

Each of these problem statements reflects the foundation salmon team's greater and greater understanding of the problem as it iterated the process with salmon management agencies, tribal groups, commercial fishing organizations, sport angler groups, salmon scientists and the conservation community. Constant iteration allows the team to hone its understanding and therefore to sharpen its strategies to achieve the desired outcome—at the same time keeping all the stakeholders onside as the process runs through time.

This evolution also points to a discussion within the foundation on the right level of aspiration to aim for. A narrower *regional* program focused primarily on salmon *management* might have been quicker to gain progress compared to a full north Pacific ecosystem level program, but also would have had less impact on the overall environment and human and ecosystem well-being. A narrower framing might also have made it more difficult to generate fundamental shifts in public attitudes toward conservation, and more challenging to attract funding from other foundations. On the other hand, any of these frames still bears the risk of being overwhelmed by bigger global environmental threats, such as climate change.

Defining the Highest-Level Problem: Steel Company Investments

The point of this is to find the right *scale and scope* in problem definition for your organization. When we worked for McKinsey, we often saw problems that benefited from redefinition to a higher level. For example, in one instance Rob's team was asked to review a $6 billion capital equipment investment plan for a large steel company. It looked straightforward: Evaluate the costs and benefits of each investment over time. But when they dug into the data, they discovered that the larger issue was one of an inability to generate cash because of an uncompetitive cost position, a much more pressing issue than the planned investments in new plant and machinery. The team's findings convinced the client to first address costs and attack the lack of cash generation by the business. They needed to lower overhead costs substantially and select only a fraction of the projects slated for investment to be successful. With these changes, the business was able to generate cash to survive.

When possible, it is advantageous to allow flexibility in the scope or width of your problem solving project. This gives rooms for the kind of discovery described in Rob's Australian steel client. But just as important, it also provides room for creative and novel solutions. Narrowly scoped projects make for fast problem solving, but they often lead to keeping the blinders on by employing conventional conceptions of the problem space. Breakthrough ideas are unlikely to emerge with old models and framing. People often wonder at the idea that newly minted MBAs employed by consulting firms can add value to organizations with veteran management teams. The answer lies in the fresh perspectives that new eyes and new analytic approaches can bring to old problems.

One of the other important principles in problem definition is to solve the problem at the *highest level* possible. The insight here is that the most granular and local solutions are often not optimal for the larger organization. In business, you often find this issue in doing capital allocation and investment decisions at the business unit level. You find what makes sense for a single unit is not what makes sense for the company overall. Wherever you can, target your problem solving efforts at the highest level at which you can work, rather than solving for the interests only of smaller units. In Rob's steel example the client wanted to solve for the right capital budget, but the higher-level problem definition was their ability to generate free cash flow to convince shareholders to reinvest in the business.

Similarly, Charles's salmon team learned that smaller regional approaches didn't work very well because salmon migrate through other regions and congregate in common far ocean feeding grounds. Solutions to reduce commercial fishing or choose more selective gear types in one area could be undone by increased fishing pressure in others. The north Pacific scale was the right scale to work this problem.

Widening the Aperture on the Problem: The Avahan HIV Project in India

Good problem definition or framing can have a huge positive impact as we have shown in our examples. The success of the Avahan HIV program in India was only achieved after a substantial reframing and rescoping. We describe in the sidebar below just how important improving the lens of problem definition can be—it ended up reducing HIV infections by a staggering 600,000 over a decade. The team followed the traditional public health (or supply side) approach at first, which led to some insights, but balanced it with what became a breakthrough effort on the demand or consumer side, in this case by involving sex workers in developing the solution. As a result of early testing of a hypothesis, the team was able to agree on a toolkit for replication across India, one that built in processes for community engagement and included the voices of sex workers that were often not heard. Exhibit 2.4 shows another example of "porpoising" between the problem statement, hypotheses, and the data, to arrive at the most accurate problem statement.

FRAMING THE PROBLEM
REDUCING HIV INFECTIONS IN INDIA

In 2003 the Bill and Melinda Gates Foundation funded the Avahan India AIDS Initiative in response to growing concern about the spread of HIV infections in India. Ten years later Lancet Global Health researchers estimated the interventions prevented over 600,000 HIV infections.[1] Framing the problem played a major role in the success of the Avahan Initiative.

The Avahan team, led by former McKinsey senior partner Ashok Alexander, reframed the problem in terms of supply and demand. They conducted field analysis to understand behavioral and causal factors and implemented actions with a strong emphasis on communications at the community level.

As Ashok put it: "We wanted to strengthen the public health approach (supply). Besides raising awareness, we were emphasizing data use by front line health workers—in effect, knowing how many condoms to distribute. We were simultaneously making efforts on the demand side, enabling workers to come together in groups to campaign for common issues such as safety. In business language, this amounted to creating a more active, aware consumer, and the demand side gathered momentum."[2]

The team then turned to the demand side and asked the sex workers for their views on the spread of HIV. They cited all too frequent examples of violence occurring with men demanding unprotected sex. The team was able to show a high correlation between violence and sexually transmitted infections (STIs). Ashok Alexander and his Avahan team saw this as a breakthrough in the work. The team then explored how they could reduce the violence perpetrated on the women. Their answer was rapid response teams of community workers, often accompanied by a lawyer and reporter from the local newspaper. The approach "went viral," as Ashok put it, as communities all over India embraced the intervention piloted in the Avahan Initiative.

Bill Gates, in his letter to Warren Buffett in early 2017,[2] wrote, "It's well documented that the decision of India's sex workers to insist on condom use for their clients kept HIV from breaking into the general population." The Lancet Global Health researchers also pointed to "a large scale increase in consistent condom use in high-risk groups since the start of the Avahan program." Importantly, they could have also added a commensurate reduction in violence against women alongside the huge reduction in HIV infections.

---

[1] Lancet Global Health article by Michael Pickles et al...
[2] Personal communication with Ashok Alexander.
[3] Gates Notes.com/2017 Annual Letter.

EXHIBIT 2.4

Porpoising to Get the Problem Statement Right

Problem statements keep on getting better when facts are brought to bear to sharpen the problem definition. We find that setting up a dialogue with questions that have to be answered is key to getting the required sharpness in problem definition. As an example, Rob was asked to help a team look at the issue of underinvestment in capacity building by nonprofits, a key finding of an enquiry by the Australian Government Productivity Commission. He asked the following questions:

1. Is it true of all or some nonprofits?

2. Is it true of large or small organizations?

3. Is it likely due to funding available or priorities?

4. Is it true for all nonprofit sectors or some?

5. Is the underinvestment in operations effectiveness or managing complex systems?

Some of these questions could be answered with known data but others required a perspective gained from interviewing sector leaders. The team was able to conclude that the issue of underinvestment was true for most but not all nonprofits; it was particularly the case for small organizations with less than fifty employees; it was due to the fact that nonprofits had little discretionary funding for capacity building; it was more acute in sectors where the service delivery model was in question; and, finally, underinvestment was especially the case in managing complex systems, even if capacity building for operations effectiveness was also underfunded. The resulting reworded problem statement went from a very broad statement to one that targeted nonprofits that had resourcing difficulties to fund capacity building, and a specific need to update delivery models for a complex systems environment. Efforts to sharpen problem statements can pay off handsomely. In the next chapter we show the link between good problem statements and good hypotheses to test. You won't be surprised to learn that sharp problem statements lead to better and more testable hypotheses.

Design Thinking and Seven Steps

One of the most common problem statements we come across relates to the *user experience*. Design thinking has developed as a powerful tool for problem solvers tackling consumer needs and the user experience, often in product or service design situations, but also outside those areas where creativity in problem solving is important to good outcomes. We are often asked where design thinking sits in relation to our seven-steps analytic problem solving process. We believe it is both consistent and complementary, especially in cases where an understanding of the user experience is essential. We present cases in the book where the user experience is at the core of problem solving and lends itself to design thinking, such as our cases on where to live, HIV in India, and whether to have knee arthroscopy surgery.

Design thinking is typically presented as a process, much like the seven steps, but with slightly different stages: empathize, define, ideate, build, test, and deliver. These six steps are illustrated in Exhibit 2.5 below as an iterative and fluid process. While the methodology is laid out in what seems like a gated, sequential process, the steps are usually not linear—they can happen in parallel and steps can be iterated and repeated as insight grows.

There are clear parallels between our steps and design thinking: The *empathize* and *define* steps correspond closely to the problem statement approach; the ideate step is akin to our process to break down a problem around hypotheses and then test; and the build and deliver steps correspond to our work planning and analysis steps. As in our approach, design thinking is highly iterative, revisiting earlier stages as knowledge accumulates.

By formalizing the methodology and values of designers, design thinking allows teams to use the creative problem solving process to find innovative solutions. A *user-centered approach* is fundamental to this kind of problem solving, where a significant amount of time is spent empathizing with and understanding the user and their "pain points." This is done through patient, sustained interactions over time, including interviewing, observing, and researching. We like the idea of integrating design thinking into the seven-steps approach, especially when novel and creative ideas are critical to the solution.

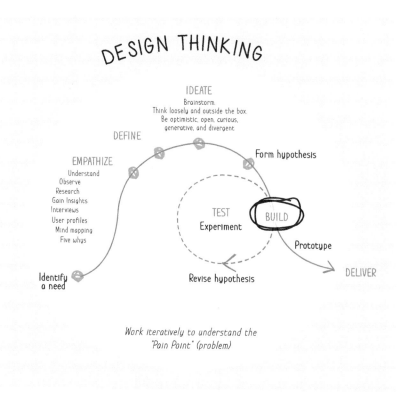

DESIGN THINKING

IDEATE
Brainstorm.
Think loosely and outside the box.
Be optimistic, open, curious,
generative, and divergent

DEFINE

EMPATHIZE
Understand
Observe
Research
Gain Insights
Interviews
User profiles
Mind mapping
Five whys

Form hypothesis

TEST
Experiment

BUILD

Prototype

Identify
a need

Revise hypothesis

DELIVER

Work iteratively to understand the
"Pain Point" (problem)

EXHIBIT 2.5

Design thinking usually starts with understanding the potential user's needs. Thus, the first step of the design thinking methodology is empathizing with the people you want to serve, learning what their needs are, recognizing why the product or solution could be relevant, and how it will be used within their everyday life. The cycle to empathize and then build-test-redefine, and build-test-redefine again, is based on an idea that you don't have to make decisions based on historical data and instinct. Rather, decisions can evolve, based on evidence from users' reactions to successful or failed prototypes. Design thinking methodology that focuses on user understanding, research, and iterating with prototypes, is a powerful tool to use in conjunction with the seven-steps problem solving approach, especially in the consumer/product space.

Putting effort into problem definition pays off. It gives you a smart start and an efficient process. Iterative re-cuts of the problem definition are highly valuable. And finding ways to challenge problem framing and scope will give you greater creativity in your solutions.

Chapter 2 Takeaways

- Defining the problem well is the starting point for great problem solving. If you don't get it right, you risk wasting your time and having an unhappy decision maker. There is an adage that says "a well-defined problem is a problem half solved"; it's worth the investment of time upfront.
- Problem definition is more than just your problem statement; you need to know the boundaries of the problem, the timeframe for solution, the accuracy required, and any other forces affecting the decision.
- Try a challenging antithesis or counterfactual to test the robustness of the problem statement. It may be around customer behavior, competitor reaction, or regulator stance on an issue.
- You should iterate and refine your problem statement as you porpoise into the data and learn more about the problem
- Bring creativity into problem definition by widening the aperture, relaxing constraints, and adding diversity to your team.
- Try to add elements of design thinking at this stage, particularly by adding active empathy for the user or decision maker.

Problems to Try on Your Own

1. Take your number one organization priority for this year and write it as a problem statement. Then test it against the criteria for a good problem statement. How different would it be if you wrote it from the CEO's perspective? Or a competitor?

2. List the top three issues in your part of the world, such as environmental decline, crime rates, employment, opioid abuse; try

preparing a problem statement for one. Set out the facts and analysis you need to know about the problem. Spend an hour collecting facts through online research and some phone calls. Then redo the problem statement as a second cut.

3. Define the problem with your banking relationship. What are the pain points in your user experience? How might they be alleviated through product or process changes?

4. Dream up an unmet consumer need and run it through the design thinking cycle.

Chapter Three

Problem Disaggregation and Prioritization

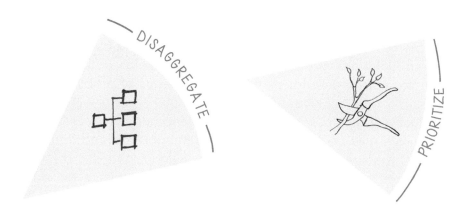

DISAGGREGATE

PRIORITIZE

Introduction

Good problem disaggregation is at the heart of the seven steps process. Any problem of real consequence is too complicated to solve without breaking it down into logical parts that help us understand the *drivers or causes* of the situation. So this is the most important step in problem solving: taking the problem apart in a way that helps us see the potential pathways to solve it. At the same time, when we can see all the parts clearly, we can determine what *not* to work on, the bits that are either too difficult to change, or that don't impact the problem much. When you get good at cleaving problems apart, insights come quickly. The magic comes in seeing which type of logic tree makes an elegant solution more obvious. It is like a plan to cut a diamond—doing it the right way really matters.

The diamond-cutting analogy is fun. But there is a risk in it. It makes the problem of cleaving seem too difficult, like it is a task for experts only. In truth, any of us can get started with an online literature review of the facets of the problem to generate ideas. This brainstorming on the shape and elements of the problem leads to an elemental logic tree to begin to cleave the problem open.

In this chapter we will cover the use of logic trees to disaggregate problems, keep track of the parts for analysis, and build insights toward solutions. We will introduce several kinds of logic trees that are appropriate for earlier or later stages of problem solving, or for different kinds of problems, including factor/lever trees, deductive logic trees, hypothesis trees, and decision trees. Some problems give up their answers in straightforward and intuitive ways. Others require more patience to yield insight. This chapter will cover the use of cleaving frameworks or heuristics for individual, organization, and social level problems that may help crack tougher problems more quickly and elegantly. We will then talk about prioritization of problem elements to prune off branches of the tree that don't contribute enough to the answer to spend time on. And finally we'll talk about team and solo processes that make disaggregation and prioritization easier and less prone to decision-making biases.

Types of Logic Trees: Getting Started

Logic trees are really just structures for seeing the elements of a problem in a clear way, and keeping track of different *levels* of the problem, which we liken to trunks, branches, twigs, and leaves. You can arrange them from left to right, right to left, or top to bottom—whatever makes the elements easier for you to visualize. There are lots of ways to do it; in fact, we almost always try two or three alternative disaggregations to discover which yields the most insights. Think of a logic tree as a mental model of your problem. Better trees have a clearer and more complete logic of relationships linking the parts to each other, are more comprehensive, and have no overlaps—but we'll get to all that.

Here is a simple example of tree construction: The task of planning to build a brick wall can be seen as either a *process* or as the sum of its *components*—both yield different insights and are helpful for visualizing the task of building the wall (see Exhibit 3.1).

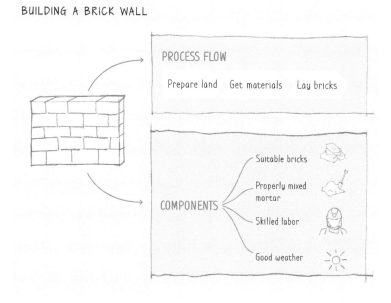

MANY WAYS TO DISAGGREGATE A PROBLEM
BUILDING A BRICK WALL

PROCESS FLOW

Prepare land   Get materials   Lay bricks

COMPONENTS
- Suitable bricks
- Properly mixed mortar
- Skilled labor
- Good weather

EXHIBIT 3.1

Exhibit 3.2 shows a number of different tree structures we have found useful in practice, and a sense of when they are best employed. Early on in the process we usually employ component or factor trees, and often work inductively (learning from specific cases that illuminate general principles later), to help us define basic problem structure. Later, after some iterations with data and analysis, we usually move to hypothesis trees, deductive logic

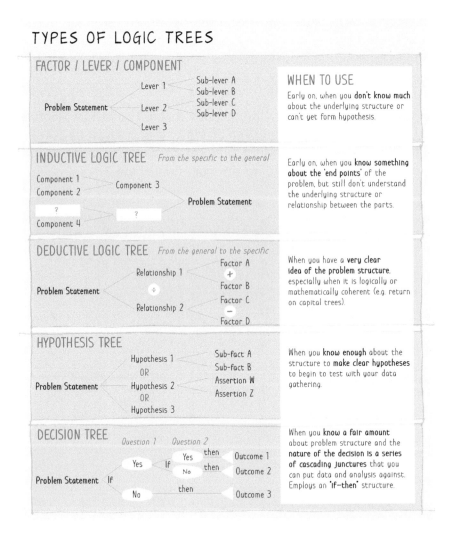

EXHIBIT 3.2

trees, or decision trees, depending on the nature of the problem. The only rule here is to move when you can from trees with general problem elements to trees that state clear hypotheses to test; vague labels do not drive analysis or action—which is the whole point.

At the very beginning, when you are able to state your problem clearly but don't yet have a detailed understanding of the problem to provide a vantage point on the solution, it usually makes sense to employ the simplest kind of tree, a component or factor tree. The goal in building logic trees is to find the levers that help us crack our problem, starting with the components that can help focus data gathering and eventually move us toward good hypotheses that can be tested. Components or factors are just the most obvious elements that make up a problem, like the bricks and mortar of our earlier brick wall example. You can usually find enough information for a logical first disaggregation with a small amount of Internet research and a team brainstorming session. Let's look at a case study to make this clearer.

Case Study: Saving Pacific Salmon—From Initial Component Tree to Refined Hypothesis Tree

Exhibit 3.3 shows an example of this kind of component or lever tree from Charles's work in salmon conservation, first introduced in Chapter 2. This tree was developed very early in the process, when the foundation he worked for knew it was committed to working on the problem, but didn't have a grasp of all the elements and relationships that defined the problem space.

So the team developed a rudimentary component tree to begin to get a handle on the problem. To get to this stage we read everything we could find about salmon and talked to a number of experts in salmon conservation. That involved days of work, not weeks—our experience is that you should only do enough initial research to generate a first-cut tree, since the tree structure will act as a guide to make further research more efficient.

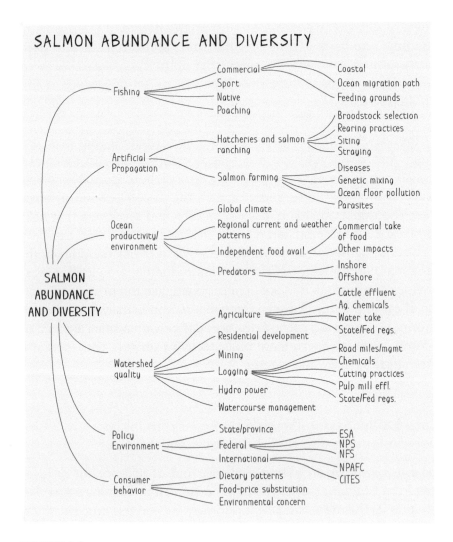

SALMON ABUNDANCE AND DIVERSITY

SALMON ABUNDANCE AND DIVERSITY

- Fishing
  - Commercial
    - Coastal
    - Ocean migration path
    - Feeding grounds
  - Sport
  - Native
  - Poaching
- Artificial Propagation
  - Hatcheries and salmon ranching
    - Broodstock selection
    - Rearing practices
    - Siting
    - Straying
  - Salmon farming
    - Diseases
    - Genetic mixing
    - Ocean floor pollution
    - Parasites
- Ocean productivity/ environment
  - Global climate
  - Regional current and weather patterns
  - Independent food avail.
    - Commercial take of food
    - Other impacts
  - Predators
    - Inshore
    - Offshore
- Watershed quality
  - Agriculture
    - Cattle effluent
    - Ag. chemicals
    - Water take
    - State/Fed regs.
  - Residential development
  - Mining
  - Logging
    - Road miles/mgmt
    - Chemicals
    - Cutting practices
    - Pulp mill effl.
    - State/Fed regs.
  - Hydro power
  - Watercourse management
- Policy Environment
  - State/province
  - Federal
  - International
    - ESA
    - NPS
    - NFS
    - NPAFC
    - CITES
- Consumer behavior
  - Dietary patterns
  - Food-price substitution
  - Environmental concern

EXHIBIT 3.3

As you can see, this first-cut tree is busy. It helps us see the big levers that affect salmon, but it doesn't have much insight coming through yet, since it is still at the component level, without clear hypotheses. We knew freshwater watershed quality and ocean environmental conditions would be important to Pacific salmon abundance and diversity, as would be the impact of commercial and other fisheries, hatcheries and fish farms, consumer behavior, and government policy. We could see some of the secondary and tertiary layers of the problem, but we didn't have a strong sense of importance or magnitude of any lever, or which ones our grant funding could affect. So we weren't in a position to develop hypotheses to guide our data gathering, analysis, and prioritization. But we did have a good list of factors affecting salmon, and we did have several layers of interventions mapped out. This gave the team better direction for the next stage of research and relationship building in salmon country. It was a good start, but only a start.

This first stage component tree for Pacific salmon is deficient in a number of other ways as well. It doesn't address the substantial regional differences in which factors are important. It doesn't show any sense of the magnitude impact of each lever. And it creates a significant confusion in the government policy element, which is shown as a separate topic area, rather than as it truly plays out by affecting *each* lever from watershed protections to fisheries to artificial propagation.

It is worth stopping here for a moment to introduce an important principle in logic tree construction, the concept of *MECE*. MECE stands for "mutually exclusive, collectively exhaustive." Because this tree confuses or overlaps some of its branches, it isn't MECE. It's a mouthful, but it is a really useful concept.

Trees should have branches that are:

Mutually Exclusive *and*	The branches of the tree don't overlap, or contain partial elements of the same factor or component. This is a little hard to get your head around, but it means that the core concept of each trunk or branch of the problem is self-contained, not spread across several branches.
Collectively Exhaustive	Taken as a whole, your tree contains *all* of the elements of the problem, not just some of them. If you are missing parts, you may very well miss the solution to your problem.

Exhibit 3.4 provides a way of seeing it visually.

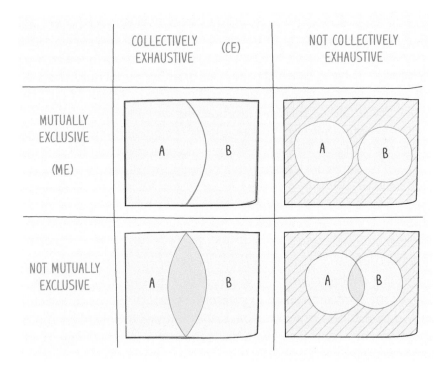

EXHIBIT 3.4

To give an example related to our Truckgear competition case from Chapter 1, if you are evaluating retailer performance with a return on capital tree, you put existing store sales on a different branch than new store sales to be mutually exclusive; to be collectively exhaustive you make sure your tree includes all sources of sales, including existing stores, new stores, and online sales. If you are having trouble getting clear hypotheses out of your tree, check to see if it is really MECE.

Constant iteration is key to making the seven steps work. After Charles's team had done a literature review, they met with many experts, forging relationships on the ground with conservation organizations, government agencies, policy personnel, fishers, and First Nations leadership. They commissioned exploratory science work with salmon researchers, and were able to refine their salmon tree and transition from a simple, components visualization to a hypothesis tree. As you can see from Exhibit 3.5, this tree is better organized and MECE, with more active questions. And it has focused the team's analysis on both specific regions and intervention types. These were not very specific hypotheses at this

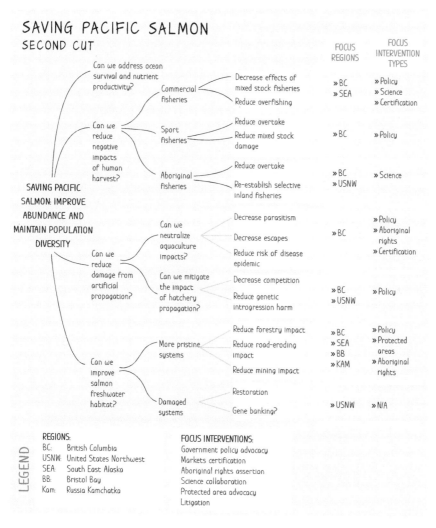

EXHIBIT 3.5

stage, but they allowed the team to work with its new partners to develop a set of initial grants to push some early outcomes (which included a ban on expansion of salmon farming further north in British Columbia) and promoted greater Foundation understanding in what became a 15-year, $275m effort to help preserve Pacific salmon. At a later stage, which will be discussed in this chapter, the team was able to prune off some lower impact or higher difficulty branches of the tree, which helped focus its problem solving on high-potential outcomes.

Deductive Logic Trees

Deductive logic trees take their name from the process of logical deduction. Deductive reasoning is sometimes called top–down reasoning, because when we apply it we argue from *general* rules or principles to conclusions via more specific data and assertions. A classic kind of deductive statement is structured like this:

- General statement: All watchmakers need glasses.
- Specific observation: Sally is a watchmaker.
- Deductive conclusion: Sally needs glasses.

Deductive logic trees are constructed similarly, with a problem statement that may sometimes be expressed in quantities, and branches that are typically logically or mathematically complete, so that the components add up to the desired objective of the problem statement. We use this kind of tree when we know a lot about the logical structure of a problem, and especially when the cleaving frame is inherently mathematical, as we saw with the return on profit levers tree in Chapter 1. A more sophisticated version of this includes the investment costs of different actions, not just the impact on profitability.

Why analyze return on invested capital? Return on invested capital (ROIC) signals how well a company can turn investments into profit. Arithmetically it is the product of two components: profit margin (sometimes called return on sales) and capital turnover (the ratio of sales to invested capital). ROIC is useful for comparing firms by understanding the levers affecting the return on company assets, irrespective of ownership structure (debt and equity) and excess cash. If you are interested in business problems, learn this tree. The next case study focuses on the use of a return on capital tree to understand the competition between two businesses. You can also find a more generic example in Exhibit 3.9.

Case Study: Battle of the Hardware Kings: Hechinger versus Home Depot

As industries change, business models are tested through tough competition and market disruption. Through the use of a ROIC tree, Charles was able to determine which levers were driving the profitability and growth of two competitors in the hardware industry. Charles worked for a consulting company that was hired by Hechinger Hardware to develop an expansion plan into new markets. The problem definition step revealed that in order to successfully expand, the business had to be able to withstand the competition of its rising peers. This tree helped the team he was on discover that an epic battle was brewing. Here is the story.

Hechinger Hardware opened its first hardware store in 1919, focusing its marketing strategy on the retail consumer, rather than contractors, fueling the growth of the do-it-yourself hardware business. While it had begun slowly expanding across its first half century, the family-owned company planned for more rapid expansion after going public in 1972. At that time the hardware industry was growing at nearly 12% annually, more than two times the US economy, and rising home prices increased homeowners' attention to upkeep and continuous improvement of their homes.

> The Company [Hechinger] has an enviable track record, including 39 consecutive quarters of positive earnings per share comparisons . . .
>
> *Alex Brown and Sons Analyst Report, FY1984*

With strong performance and promising industry predictions, Hechinger was looking to expand into new markets. It had

$130 million of cash available for expansion on its books and strong employee seniority—150 managers across the chain had nine years or more of experience—so company management felt confident in their ability to build market share.

However, the consulting team's analysis uncovered a problem for Hechinger that it didn't see coming. A small southern competitor, Home Depot, had opened three new warehouse-style stores starting in 1979, a novel idea. In contrast to Hechinger's spotless stores, extensive backrooms for inventory storage, and relatively high prices, Home Depot built a warehouse hardware superstore model intended for both retail shoppers and contractors. Going public in 1981 they began to rapidly expand from their Atlanta base, coincident with Hechinger's expansion from Washington, DC, setting up a showdown. While Hechinger undoubtedly had excellent management and a strong record of historical success, at the time they didn't see that Home Depot was changing the industry's competitive dynamic.

Faced with a competitive player in a number of promising expansion markets, Charles and his team set to work with a comparative analysis of Hechinger and Home Depot and were startled by what they found: What appeared to be similar businesses externally were radically different internally. To do this problem solving the team employed a return on invested capital tree, which turned out to be a powerful problem solving tool. What it showed is that while return on capital was similar for the two businesses, the drivers of success were different. Using publicly available accounting data, Exhibit 3.6 shows:

- Home Depot had lower overheads and lower costs of goods sold, but it also had lower gross margins (selling price minus cost of goods)—it was following a low-cost/low-price strategy.
- Home Depot had much higher asset productivity, meaning it generated more sales per dollar invested, including higher sales per square foot of store space and higher inventory turns.
- Home Depot was growing much faster, although it was of similar size in 1983.

RETURN ON INVESTED CAPITAL ANALYSIS
HECHINGER VS. HOME DEPOT

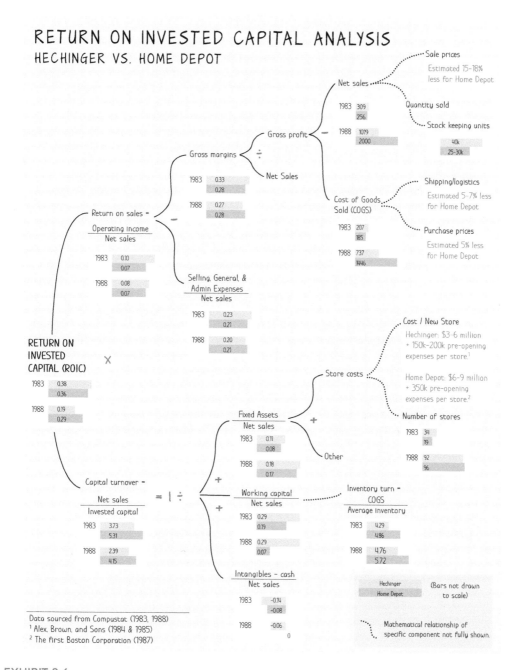

Data sourced from Compustat (1983, 1988)
[1] Alex, Brown, and Sons (1984 & 1985)
[2] The first Boston Corporation (1987)

EXHIBIT 3.6

Clearly, Home Depot was making up for lower margins by having lower overhead costs and higher asset productivity, generating a similar return to the long-established Hechinger. The team decided to dig deeper. What it discovered was remarkable. Home Depot was growing so quickly because it had *much* lower prices. Charles's team conducted secret shopper pricing analysis and found that Home Depot's prices were 15 to 18% lower for comparable products. How could it possibly operate at such low prices?

The ROIC tree was the central framework to guide the analysis. What the team learned was that Home Depot had built a state of the art inventory management system, and had developed a store design that housed inventory on 20-foot racks on the retail floor (versus Hechinger's 8-foot racks), therefore doing without backroom storage and labor intensive restocking. Moreover, instead of storing goods mainly in a central company warehouse, it negotiated with suppliers to direct ship to Home Depot stores, or cross-dock goods (a procedure in which a truck from a supplier is quickly unloaded and the goods go straight to store delivery trucks without being double handled). The team estimated that Home Depot was able to operate with 5–7% less shipping and logistics costs than Hechinger, and negotiate as much as 5% lower costs for the same goods by concentrating volume on orders of fewer retail items (sometimes called stock keeping units, or SKUs).

> Cross-docking or breaking up manufacturers' shipments to go to the various stores is undertaken on a small scale, but for the most part, suppliers are more than willing to drop ship to the stores because the individual locations order by the trailer load. Home Depot's average sales per store run around $20 million, or more than double Hechinger's or Builders Square's.
>
> *Analyst report, The First Boston Corporation*

So Home Depot was generating the same return on invested capital, but able to make up for much lower prices with a combination of lower distribution costs, cheaper sourcing, lower store and central overheads, and much higher asset productivity. Lower prices were driving much higher sales per store and a much higher company growth rate. Trouble had quickly arrived for Hechinger: Could it adopt some of Home Depot's competitive practices and regain its regional lead based on its strong brand?

Although Hechinger tried to lower its costs and increase its asset productivity, over time the differences magnified, and by 1988 the businesses had diverged (see Exhibit 3.7). Home Depot's sales were accelerating as it opened new markets and drove nearly twice the sales per store than Hechinger, and its asset productivity continued to climb.

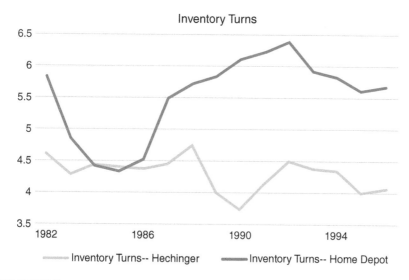

EXHIBIT 3.7

As Hechinger tried to compete with Home Depot's prices, they offered sales and promotions, but—despite the acquisition of Home Quarters, a similar warehouse chain—the company failed to make the deep business model changes required to compete. With new entry on many fronts across 19 states, including their long-time, dominant Washington, DC home market, they began to close stores. By 1997 Hechinger was out of business[1] (see Exhibit 3.8).

---

[1]Margaret Webb Pressler, "The Fall of the House of Hechinger," *Washington Post*, July 21, 1997.

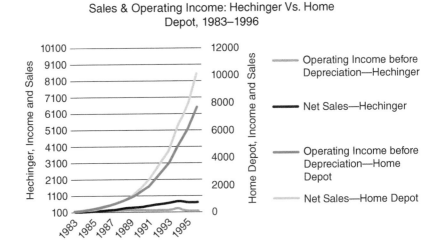

EXHIBIT 3.8

The return on capital tree shows the fundamental differences in business models that led to this competitive result. It demonstrates the value of a component disaggregation problem solving approach applied in a business setting.

Exhibit 3.9 is a more generalized version of a return on invested capital tree. We have expanded several branches out to highlight the levers that impact the return on capital metric that might help you with your other business problems.

In the hardware company comparison, the objective of the tree was return on invested capital, and the branches included profitability and asset productivity, drivers that mathematically led to the difference in operating and financial results between competitors Home Depot and Hechinger. This helped us understand the two companies' prospects in the market by highlighting how their two different business models ultimately led to different levels of financial success. (One thing to be careful about in using return on capital trees is that the definition of capital and profit typically employed is an accounting one (so subject to accounting rules on things like depreciation), rather than a cash or replacement cost

LEVERS THAT IMPACT RETURN ON INVESTED CAPITAL (ROIC)
IN A RETAIL BUSINESS

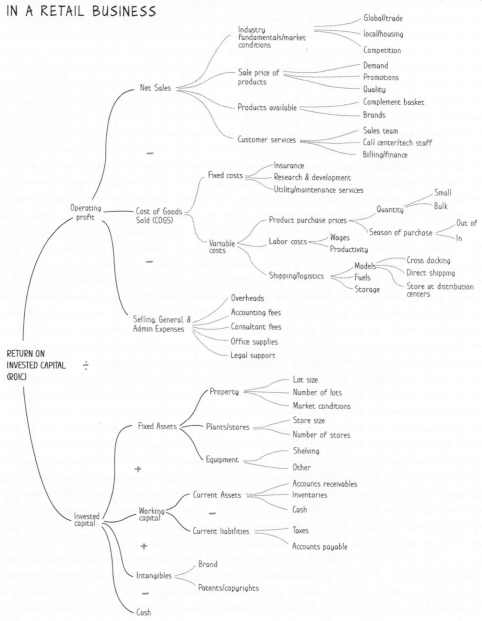

EXHIBIT 3.9

definition. You may benefit from cross-checking your numbers with a replacement cost calculation for core assets like stores and using cash profitability.)

Case Study: Bay Area Nursing Related Patient Outcomes

To show the clarity deductive logic trees can bring, let's introduce a new example, this time around improving nursing in hospitals in the San Francisco Bay Area. Charles observed a team working on this problem at the foundation he worked with. The team wanted to improve nursing-related patient outcomes in the Bay Area in California. Nurses provide upwards of 90% of patient care in hospitals. More than 100,000 lives a year are lost in the United States from mistakes in patient care from many sources, especially from sepsis, ventilator acquired pneumonia, hospital acquired infections, and medication errors. There is a substantial shortage of nurses in California and beyond, and studies show that for each patient added per registered nurse (RN), mortality rates increase. Every one of us has a lot to gain from making progress on this problem.

Early on in the project the team constructed a relatively straightforward deductive logic tree focused on increasing both the number of skilled nursing graduates, and on improving the skills and practices of existing RNs.

By developing this deductive logic tree, shown as Exhibit 3.10, and more sophisticated versions that followed, the foundation nursing team was able to focus its attention on the key drivers of nursing numbers and skill levels. This allowed the team to use data and analysis to determine which levers were most powerful in improving patient outcomes, and which were cost-effective to address. They developed a series of strategies to address these levers, including:

- Increasing the workforce of well-trained nurses via new nursing schools
- Implementing evidence-based nursing practices in hospitals
- Supporting frontline nursing leadership
- Improving patient transitions from hospitals

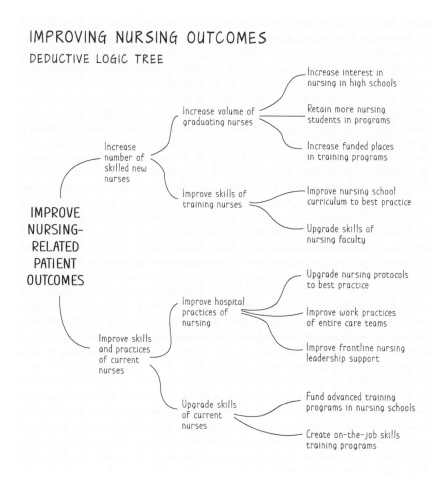

IMPROVING NURSING OUTCOMES
DEDUCTIVE LOGIC TREE

IMPROVE NURSING-RELATED PATIENT OUTCOMES

- Increase number of skilled new nurses
  - Increase volume of graduating nurses
    - Increase interest in nursing in high schools
    - Retain more nursing students in programs
    - Increase funded places in training programs
  - Improve skills of training nurses
    - Improve nursing school curriculum to best practice
    - Upgrade skills of nursing faculty
- Improve skills and practices of current nurses
  - Improve hospital practices of nursing
    - Upgrade nursing protocols to best practice
    - Improve work practices of entire care teams
    - Improve frontline nursing leadership support
  - Upgrade skills of current nurses
    - Fund advanced training programs in nursing schools
    - Create on-the-job skills training programs

EXHIBIT 3.10

After 12 years of investment in this challenging problem, the foundation's grants helped substantially increase the nursing supply in the Bay Area, with more than 4,500 RNs added, nursing school curriculums improved, bloodstream infections and readmissions rates reduced, and an estimated 1,000 lives saved a year from sepsis. Good problem solving matters.

Inductive Logic Trees

Inductive logic trees are the reverse of deductive logic trees. They take their name from the process of inductive reasoning, which works *from* specific observations *toward* general principles. Here is an example of inductive reasoning:

- Observation: Sally is a watchmaker and wears glasses.
- Observation: Shaun is a watchmaker and wears glasses.
- Observation: Steven is a watchmaker and wears glasses.
- Inductive assertion: Watchmakers typically wear glasses.

We employ inductive logic trees when we do not yet know much about the general principles behind the problems we are interested in, but we do have some data or insights into specific cases. Inductive trees show probabilistic relationships, not causal ones: Just because all the swans you have seen are white, does not mean all swans are white (there are black swans in Australia.[2]) In many cases you will actually work on your initial tree *both* inductively and deductively. You will have a sense of some of the bigger drivers and general principles, and you will have good case examples of successful projects in the space you are looking at. So you work both from the trunks of the tree *and* from the leaves, slowly and iteratively figuring out which is which.

Case Study: Dealing with Contested Historical Legacies—from Inductive Thinking to a Decision Tree

As we have seen in recent news stories focused on controversial statues and public monuments, there has been a lot of public interest in historical artifacts that chronicle or memorialize historical leaders whose views are out of step with current values, initially sparked by activism on university campuses, but now including municipalities and other institutions. As the head of the Rhodes Trust, one of many institutions with a complicated historical legacy, Charles had been grappling with these issues.

What Charles observed is a lot of ad hoc approaches to each historical artifact. Under pressure from interest groups and external commentators, institutional decision makers have been lurching from decision to decision, and often reversing course, with no

---

[2]See Nassim N. Taleb, *The Black Swan: The Impact of the Highly Improbable* (New York: Random House, 2007), for a deeply insightful discussion of probability and decision-making errors.

clear set of principles to guide their actions. Good moral reasoning requires, well, *reasons*, and Charles thought that the debate would be improved by developing some principles for how to deal with artifacts of historical characters. This is complicated by the fact that even our favorite historical characters held views that we would find abhorrent today. So the framework had to accommodate heroes, such as Frederick Douglass, Thomas Jefferson, Walt Whitman, and Gandhi, not just historical bad guys.

This turns out to be an important insight. The team began an inductive-reasoning exercise where we took a large range of historical characters about which there is rich information and even some agreement on how to assess them. For example, we compared Thomas Jefferson with the reputations of other presidents who owned slaves, and we looked at the legacies as varied as John C. Calhoun at Yale, to Aulus Plautius, the Roman general who invaded Britain in 43AD. By working backwards from how people think about individuals, the team began to tease out some general principles of judgment. At first all they had was a list of threshold questions that underpinned the judgments or assessments, but no clear hierarchy of what questions were most important, as seen in Exhibit 3.11.

ARTIFACTS AND CONTESTED CHARACTERS:
THRESHOLD QUESTIONS

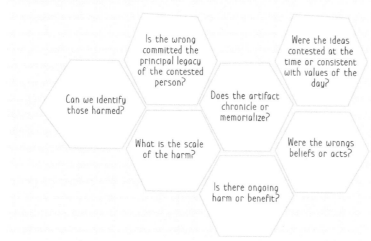

Is the wrong committed the principal legacy of the contested person?

Were the ideas contested at the time or consistent with values of the day?

Can we identify those harmed?

Does the artifact chronicle or memorialize?

What is the scale of the harm?

Were the wrongs beliefs or acts?

Is there ongoing harm or benefit?

EXHIBIT 3.11

After some intensive whiteboard sessions to figure out the hierarchy or order of the principles, the team came up with the following **decision tree** for how to address these artifacts of difficult historical legacies (see Exhibit 3.12).

ARTIFACTS AND CONTESTED CHARACTERS:
DEALING WITH DIFFICULT HISTORICAL LEGACIES

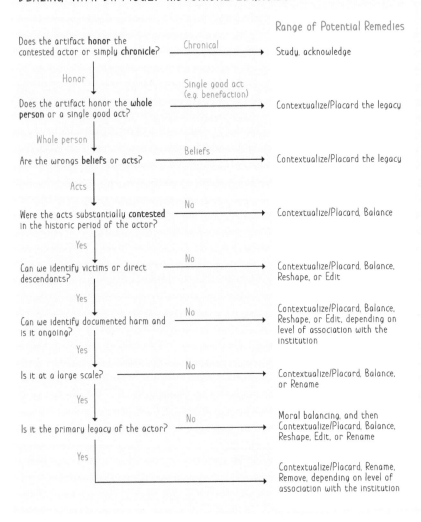

Range of Potential Remedies

Does the artifact **honor** the contested actor or simply **chronicle?** — *Chronicle* → Study, acknowledge

Honor ↓

Does the artifact honor the **whole person** or a single good act? — *Single good act (e.g. benefaction)* → Contextualize/Placard the legacy

Whole person ↓

Are the wrongs **beliefs** or acts? — *Beliefs* → Contextualize/Placard the legacy

Acts ↓

Were the acts substantially **contested** in the historic period of the actor? — *No* → Contextualize/Placard, Balance

Yes ↓

Can we identify victims or direct descendants? — *No* → Contextualize/Placard, Balance, Reshape, or Edit

Yes ↓

Can we identify documented harm and is it ongoing? — *No* → Contextualize/Placard, Balance, Reshape, or Edit, depending on level of association with the institution

Yes ↓

Is it at a large scale? — *No* → Contextualize/Placard, Balance, or Rename

Yes ↓

Is it the primary legacy of the actor? — *No* → Moral balancing, and then Contextualize/Placard, Balance, Reshape, Edit, or Rename

Yes ↓

→ Contextualize/Placard, Rename, Remove, depending on level of association with the institution

EXHIBIT 3.12

You may agree or disagree with the threshold questions and range of sanctions the team came up with,[3] but hopefully you find useful the idea of brainstorming some pragmatic principles by a combination of inductive reasoning about contested individuals and reference to historical philosophical maxims, and then using this output to generate a decision tree to guide action in a more systematic way.

Step 3: Prioritization—Pruning Your Logic Trees

Good problem solving is just as much about what you don't do as what you do, and good prioritization in problem solving makes solutions come faster and with less effort. We want our initial trees to be MECE, so that we know we have all the parts. But we don't want to retain elements of the disaggregation that have only a small influence on the problem, or that are difficult or impossible to affect. Before we start to invest significant time and effort into work planning and analysis, we have to prune our trees.

We have found the 2×2 matrix in Exhibit 3.13 to be a useful forcing device for prioritization of which levers to work on, here shown for the Pacific salmon case study. The left-hand axis is whether or not your efforts could have an impact on the problem lever or branch.

---

[3]*Remedy Definitions*

Contextualize/Placard: Leaves artifact in place, but tells the story of the actor's role in offensive acts.

Balancing: Brings into the physical or digital space the voices/images of others, including those wronged, may include balancing restorative justice actions.

Relocation: Removes the artifact, but to a place it can be studied.

Reshaping or editing: Original monument is left in place, but altered in a way to highlight offensive aspects.

Destroying or removing (as it sounds).

Renaming (as it sounds).

Moral Balancing: Applying a moral calculus to determine the principal legacy of the figure.

Reparations and/or restorative justice.

PRIORITIZATION

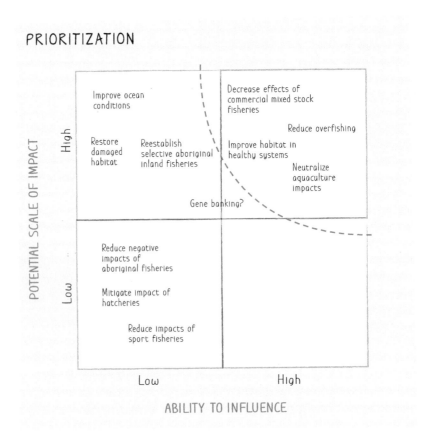

EXHIBIT 3.13

The bottom axis is how important that lever is in affecting the overall problem you are trying to solve, in this case the impact on salmon abundance and diversity.

As you can see from the matrix, some prioritization decisions are relatively straightforward: Even with the resources of a large foundation, our team couldn't hope to influence climactic conditions, which are the main driver of ocean productivity—providing the food for juvenile salmon at sea. Although this lever has a significant impact on salmon diversity and abundance, we have to lop it off.

Second, the impact of hatcheries and "ocean ranching" (putting artificially raised salmon into the ocean hoping they will return to be captured) is not insignificant—these fish compete with wild fish for food, and may cause genetic introgression via inbreeding—but in the initial cut at the problem we left it off our priority actions. While there is little evidence of net supplementation or cost-effective returns, hatcheries are big job providers and have huge support from indigenous groups and sports and commercial fishers. It is a tough lever to move.

As you will see in Exhibit 3.13, the team also did not prioritize investments to repair damaged ecosystems in the southern end of the salmon's range. We agonized over this decision, but the cost of restoration compared to the costs of protection of more pristine northern systems was not favorable. And the growing impact of climate change on water temperatures in these southern systems meant there was no guarantee of durability of any results.

In the spirit of iterating steps, it may also be valuable to revisit the problem context to see if relaxing constraints in the problem statement would make a difference to which branches you prune. As the Pacific salmon project progressed through its 15-year life, we did make targeted investments in limiting the spread and impact of hatcheries, although it never became a major focus. In general, problem definitions with tight constraints on the solution space yield answers more quickly, but sometimes at the expense of creativity. One approach is to relax each constraint and see if the solution set opens up in a substantial enough way to be worth the extra work, time, and investment required to make those options viable.[4]

Advanced Class: Using Cleaving Frames to Take Apart Problems

In the previous sections we explored different types of logic trees, the basic structures for problem disaggregation, and problem prioritization. We addressed cases early on in problem

---

[4]J. Hammond, R. Keeney, and H. Raiffa, *Smart Choices* (Broadway Books, 1999), 48–49.

solving where we only knew enough to break problems into basic factors or levers, or where we had to work inductively from specific cases to move toward general principles of understanding. And we examined problems where we had enough information to drive from specific hypotheses, where we could use deductive logic trees and decision trees. As we saw, there is no absolute right or wrong way to construct trees—aside from aiming for MECE trees—and tree types often overlap. Hypothesis trees can be deductive in logic, and inductive reasoning can generate effective decision trees.

Now we are going to take the conversation to the next level. Expert practitioners of problem solving often employ existing frameworks or theories to more quickly and elegantly cleave problems into insightful parts. We have seen an example of this already with the hardware company competitive battle case study that employed a particular kind of deductive logic tree, a return on capital tree. In fact many business problems benefit from this particular type of problem disaggregation, because it shows the levers of revenue (price, volume, market share), costs (fixed, variable, overheads), and asset utilization so clearly, and in mathematical relationship to each other. This kind of tree also makes "what if" competitive scenario analysis easy. For example, it is easy to model both niche and broad market product strategies, and for your team to debate how realistic the assumptions are that generate results. We often call this kind of work "what you have to believe" analysis.

Just as return on capital trees are often an incredibly insightful type of problem disaggregation for business problems, other theoretical constructs or frameworks can be powerful cleaving tools for other kinds of problems. Exhibit 3.14 shows a toolkit of what we call cleaving frames for different kinds of problem. Good problem solvers have toolkits like this that act as lenses to visualize potential solutions. They try on one or more theoretical frames to see which one is likely to be the best fit for the problem at hand. Often they combine more than one frame to make progress on particular

CLEAVING FRAMES
BUSINESS

Frame	Elements	Example
» Price/Volume	» Market share, awareness, trial, repurchase, elasticities	» Product entry strategies
» Collaborate/Compete	» Where to play, how to fight, acquiring a reputation, signalling	» Any competitive situations » CSIRO WiFi
» Market/Ability to compete	» Opportunity, competitive position, capabilities, resources	» Entry/start up » BHP
» Invest/Harvest	» Growth/Share, explore vs exploit, disruptive entrants	» Portfolio of activities » BHP
» Margins/Asset turns	» Return to capital, valuing options	» Business model construction » Home Depot–Hechinger
» Scale/Scope	» Size vs breadth	» Social media platforms
» Capital/Noncapital	» Rent, own, borrow, share, zero-basing	» Asset efficiency » Uber, Airbnb
» Principal/Agent	» Aligning incentives, monitoring	» Compensation, insurance, second-hand markets
» Asset/Options	» Valuing potential (real and potential), puts/calls	» Multi-play investment games
» Customer/ Shareholder	» Competing perspectives	

EXHIBIT 3.14

problems. Let's spend some time highlighting a few of these to make this notion clearer.

Continuing with the focus on business problems for a moment, many company performance and competition questions benefit from a series of frames that help highlight the likely solution paths quickly.

This list isn't meant to be exhaustive, as many problems combine elements from more than one frame. Some example frames:

- **Price/Volume**: One of the key elements of our return on capital tree is the revenue drivers branch that focuses on product pricing and volume. This frame raises questions about the nature of the competitive game: Are there differentiated products or commodities? Are there competitive markets or oligopoly markets controlled by a few players? Each has different dynamics and good business problem solvers build these into their disaggregation and research plans. The kinds of elements here often include assumptions about market share, new product entry, rate of adoption, and price and income elasticities.

- **Principal/Agent**: Principal/agent problems occur where certain activities are done by agents (think contractors or employees) on behalf of principals (think investors or managers), and are very common in business. At the core of this kind of problem is the need to create incentive structures to align the interest of the principal and the agent, when the principal has incomplete visibility or control over the work of the agent. The best structures provide good, checkable results for the investor and fair incomes for the contractor. It sounds easy but it isn't. This kind of problem appears not just in contracting situations, but also in any second-hand asset sale and in any insurance problem.

- **Assets/Options**: Every asset a company controls, or could purchase, creates options for future strategic moves that may have substantial value. Rob worked for an Australian mining company that asked his team to evaluate an investment in a particular property. What the team discovered was that the investment in the port and the railway infrastructure to exploit that particular property created hugely valuable options for a whole range of other sites. It made his client the "natural owner" (a powerful asset/option concept developed by Rob and another colleague John Stuckey) for other sites worth billions of dollars in option value. This case is outlined in more detail in Chapter 8.

- **Collaborate/Compete**: Any business strategy needs to take account of the potential reaction by rival firms. Each company needs to decide where it is willing to engage in intense competition (say based on pricing or large investments) and other cases where it is not, either because of the nature of the market or the nature of the other competitors. The tools and elements in this frame are those from game theory, and include concepts such as multi-play games and reputation. Our CSIRO Wifi example, shown later, employs this frame to decide whether to go to court to protect intellectual property.

At the level of societal problem solving, in the policy space, there are many other useful frames, shown here in Exhibit 3.15, most of which will be familiar to you.

CLEAVING FRAMES
SOCIAL / CITIZEN

Frame	Elements	Example
» Demand/Supply	» Can we get more? Use less.	» Water, CO_2 energy, traffic
» Incidence/Severity	» Social risk; type, level, and risk of harm	» Terrorism, health care, bird flu
» Create/Redistribute	» Incentive, produce vs. tax	» Tax, tax credits, capital gains, ownership
» Mitigate/Adapt	» Reduce harm, address harm, resilience	» Environment, climate change, violence, drug use
» Regulate/Incentives	» Market design, property rights, regulatory design	» Cap and Trade vs. carbon tax, water rights, in-stream reservation
» Equality/liberty	» Community needs, individual rights	» Gun control, drug policy

EXHIBIT 3.15

- **Regulate/Incent:** Policy makers often face the choice of adding legal regulation to address a problem, or using taxation, subsidies, or nudging policies that provide incentives for people or firms to adopt the desired behavior. This frame frequently comes into play around pollution and other externalities.

- **Equality/Liberty:** Many policy decisions to address social problems face the fundamental frame choice of encouraging more equality among citizens, versus allowing more individual freedom. All policies that involve taxing/spending have elements of this frame.
- **Mitigate/Adapt:** This frame contrasts policy efforts to reduce harm from some causal factor, with efforts to adapt to the factor. This is often the axis in the climate change debate.
- **Supply/Demand:** This frame addresses questions such as "Can we get more?" versus "How can we use less?" and is often the lens employed for dealing with problems like water supply, health care, and energy.

Case Study: Climate Change Abatement and the Cost Curve

Climate change is a particularly thorny problem and often is cleaved around mitigation and adaptation, or incidence and severity (think of Kiribati less than a meter above the ocean!). The cleave Charles and Rob think is particularly powerful is along demand/supply lines where the returns from, or costs of, abating CO_2 are shown by the type of activity and the tons abated. This is called a cost curve, and it reads from left (lower cost) to right (higher costs).[5]

What you see very quickly in Exhibit 3.16 is that there are a large number of abatement activities for which there are positive returns to private companies and individuals. This means that a huge amount of CO_2 reduction can occur with good education efforts and perhaps supporting tax credits for the investment costs. There is a second class of actions, mostly in the agriculture and land use space (reforestation, degraded land recovery, avoided deforestation), where the investment costs are relatively small compared to

---

[5]McKinsey & Company, *Pathways to a Low-Carbon Economy: Version 2 of the Global Greenhouse Gas Abatement Cost Curve*, September 2013.

the CO_2 reduction benefits. The third bucket captures actions that are longer term and that will require substantial private and social investment in new technology and markets. In our opinion, this cleaving frame provides a useful counterpoint to the mitigate/adapt lens on the problem. When we look only at individual (see Exhibit 3.17) or corporate carbon footprints, we often miss the opportunity to aggregate actions across players and achieve larger results.

CLEAVING THE PROBLEM
USING SUPPLY AND DEMAND

Global GHG Abatement Cost Curve beyond business as usual – 2013

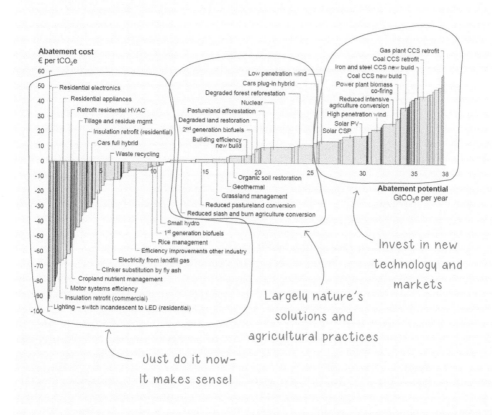

EXHIBIT 3.16

CLEAVING FRAMES
INDIVIDUAL

Frame	Elements	Example
» Work/Play	» Leisure vs. effort	» Choosing a career » Weight loss
» Near Term/Long term	» Spend vs. invest	» Education » Solar panels » Retirement savings
» Financial/Non-financial	» Values	» Where to live

EXHIBIT 3.17

Problem solving in the individual or personal space can also benefit from cleaving frames. Many of the frames we employ in businesses around investment decisions work equally well for personal decisions, such as Rob's solar panel decision. Other frames useful for personal problem solving include:

- **Work/Play:** How much/how long to work set against non-work interests (for example, when to retire and whether your savings are adequate).

- **Near term/Long term:** Another related category of personal decisions focuses on trading off relatively certain near term decisions (for example, investing in education) against longer-term and more uncertain future possibilities (what skills will be required in two decades?).

- **Financial/Non-Financial:** Another cleaving point around decisions like moving to a new house or changing jobs is those elements of the decision that are financial (how much do houses cost in the new city?) versus those that are non-financial (are the schools good enough?).

The most powerful way to reach a useful disaggregation of a problem is to start with a particular cleaving frame and then do some back of the envelope calculations to confirm that it would provide insight, as the CO_2 abatement cost curve so clearly does to support a supply/demand split.

In an example of this approach, Rob was arguing to his team at The Nature Conservancy Australia (TNCA) that they should focus on Western Sydney to assess the role of *urban green spaces* in asthma hospitalizations. His hypothesis, based on some early comparative data, was that parks and other green spaces led to lower incidence and severity of asthma. He decided to use the incidence/severity cleaving initially for no other reason than it was a familiar frame for accident and injury reporting on other boards he has served on. He had to make the case to the team that this cut on the asthma problem would be insightful. With available data he was able to show that Western Sydney warranted attention for the following reasons:[6]

1. The incidence of asthma was 10% higher for Western Sydney than Northern Sydney for adults 16 years and over. Australia has among the highest levels of asthma in the OECD.

2. The severity of asthma, measured by the hospitalization rate was 65% higher in Western Sydney and the death rate from asthma 54% higher—so incidence is higher, but severity is much higher.

3. Evidence pointed to a lack of urban green spaces as a potential driver of severity. Tree cover in Western Sydney was estimated at 15–20% compared to 30–40% in Northern Sydney. In addition, particulate matter levels (PM2.5 maximum) are 54% higher in Western Sydney. Tree respiration appears to play a role in absorbing particulate matter, a topic we illustrate in Chapter 6 in the case of London's air quality.

---

[6]*Health at a Glance 2017: OECD Indicators*, Health Stats NSW, EPA NSW, iTree assessment of canopy cover, Figure 6, UTS, Institute for Sustainable Futures, May 2014.

As a result, the team is developing an experimental design to systematically explore the green space issues raised by the incidence/severity cleaving.

Again, the point in all of this discussion of using theoretical frameworks or concepts to aid problem disaggregation is to find a cut through your problem that exposes insight. Different frames often yield different insights, so it makes sense to test several. And you can often try a social frame on a business problem, or vice versa. While it is always impressive to watch experienced problem solvers quickly disaggregate difficult problems into insightful chunks, there is also a risk in assuming "I have seen this one before, it is an X problem." We often see the world via mental models (another term for frames) that have worked for us before. When we encounter genuinely novel problems, we sometimes persist in using frames that are unhelpful or misleading in the new and different context. For centuries, astronomers thought the sun revolved around the earth, and scratched their heads when important navigation problems weren't easy to solve! The next section addresses team processes that can help speed problem solving while avoiding the potholes of false pattern recognition.

Team Processes in Problem Disaggregation and Prioritization

These problem solving steps benefit substantially from teamwork, and solo practitioners should consider enlisting family or friends to assist them here. Because it is often difficult to see the structure of the problem, team brainstorming is hugely valuable, especially when trying different lenses or cleaving frames. One technique we have both found valuable is to use large yellow Post-it notes to capture team member ideas on early logic tree elements, as shown in Exhibit 3.18. These can then be moved around on a whiteboard as the order and hierarchy of trunks, branches, twigs, and leaves becomes clearer.

TEAM PROCESSES

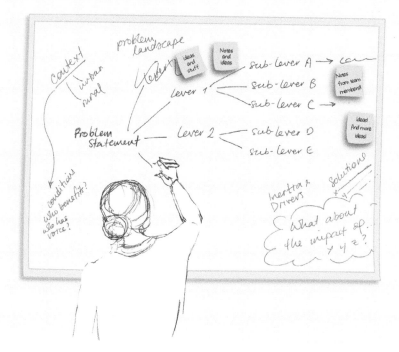

EXHIBIT 3.18

While it is a good idea to consult the literature and look for best practices around your problem, it is not uncommon for individuals to get attached to their initial cut through the problem, and as mentioned earlier, reliance on external views creates a risk of applying incorrect frames. This is even—or especially—true of experts. Use of constructive challenging and "what you'd have to believe" questions can help get the process out of ruts, and foster more creativity in solution paths. Team brainstorming sessions can really help avoid attachment in problem prioritization. Another technique we have used is giving every team member 10 sticky notes and let them allocate them in a voting process for priority analyses (see Exhibit 3.19).

VOTING PROCESS

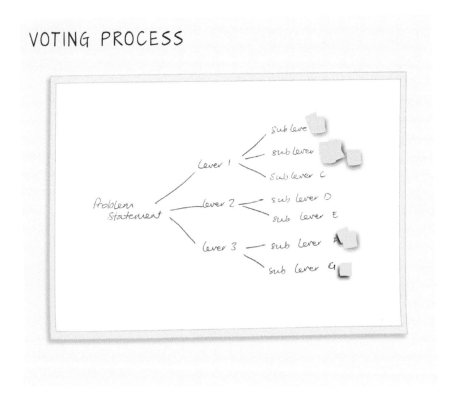

EXHIBIT 3.19

Problem disaggregation is central to good problem solving. We have illustrated the different type of logic trees that you can use when you have a problem to solve. We encourage getting started with a tree and filling it out with what you know already. We have shown the improvements you can make with further iterations of the tree.

Your creativity is often likely to come from how you cleave a problem. Cleaving brings elements of art and science to your problem solving as we show by way of example. In reflecting on how we chose to cleave a problem in a particular way, we have been able to develop a comprehensive list of ways to cleave business problems and those encountered in life.

Chapter 3 Takeaways

- Problem disaggregation is critical to good problem solving; it gives us manageable chunks to work on and allows us to begin to see the structure of the problem.

- Start with simple factor or component trees when you are just starting out and don't know much; later, work toward more complete deductive logic trees and decision trees.

- It often helps to solve trees backwards, inductively, when you know more about the detailed issues (think of these as the leaves on the tree) than you do about root causes.

- See if you can make your tree structures both mutually exclusive (no overlapping branches) and collectively exhaustive (no missing branches).

- For business problems it almost always makes sense to start with a profit lever or return on capital tree.

- As you get more experienced, try the broader set of cleaving frames from the later part of the chapter; different slices through the problem yield different insights.

- Prioritization is really important once you have a good tree structure; try putting all your twigs and leaves on a matrix of the size of potential impact and whether you can affect it. Focus your early efforts on the big levers that you can pull!

Problems to Try on Your Own

1. Take a growth opportunity for your business or nonprofit and prepare a logic tree to make the case, first using inductive logic then deductive logic.

2. Try creating a logic tree for the growth opportunity expressed in arithmetic relationships.

3. Set up a priorities matrix for the top half dozen priorities in your business plan. Which ones should you ramp up with resources and slow down or terminate based on your assessment?

4. How else might you cleave the nursing supply problem?

5. Would you cleave the airport capacity problem in a more compelling way than outlined in Chapter 1?

Chapter Four

Build a Great Workplan and Team Processes

WORKPLAN

Solving some problems is easy. All you need is a piece of paper or a whiteboard, a calculator, and an Internet connection to get data or access expert opinion. The Where-to-Live problem we presented in Chapter 1 is pretty much like this. You have a family meeting to talk about what characteristics in a town are important to each family member, you agree on some rough weightings (Is trail running availability more important than access to fly fishing? What about the commute to work?), you go online to figure out what data is available that correlates reasonably well with those variables, you normalize the data to a 1–100 scale, pop it in a spreadsheet, and see what comes out. It is an important decision, to be sure, but not a very complicated one to think through logically.

But even reasonably straightforward personal-level projects can get complicated quickly. Look at Rob's Should-I-Put-Solar-on-My-Roof logic tree and analysis. He had to calculate the potential value of the cost savings compared to the utility's rates and the investment required; he had to project whether the feed-in tariff (what the utility would pay him for excess power) would change and whether solar panels would continue to get cheaper; and he had to estimate his own carbon footprint to calculate whether this investment would substantially decrease his climate impact! As we saw back in Chapter 1, none of those analyses is beyond a smart homeowner, but Rob could have wasted a lot of time and effort if he didn't plan these analyses with some thought.

Maybe you think you would like to skip this chapter—it seems boring compared with the logical disaggregation trees of the last chapter, or the exciting use of big data techniques of Chapter 6. Don't do it! Having fun instead of drudgery in problem solving means finding the *critical path*. The critical path is the continuation of the prioritization process we described toward the end of Chapter 3. It means high-grading the analysis you use to solve problems so that you are always working on the parts that have the highest probability of yielding insight. Workplanning and the frequent iterations that follow the initial plan are the way you stay on that critical path.

If you are working with a team, or can mimic that with input from family and friends, the workplan is the place to get specific about your initial hypotheses, clarify what outputs you want from analysis, and assign the parts so that everyone knows what they are doing and by when. This is also the time to further establish and reinforce good team processes to avoid confirmation bias and other common problem solving mistakes.

This chapter covers best practices in work planning and project management, with examples of how you link your logic tree hypotheses to a plan for analysis. We discuss best practice in one-day answers, driving from your hypotheses. Finally, we introduce more team processes and norms to aid creativity and fight biases and cognitive errors in problem solving.

Workplanning and Project Management

Lots of people have experience with workplanning and project management. Let's face it, a lot of those experiences are probably bad. Workplans are typically endless in length and full of quickly outmoded detail. Responsibilities and timing expectations are vague and often violated, and unpleasant surprises in team follow-up meetings are all too common ("I thought you were going to interview John Snow" or "That isn't what I expected it to look like!").

For these reasons, we learned at McKinsey to do our workplanning with some twists (see Exhibit 4.1).

These best-practice approaches to workplanning mean that we don't do any analysis for which we don't have a hypothesis. We never go off and build a model without a very good idea about what question it answers. We sharpen our thinking even more by requiring that we can visualize what form the output might take (we call this *dummying* the chart), so we know if we would want it if we had it. We order our analyses logically, so those that can knock out, or obviate later analyses, are done first. And we are painfully explicit about who is expected to do what analysis by what date and time. By being specific here, we save tons of time in wasted work.

WHAT	WHY
1. We don't do any analyses that aren't guided by very clear and testable hypotheses	There is no vague "I'll look into X or Y"
2. We often work backward from clearly visualized and 'dummied' outputs	Every analysis is driven by a specific contribution to the solving of the problem
3. We are very careful about the order in which we do analyses	Do knock-out analyses first
4. We are very specific about who is doing what by when	No confusion about responsibilities or deadlines
5. We have workplans that go out only 2-3 weeks, and longer term study plans to rough out later periods	Early analysis always changes the plan

EXHIBIT 4.1

Done well, it looks like Exhibit 4.2.

We introduced the Bay Area Nursing example in Chapter 3. Let's take a look at an example workplan from that bit of problem solving. You can see in Exhibit 4.3 the specificity at each level, issue, hypothesis, analysis, source of data, responsibility, and end products.

There is a human inclination to just jump in to analysis without being crystal clear about what output is needed to solve the problem. Team members seem more prepared to spend time building models and conducting complex analyses than they are in carefully specifying what they *really want* from this work. With even more powerful analytic tools now available, including the learning algorithms of artificial intelligence techniques we'll talk about in Chapter 6, the urge to wade prematurely into data without doing the thinking on the underlying structure of the problem is even stronger than in the past. You should avoid this tendency. We encourage you to think

MODEL WORKPLAN

	Issue	Hypothesis	Analysis	Source	Responsibility +Timing	End Product
Definition	» Starts with end points (or 'leaves') from logic tree » The definition of an issue varies from 'an important question' to 'an unresolved question'. It is phrased so that it can be answered yes or no and on which a specific action depends.	» The hypothesis is a statement of the likely resolution of the issue. It includes the reason for answering yes or no.	» The analysis of a statement of the 'models' that will be explored in order to prove or disprove the hypothesis, and hence resolve the issue.	» The source identifies the likely locations, or means of obtaining data to undertake analysis.	» The team member and timing of delivery of end product or intermediate output	» The design of the chart or table or other graphic that will show the relationship or lack of relationship
Action	» Make sure each issue is stated in as detailed a manner as possible » Define sub-issues where necessary	» List all hypotheses; use: » Front-line ideas » Own ideas » Colleagues' ideas » Discuss with team members » Refine hypotheses » Readjust priorities for analysis	» Identify decision making » Determine extent of analysis required » Simple case » Complex justification	» Identify readily available data » Decide on methodology	» Decide who will help collect the data and do analysis » Decide on time frame, with milestones	» Draw 'ghost' exhibits » Develop story-line

EXHIBIT 4.2

hard about problem structure and desired outputs before you start running numbers.

As we discuss earlier, the order in which we do our analyses matters. If you set up your workplan carefully, you'll do the knock-out analyses first, the really important analyses next, and the nice to have analyses last. In Rob's solar case, the *years to payback* for his investment under a likely case power-pricing scenario was the knock-out analysis. If the payback was too long or uncertain, it just didn't make sense to continue to the other analyses. Rob's question

WORKPLAN DETAIL: BAY AREA NURSING

Issue	Hypothesis	Analysis	Source	Responsibility +Timing	End Product
Why are fewer students enrolling in nursing school?	» Demand for nursing school remains high, but program capacity has declined.	» Assess number of qualified students applying to nursing school, number enrolled, and number turned away. » Inventory number and size of nursing schools in the Bay Area. » Identify reasons for declines in program enrollment.	» California Board of Registered Nurses. » American Association of Colleges of Nursing. » Interviews with nursing school deans.	» Liz (Monday 9am – have a fun weekend!!) » Ray (end of week). » Amory (Tuesday next week).	» Longitudinal charts of nursing places, applications, acceptance rates by school. » Factor analysis of declines in enrollment. » Interview results.
Why is the turnover rate for hospital Registered Nurses (RNs) high?	» Hospital RNs are retiring earlier than expected and/ or leaving hospitals for other sites or professions.	» Compare average age of hospital RNs retiring to other RNs and professions. » Assess primary reasons for RNs turning over.	» California Board of Registered Nurses. » State-wide nurse survey.	» Margaret (end of March). » Paul (end of March).	» Longitudinal chart of retirement ages. » Factor analysis of reasons. » Survey results.

EXHIBIT 4.3

of next importance was whether it *made sense to wait*, due in this case to declining solar PV panel costs. In investment decisions, timing is often critical even when the overall case for investment is strong. Rob and Paula are committed conservationists, but estimating the *reduction in carbon footprint*, the third question, is really a nice-to-have in this case. On pure investment grounds this investment has a 25% return, better than any interest rate out there. If the investment case was weaker, the carbon reduction might have pushed Rob to install the panels in any case, so it was important to include it in the tree—and it provides some emotional downside protection if some of the cost savings don't materialize.

Knock-out analysis involves making estimates of the importance of a variable and the influence you can have on it, an estimate of expected value, the first cut of which comes out of our prioritization matrix from Chapter 3. As a result of a rough knock-out analysis, you typically conclude that some lines of enquiry aren't worth pursuing. For example, in reviewing business units in one of Rob's client's cost reduction exercise, a knock-out analysis concluded that a 50% gain from outsourcing was possible, which sounds great. But the contribution to that group to the overall company's cost reduction target was only 5%. As a consequence no effort was focused on that particular unit, with the attention placed on units that would make a larger contribution to the target. This is consistent with the 80/20 rule we will discuss in the next chapter: Focus your work on the 20% of the problem that yields 80% of the benefit.

Chunky Workplans and Lean Project Plans

Tools like Microsoft Project can be extremely helpful in workplanning. But they can also end up being like a beast that needs to be fed, generating enormous detail in workplanning that stretches out in time. As a new McKinsey engagement manager, before he developed the seven steps discipline, Charles was famous for working all night to generate 30 page workplans for his teams. But with this much detail, they were at risk of being swallowed up by all the analyses that *could be done*, without any sense of critical path. These encyclopedic workplans were quickly outmoded when the first few analyses pointed to promising new avenues in the work. The way we do problem solving now—driving from hypotheses, using rough and ready analysis approaches wherever possible, frequent porpoising into the data, and constant iterations to refine the problem statement and logic tree understanding—we find that long workplans are unnecessary and unhelpful.

Our approach is to do short, but highly specific, workplans that focus on the most important initial analyses, perhaps stretching out two to three weeks, and constantly revise them as new insights come from the team's work. We couple these with rougher project plans, usually in Gantt chart format, that cover the fixed milestone dates and to ensure the overall project stays on track from a time perspective. We call them chunky workplans and lean project plans (see Exhibit 4.4).

USE CONCISE 2-3 PAGE WORKPLANS TO GUIDE PROBLEM SOLVING 2-4 WEEKS OUT

Chunky Workplan

Sub-Issue	Hypothesis	Analysis	Source	Responsibility/Timing
What situation prevailed before the performance deterioration?	» Refinery enjoyed niche market conditions, but had little growth	» Assess transportation cost differential for imported products (net of crude disadvantage) » Compare PDQ crude cost advantage to alternative » Estimate tripoly impact (residual price differentials?)	» Petroleum supply annual » Oilco World crude price data (Oil Institute Centre) » Residual analysis » Get Bluebeard price slate	» Chris (Monday) » Chris (end of week) » Ned (Tuesday next week)
What caused the decline in performance?	» Market niche position did not erode much, but operating costs, SG&A and CapEx all grew faster than margins	» Conduct complete costs assessment by component 1988-1992 » Review CapEx plans » Test both against industry best practice	» Year-end products » John Doe » Call Houston experts » Soloman report » PIRA	» Duncan (end of June) » Ned (Wednesday) » Chris (next Thursday)

USE GANTT CHARTS TO MANAGE PROJECT DELIVERABLES OVER LONGER TIMEFRAMES

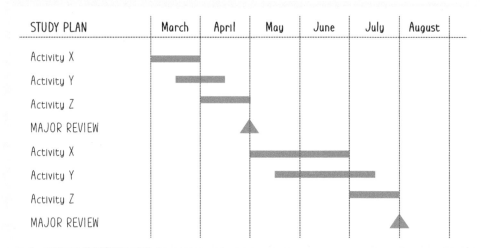

STUDY PLAN	March	April	May	June	July	August

Avoid super detailed, encyclopedic "full project" work plans.
No one reads them, they are out of date in 3 weeks, and no one wants to revise them.

EXHIBIT 4.4

One-Day Answers

We find there is great clarity in stating what you know about your problem at any point in the process. It helps bed down what understandings are emerging, and what unknowns still stand between the answers and us. We call this a one-day answer, and they convey our current best analysis of the situation, complications or insightful observations, and our best guess at the solution, as we iterate between our evolving workplans and our analysis. By working this way we can divert resources to areas where we have the biggest gaps in problem solving and shut down analysis that is not taking us anywhere. We contrast this approach with typical efforts that encourage gathering huge data sets and endless interviews before problem solving starts. As analysis results come in, we can refine our one-day answers and begin to synthesize our evidence into more complete stories. We'll talk below about how we use other team processes to avoid the potential for confirmation bias that comes from early hypothesizing.

There are many ways to structure one-day answers, but the classic way employed in McKinsey and elsewhere is to organize them in three parts:

1. A short description of the situation that prevails at the outset of problem solving. This is the state of affairs that sets up the problem.

2. A set of observations or complications around the situation that creates the tension or dynamic that captures the problem. This is typically what changed, or what went wrong that created the problem.

3. The best idea of the implication or resolution of the problem that you have right now. At the beginning this will be rough and speculative. Later it will be a more and more refined idea that answers the question, "What should we do?"

We usually use this order of situation–observation–resolution in our team processes, but later on as you begin to synthesize your findings, you may reverse these and lead with "You should do this," then followed by supporting reasons. Chapter 7 explains this in more detail.

One-day answers should be crisp and concise. This is not the place to have 40 bullet points of unorganized facts. Exhibit 4.5 gives some best-practice thoughts.

WHAT ONE-DAY ANSWERS ARE NOT

	THIS	NOT THIS
Situation	» The problem or opportunity at the core of the decision-maker's dilemma	» Issue history or masses of facts unrelated to the core opportunity/problem
Observation	» The critical insight or leverage point that is emerging	» Vague description of the complication (rehash of problem statement) or another bunch of facts masquerading as insight
Implication	» The 'logical high ground' » Implied set of actions » Options we see at this point	» 'The' one and only answer » Unsupported prejudices or preconceived ideas not related to steps 1 and 2

EXHIBIT 4.5

Let's look at a short example from our hardware company case study.

Situation: Hechinger is a dominant player with a long and successful history in one region and seeks to expand.

Complication: A new competitor, Home Depot, has emerged with a warehouse superstore model that appears to be growing much faster, driven by substantially lower pricing. Their business model is different, and compensates for lower prices by sourcing economies, lower cost logistics, and higher asset productivity. They will soon have geographic overlap with Hechinger.

Resolution: To remain competitive, Hechinger needs to quickly reform its inventory management and logistics systems, and develop lower-cost sourcing models, to allow lower pricing—or it will face a real threat even in its core markets.

As you can see, this is a concise summary of where the problem solving effort sits at a moment in time. It guides the analysis that still has to be done (in this case particularly the answer to the question "What should Hechinger do?"). It provides a strawman that can (and should) be attacked and stress tested for faulty thinking. And it gives you something to say if you find yourself in an elevator-test moment!

Great Team Processes for Workplanning and Analysis

Nearly everyone has experience working in teams, and we're willing to bet you have worked on good ones and bad ones. Our task is focused on problem solving, not good management practices more broadly, but there is lots of overlap. We have found that the best teams have relatively flat structures, good processes and norms, and explicit approaches to avoiding bias. Let's take each of these in turn.

Team Structure and Leadership

Good problem solving teams usually have an excellent lead or coordinator—somewhere between a musical conductor and an air traffic controller—who makes sure that the basic elements come together and on time. But the best teams typically have relatively little hierarchy in the structure of brainstorming and ideation. This kind of structure can be challenging to create inside larger organizations that have conventional hierarchical roles. When we work within large organizations, we nearly always set up temporary teams that act outside the normal reporting structures and deliberately have limited lives. This allows for non-hierarchical and creative team processes that are more likely to generate good solutions.

Of course, these same principles apply to working on family-level problems, and to social-scale problems with decision makers inside political hierarchies. In every case we try to make conventional authority figures play a different and less directive role in problem solving to get fresh and creative answers.

We will deal with some important insights on team composition next.

Team Norms

Over the course of our careers, we have seen some teams that problem solve in a highly efficient way and others that flail around, miss deadlines, and fail to develop compelling solutions. This can happen even after good work on problem definition, disaggregation, and prioritization. What is it that good problem solving teams do better in their approach to workplanning and analysis? A number of things stand out in our experience:

1. *They are hypothesis driven and end-product oriented.* They use strong hypotheses to guide workplanning and analyses. This doesn't mean they are trying to prove the hypothesis in spite of the facts. Just the opposite: Strong hypotheses are easier to challenge and pressure test. The end products we are describing are typically analyses that will unambiguously resolve an issue or sub-issue. For Rob's knee arthroscopy, discussed in the next chapter, he framed the hypothesis that he should have surgery now and then set out the supporting analyses. He set a clear threshold for those: that the outcome would be better than doing nothing and that no improved technology solution was imminent. The end product of his analysis was the completed decision tree where he compiled research studies and the latest timing of new treatments such as stem cells for meniscal repair.

2. *They porpoise frequently between the hypothesis and data.* They are flexible in the face of new data. This means they are ready to cease analysis where it has reached a dead end and start work on promising new lines of inquiry. In the Avahan HIV project in India that we introduced in Chapter 2, the team started with an initial hypothesis that was directionally useful but provided no leverage for action. What did they do? They took a new tack based on what they had learned that focused on female sex workers and the communities in which they lived. This hadn't previously been explored as part of a disease problem, and it ultimately yielded insight and a course of action of profound impact.

3. *They look for breakthrough thinking rather than incremental improvements.* They do this by asking about performance limits and reference points for best practice, and the distance they are from those limits. A mining company using large, heavy vehicles was exploring whether they could do tire changes more quickly. They asked who did tire changes fastest and had the most experience in the world. The answer was Formula 1. The mining team then visited Formula 1 racing pits to learn about how they could improve their processes. That is creativity!

Team Behaviors to Avoid Bias and Error

Many of you will be familiar with the notion of type 1 and type 2 thinking patterns, introduced to the general public in Nobel Prize winner Daniel Kahneman's *Thinking, Fast and Slow*.[1] Type 1 thinking is automatic and intuitive, and governs much of our behavior. Perhaps to save us from being eaten by jackals, many of our decisions are essentially automatic, without the conscious logic of type 2 considered, rational thinking. Any time we have done something before and had it be successful, it is more likely that our brains will quickly choose this path again, without conscious thought. Just like learning to say a foreign phrase, the first time is labored and

---

[1]Daniel Kahneman, *Thinking, Fast and Slow* (New York: Farrar, Straus and Giroux, 2011).

painfully self-conscious. With time it becomes, literally, second nature and disappears into our automatic mental systems.

This is great for speaking a new language or riding a bike or tying your shoes . . . but not so great for systematic problem solving. Our kind of problem solving can and does benefit from pattern recognition, of course. When you correctly see that a particular business problem is best cleaved by a return on capital tree or a supply curve, it makes problem solving faster and more accurate. Philip Tetlock reports that grandmasters at chess have 50,000–100,000 patterns stored in this deep memory system.[2] But when we incorrectly see a familiar framing for a *new* kind of problem, we risk disastrously wrong solutions or endless work getting back on track. This kind of mistake is sometimes called an availability heuristic (you use the framework you happen to have handy, not the right one) or substitution bias (you substitute a simple model you know rather than understanding the more complicated actual model). And even when there is no absolute cognitive mistake in problem framing, excessive problem patterning is a block on novel solutions and creativity in problem solving.

Now here is the bad news. Depending on who is counting,[3] there are upwards of one hundred different kinds of cognitive biases and mistakes that humans are prone to make in problem solving, some related to type 1 *fast* thinking errors, some driven by other processing biases, including many related to our relationship with resources. The enumeration of cognitive biases in decision making coming out of experimental psychology and behavioral economics is both interesting and important for anyone who cares about problem solving. But to believe some of the literature, these biases render people incapable of rational thought entirely! In our experience good problem solving design and team processes can address most of these, and in addition encourage creativity. This is what the seven steps process is all about.

---

[2]Philip E. Tetlock and Dan Gardner, *Superforecasting: The Art and Science of Prediction* (Crown Publishing, 2015).
[3]See Rolf Dobeli, *The Art of Thinking Clearly* (Sceptre, 2013).

A Practical Way to Deal with Biases

Lets talk about the main sources of bias and error in problem solving. In conversations with our former colleague and Kahneman collaborator, Professor Dan Lovallo, he suggests that the most important to address are confirmation bias, anchoring bias, and loss aversion.[4] We will add in availability bias and overoptimism as additional issues to address in your team processes. Indeed, as Exhibit 4.6 shows, many of the other biases described in the literature are forms of these five underlying issues.

1. *Confirmation bias* is falling in love with your one-day answer. It is the failure to seriously consider the antithesis to your thesis, ignoring dissenting views—essentially picking low hanging mental fruit.

2. *Anchoring bias* is the mistaken mental attachment to an initial data range or data pattern that colors your subsequent understanding of the problem.

3. *Loss aversion*, and its relatives, the sunk cost fallacy, book loss fear, and the endowment effect, are a failure to ignore costs already spent (sunk) or any asymmetric valuing of losses and gains.

4. *Availability bias* is use of an existing mental map because it is readily at hand, rather than developing a new model for a new problem, or just being influenced by more recent facts or events.

5. *Overoptimism* comes in several forms including overconfidence, illusion of control or simply failure to contemplate disaster outcomes.

There are a number of team process-design approaches that can lessen the impact of most of these cognitive biases and errors, and that can simultaneously encourage more novelty and creativity in problem solving.

---

[4]Daniel Kahneman, Dan Lovallo, and Olivier Sibony, "The Big Idea: Before You Make the Big Decision," *Harvard Business Review*, June 2011; Private conversation with Professor Dan Lovallo, University of Sydney.

DEALING WITH BIASES

Principal Bias	Related Bias	What is it?	How to deal?
CONFIRMATION BIAS	» Affect heuristic » Group think » Self-interest bias » Authority bias or Sunflower bias	Falling in love with your one-day answer; failing to look at alternatives and antitheses; not hearing dissenting views	» Constructive confrontation » Dialectical argument; thesis, antithesis, synthesis » Team composition—diversity (views/background) » Role playing
ANCHORING BIAS	» Saliency bias » Neglect of reversion to mean/compounding	Assuming an initial data range or increased/decreased pattern is the whole range or will continue (mental numerical stickiness)	» Develop alternative hypotheses (antitheses) » Hard-core data gathering and analysis, including scenario modeling » What you have to believe—team process
LOSS AVERSION BIAS	» Sunk cost fallacy » Endowment effect » Accounting book loss fear	Mental numerical stickiness or any kind of asymmetric valuing of losses or gains	» Clear forward-looking mind-set » Good analytic tools (NPV analysis valuing options, Bayesian thinking)
AVAILABILITY BIAS	» Substitution bias » Overemphasis given to current events	Use the map or story we have at hand rather than investing in understanding the new complex situation	» Value of additional information » Explicit options to wait vs. decide now
OVEROPTIMISM BIAS	» Overconfidence » Illusion of control » Disaster neglect	Underestimating low probability events	» Explicit extreme downside case » Premortems

EXHIBIT 4.6

Diversity in team members: Building a team with different backgrounds and viewpoints really helps create an environment of active openness to new ideas and approaches. This is a great source of creativity in problem solving and often overlooked. If you are solving your problem solo, find a way to brainstorm your ideas with a diverse range of others, insiders and outsiders, at each stage of the process. Phillip Tetlock's work on forecasting shows that teams always outperform individuals in this form of problem solving, even very high-performing solo practitioners. And the best superforecasting teams even beat crowd-sourcing and prediction markets.[5]

Always try multiple trees/cleaves: Even when a problem seems perfectly designed for your favorite framework, try multiple cleaving frames to see what different questions and insights emerge. When we decided to look at obesity as a wicked problem, discussed in Chapter 9, we had a team meeting where we tried out various alternative-cleaving frames. In only half an hour we outlined a number of possible cleaving frames and argued the case for each—such as incent/regulate, individual behavior/public health, incidence/severity and supply/demand, before settling on supply/demand. Don't settle on your first cut through the problem.

Try adding question marks to your hypotheses. We are committed to being hypothesis driven, but our former colleague Caroline Webb's work reports behavioral research suggesting that active questioning moves our brains into discovery mode, away from confirmation mode.[6] A number of the best problem solvers we've met use active questioning as their prime problem solving tool. The answers they get lead to the next set of questions until finally the hypothesis is sharpened or challenged in its present form.

Team Brainstorming Practices: The values your team establishes early on contribute enormously to the quality of your problem solving. Here are some practices we have found especially conducive to fighting biases and promoting creativity:

- Obligation to dissent
  A core value of McKinsey is the *obligation to dissent* and it is baked into even the greenest business analysts from induction. This means not only is it okay for a junior team member to speak

---

[5]Philip E. Tetlock and Dan Gardner, *Superforecasting: The Art and Science of Prediction* (Crown Publishing, 2015).
[6]Caroline Webb, *How to Have a Good Day* (Random House, 2016), 167.

up when they disagree in a brainstorming session—or in front of the client—it is an absolute obligation. Senior team members who don't adhere to this value can be fired. Team members typically respect hierarchy and need team leaders to encourage them to speak up if they have a different view, whether they have been employed for a day or ten years.

- Role playing
  Try acting out your interim solutions from the perspective of clients, suppliers, other family members, citizens . . . whoever isn't you. Then switch roles and play a new character. It sounds embarrassing—and it is at first—but it is remarkably clarifying. Caroline Webb also recommends drawing, mapping, or verbalizing solutions as alternatives to conventional discourse to generate different and more creative results.[7]

- Dialectic standard
  Establish the classical argument form as your team norm: thesis, antithesis, synthesis. This means every idea or hypothesis must be met with its antithesis and challenged, before joining the learning together in synthesis.

- Perspective taking
  Perspective taking is the act of modeling another team member's assertion or belief (especially if you don't agree) to the point that you can describe it as compellingly as the other.[8]

- Constructive confrontation
  To disagree without being disagreeable is the heart of great problem solving team process. One of the great tools we both used in McKinsey is "What would you have to believe?" to accept a particular thesis or viewpoint. This involves spelling out all of the assumptions implicit in the perspective, and all the implications. One example of "What would you have to believe?" involved looking at a growth company's share price during the dot-com era. To justify the share price earnings had to grow at 40% compound for the next five years, then at double the US GDP growth

---

[7]Caroline Webb, *How to Have a Good Day* (Random House, 2016), 170–172.
[8]Philip E. Tetlock and Dan Gardner, *Superforecasting: The Art and Science of Prediction* (Crown Publishing, 2015).

rate in perpetuity! That is an unbelievably high growth expectation . . . and was not achieved, leading to a stock price crash for the company.

- Team distributed voting
  There is often disagreement when pruning branches on a logic tree, or when assigning priorities in the analysis work planning. If you aren't careful, the most articulate or senior team member can inappropriately sway the conversation. As described in Chapter 3, one approach we have used is to assign each team member 10 votes, represented by sticky notes, and have each team member use them to vote on their favorite (or least favorite) analysis, allowing cumulative or bullet voting—most senior person votes last, so as not to bias the choices of more junior members.

- Solicit outside views (but be careful with experts)
  It is easy to breathe your own exhaust in intensive problem solving, especially when you are working in a space or business that is familiar. It is critical to engage outside data and perspectives to refresh your view of the problem. The normal thing is to interview experts—but the risk is that they just reinforce the dominant or mainstream view and therefore smother creativity. Try talking to customers, suppliers, or better yet players in a different but related industry or space.

Explicit Downside Scenario Modeling and Pre-Mortem Analysis: Nicolas Taleb's wonderful book *The Black Swan*[9] reminds us of the dangers of assuming normal distributions. Improbable jumps or discontinuous events do occur, and long-tailed distributions (irregular-shaped statistical distributions with a long tail on one side, indicating small but measurable probability for even extreme events) mean we should take these into account in our problem solving and modeling. This means that we should explicitly model not just a narrow band (expected case, downside case) of values, but more extreme downside cases. A related idea is to do pre-mortem

---

[9]Nassim Nicholas Taleb, *The Black Swan: The Impact of the Highly Improbable* (Random House, 2007).

analysis, where the team works through all the implications of even unlikely failure cases.[10]

Good analytic techniques: Humans are prone to a number of errors around money. These include paying attention to sunk costs, unreasonably high discount rates on future events, and treating losses and gains asymmetrically. One way to avoid these errors is to use good analytic techniques, including problem/model design, net present value analysis, marginal analysis, and use of cash flows rather than accounting book values. We will cover these in Chapter 5.

Broaden your data sources: In every area of life, individual/ workplace/society, there are core government and private data sets that everyone has access to. Sometimes these are terrific, but everyone has them, including your competitors, and there are often methodological issues in their collection. It is worth considering whether there are options for crowd sourcing alternative data, whether prediction markets cover your topic or could be induced to, or whether your interest area is amenable to some form of A|B testing or randomized controlled trials. Custom data collection costs have come down substantially and new data sets can yield insights very different from the obvious mainstream analyses. Tools such as Survey Monkey are simple to use and can bring customer, competitor, and supplier perspectives that may be especially insightful.

How does this all get put in place in real-life settings in your teams? Often by the cues and behaviors of the team leader, like the case in Exhibit 4.7.

Agile Team Processes

In the Introduction we argued that many organizations are responding to demands to be become better problem solvers by taking on the persona of problem solving corporations. They do so by seeking to become lean and agile and often employ the language

---

[10]Daniel Kahnemann, Dan Lovallo, and Olivier Sibony, "Before You Make That Big Decision," *Harvard Business Review*, June 2011.

TACKLING BIASES IN MINERAL EXPLORATION

Rob saw a powerful way to address major biases in a McKinsey team setting some years ago in a project led by Bob Waterman, co-author of the best-selling book *In Search of Excellence*. The team was reviewing the exploration strategy of an Australian mineral resource company that hadn't made a major discovery in a decade, despite significant spending on exploration. Prior to this they had made numerous world-class discoveries.

Loss Aversion versus Big Bets

The team reviewed and gathered results for the client's failing exploration strategy (selection of prospects, funding allocations, sampling and drilling). Nothing definitive was emerging to explain what was happening. In interviews with the management team, however, Bob detected a difference between the stated goal—to locate scarce resources that could become long-lived mines in the bottom quartile of operating cost (which requires a big bet mentality)—and the way they were approaching exploration. They had shifted away from making big bets because of a fear of losses (loss aversion), to making small bets where there was a low probability of loss (typically around known mineralization where technical successes were more likely). Bob then proposed the team look outside the group where success and failure could be contrasted.

Anchoring Outside versus Inside

Companies that anchor outside their own teams and take a scientific view of the odds rather than limit themselves to internal data or the case at hand, unlock a different perspective. With the client's help, the team surveyed a dozen mineral exploration companies, half of whom had been very successful and the other half unsuccessful. While a small sample, it represented more than 75% of Australian mineral exploration in a year. The client agreed to share its findings with all participants. What became clear from the survey was that the successful companies had big bet cultures and were science led, quickly testing their concepts through drilling. Based on those drilling results they either doubled down or abandoned the mineral prospect. Unsuccessful companies were less hypothesis-driven, sticking with unsuccessful prospects for longer. Anchoring outside became a new best practice in exploration.

Authority Bias

Bob presented the team's findings at a meeting with the CEO, senior management, and the exploration team. As soon as Bob finished the presentation, the CEO began speaking. Bob thought this would be the case and was worried it might stifle dissenting views. He intervened, suggesting instead that each person at the table give their views first and that the CEO then make concluding remarks and summarize the discussion. As they went around the table, each person voiced their support for a new finder mentality and rigorous science-based processes. They were able to speak their minds without fear of opposing the CEO. This simple technique reduced the prospect of authority bias, a subset of confirmation bias. The client successfully implemented changes to elevate the importance of exploration and their science capability. Not long after, they ended their drought with exploration success.

EXHIBIT 4.7

of scrums, a term from rugby. They seek to work on the right problems, address root causes of problems, and organize around teams with short duration work plans and clear accountability (see Exhibit 4.8). All this is consistent with the approach we have outlined in this chapter.

AGILE ORGANIZATIONS, SCRUMS AND SPRINTS

The language associated with teams is changing to embrace agile, lean, and scrums. We have daily scrum events, scrum masters, sprint planning, sprint reviews, and sprint retrospectives—all within a month. Teams and organizations who have had success in applying the principles point to a focus on priorities, timely outcomes, accountability, transparency, and a bias for action. As the metabolic rate of organizations quickens the need for agile organizations and scrum teams can be expected to rise further.

There is commonality and difference between what is termed lean, agile and scrum. Lean has a focus on decreasing waste as did its predecessor, kanban. Agile has a focus on increasing velocity. Scrum is described as a framework for developing complex products. All three use team structures to bring openness and accountability to tasks through project planning descriptors.

Some see the rise of agile and scrums as heralding a new organization paradigm and providing a framework to address complex adaptive problems (Dr. Jeff Sutherland, 1995). To meet that expectation organizations will need to become problem solving corporations as we discussed in the Introduction, displaying mental muscle and machine muscle. They will need to embrace bulletproof problem solving as a requirement. At the team level, agile and scrum teams have to ask themselves the following questions if their problem solving is to be as good as it can be:

» Are we working on the right problem?	(Step 1)
» Have we broken down the problem into key issues to analyse?	(Step 2)
» Are our priorities right in terms of short and long-term impact?	(Step 3)
» Have we balanced the scrum deliverables against burn-out risk of team members?	(Step 4)
» Have we brought outside perspectives and expertise to bear?	(Step 4)
» Are complex problems that require analysis getting the right share of resources?	(Step 5)
» Are we carefully synthesizing our findings?	(Step 6)
» Are we presenting our findings in a compelling narrative?	(Step 7)
» Is there adequate iteration between progress and goals?	(Steps 1–7, again)

We see great potential for organizations to build on the tenets of agile, lean and scrums to become problem-solving corporations. To do so it means that the key elements of the way teams do bulletproof problem solving that we have outlined need to be inculcated into the organization.

EXHIBIT 4.8

PSYCHOLOGICAL PROFILE OF SUPERFORECASTERS

Philosophy	Style	Methods
Cautious	Actively open-minded	Pragmatic
Humble	Intelligent & well-read	Analytical
Non-deterministic	Reflective	Dragonfly-eyed (multiple lenses)
Growth mindset	Introspective	Probabilistic
Lots of grit	Self-critical	Thoughtful updaters
	Numerate	

EXHIBIT 4.9

Above all, there is an orientation or attitude that is found in the best problem solvers that reflects an *active openness* to new ideas and data, and a suspicion of standard or conventional answers (see Exhibit 4.9). Tetlock describes it well in profiling the superforecasters.

In closing, good workplans make an enormous difference in problem solving. We have explained how they are a necessary but not sufficient condition for problem solving success. One-day answers help sharpen our hypotheses and make our analysis focused and efficient. Knock-out analyses provide focus on the critical path in problem solving. Finally, there are a host of team effectiveness disciplines that accompany the workplan that can help you produce great outcomes and guard against the pitfalls and biases that we hear so much about.

Chapter 4 Takeaways

- Good discipline and specificity in workplanning will save you a huge amount of work—take the time to do it right up front!
- To be on the critical path in problem solving, make sure you get the order of your analyses right and do the knock-out analyses first.

- Make your workplans chunky: short and specific; and your study plans lean: capture key milestones so you deliver on time.
- One-day answers clarify where you are and what work is left to do—and provide a strawman for pressure-testing your work.
- Tools like pre-mortems can help highlight risks to focus on with big decisions where a lot is at stake.
- Good team structure and norms help foster creativity and fight bias in problem solving.
- Short-circuit hierarchy wherever you can—foster an obligation to dissent.
- Try role-playing for creativity to bring in outside perspectives.
- Great problem solvers are well read, open to new ideas, reflective, self-critical, persistent . . . and use teamwork wherever they can
- Agile team processes are increasingly the vehicle for problem solving efforts; try to build agile characteristics into your teams.

Problems to Try on Your Own

1. For the problem "Should I buy an electric car?": Design a logic tree of questions in the best knock-out order; show how it is MECE.

2. Write up the one-day answer for the electric car decision.

3. Try role-playing support for Brexit; then switch sides and make as compelling a case for Remain.

4. Re-read the nursing case study and make the conclusions in a deductive logic form then an inductive logic form.

5. List out the most common biases that affect problem solving and how you plan to address them in your problem solving.

6. Take whatever your current problem is and dummy up 10 exhibits you would like to have real data and analysis for.

7. Prepare a one page, agile plan for the next month for a project you're working on that incorporates the seven-steps process.

Conduct Analyses

ANALYZE

How you go about gathering facts and conducting analysis to test your hypotheses often makes the difference between good and bad problem solving, even when the earlier steps have been followed carefully. Good problem solvers have a toolkit at their disposal that helps them work efficiently, starting with heuristics and rules of thumb to understand the *direction and magnitudes* of relationships that allows them to focus attention on the most important issues. They don't jump right into building giant models until they have a clear understanding of whether and where complex tools are required.

The analysis stage is critical to the objectivity of your problem solving. There are many jokes about torturing the facts until they speak the truth you want to hear. There was even an old *New Yorker* cartoon that showed a person reaching into a filing cabinet with drawers marked "His facts. Her facts. Your facts."—and this was well before the advent of fake news. Following a structured problem approach, where we use good analytic techniques to pressure test our hypotheses and good team processes to limit bias, allows us to avoid torturing the facts.

In this chapter, we focus on how to do powerful analyses quickly and efficiently, starting with heuristics, shortcuts, and rules of thumb. We illustrate how you can structure and resolve many analytic issues you face with straightforward heuristics well before any use of the complex "big guns" analysis we introduce in Chapter 6.

Heuristics and Rules of Thumb

Heuristics are powerful tools that act as shortcuts in analysis. They help you size the different elements of the problem to determine the efficient path in further analysis. They can be dangerous when incorrectly applied, of course. Author Nicholas Taleb describes how simple rules based on past success can lead you astray in settings where low probability events can produce outsized errors.[1] We'll show you how to avoid these mistakes.

We use the term heuristics, rules of thumb, and shortcuts interchangeably. In Exhibit 5.1, we explore a range of heuristics that are useful for individuals, enterprises, and citizens. When you are asked to list your top 10 songs of all time, it's hard to leave some classics

---

[1]Nassim Nicholas Taleb, *The Black Swan: The Impact of the Highly Improbable* (Penguin, 2007).

HEURISTICS & SHORT CUTS

Tool	What it is	When to use it	Watch out
Occam's Razor	» The simplest solution that requires the fewest assumptions	» Always	» Don't get committed to the first cut answer
Order of Magnitude cuts: bounding the market	» What is maximum potential value?	» Always! Never start a problem without order of mag analysis	» Don't fall in love with the maximum
80/20 Thinking	» Finding the 20% of the problem that drives 80% of the value » Finding the big levers	» Scoping problems under constraint	» Don't miscalculate risks in large scale, interconnected settings
Rule of 72	» Divide growth rate into 72 to get doubling period	» Any growth or compounding problem	» Step change process
S-Curve / Adoption Curve	» Typical model of adoption	» Adoption of new technologies and products	» Slow then rapid diffusion
Expected Value	» Expected value is the value of an outcome multiplied by its probability of occurring	» Any time you have a future uncertain event involving value	» Other/better disruptive technologies
Bayesian Thinking	» Conditional probability	» When you need to think probabilistically	» Care to assemble data for calculations
Reasoning by Analogy	» Creating reference classes	» When order of magnitude varies widely depending on comparator	» Outlier cases
Break-even Point	» Break-even volume	» Quick check on business model viability	» Fixed costs with scale behavior
Marginal Analysis	» Economics of the next unit	» Production, consumption, and investment problems	» Step jumps in cost
Distribution of outcomes	» The possible range of outcomes	» Project cost estimates » New business revenue » M&A	» Mean reversion » Non-normal distributions

EXHIBIT 5.1

off the list. So too it is with our top heuristics. We didn't invent them, we just make good use of them and so can you.

The oldest of these is definitely *Occam's Razor*—favor the simplest solution that fits the facts—which originated in the fourteenth century. It tells us to select the hypothesis that has the fewest assumptions. One way of seeing why this make sense is a simple math example: If you have four assumptions that are independent of each other, with an 80% separate chance of being correct, the probability that all four will be correct is just over 40%. With two assumptions and the same probabilities, it is 64%. For many problems the fewer the assumptions you have the better. Practically speaking, this means avoiding complex, indirect, or inferential explanations, at least as our starting point. Related to Occam's Razor are one-reason decision heuristics, including reasoning by elimination and *a fortiori* reasoning, where you eliminate alternatives that are less attractive.[2] The important reminder is not to get committed to a simple answer with few assumptions when the facts and evidence are pointing to a more nuanced or complex answer (remember the availability and substitution biases from Chapter 4).

Order of magnitude analysis is used to prioritize team efforts by estimating the size of different levers. In business problems, we typically calculate the value of a 10% improvement in price, cost, or volume to determine which is more important to focus on (assuming, of course, that each is similarly difficult or easy to change). It applies to analyzing social issues as well. The nursing case in Chapter 3 showed the difference in outcomes from improvements in nurse quality and quantity. Doing an order of magnitude analysis should provide a minimum, most likely, and maximum estimate, not simply the maximum. Often the best knock-out analysis, which we referred to in the previous chapter, is an order of magnitude analysis to show how changes would improve an outcome or make little difference.

Efficient analysis is often helped by the 80:20 rule, sometimes called the *Pareto Principle* after the Italian economist Vilfredo Pareto, who

---

[2]Gerd Gigerenzer, Peter M. Todd, and the ABC Research Group, *Simple Heuristics That Make Us Smart* (Oxford University Press, 2000).

first noticed this relationship. It describes the common phenomenon that 80% of outcomes come from 20% of causes. If you plot percent of consumption of a product on the Y-axis and percent of consumers on the X-axis you will often see that 20% of consumers account for 80% of sales of a product or service. The point of doing 80:20 analyses is again to focus your analytical effort on the most important factors. Many business and social environments feature market structures where 80:20 or something close to that ratio is the norm, so it's a handy device to use. For example, in healthcare 20% of the population often account for 80% of healthcare costs, a fact that provides huge difficulty for insurance plan-rating models. The 80:20 rule may also apply in complex system settings. For example, when Rob visited Myanmar in 2016 he learned that only one-third of the population have access to electricity, yet the country has the potential to produce 100 GW from hydropower. A team explored the trade-offs between fishery support and hydropower by looking at portfolios of projects on a tributary of the great Irrawaddy River.[3] They showed you could get almost 95% of potential power for a 20% reduction in fishery supports. To achieve 100% of power entailed losses of one half to two-thirds of fishery support. This extreme version of the 80:20 rule starkly highlights the dilemma for policymakers, in this case between energy, livelihoods, and the environment.

Compound growth is key to understanding how wealth builds, how enterprises scale quickly, and how some populations grow. Warren Buffett said: "My wealth has come from a combination of living in America, some lucky genes, and compound interest."[4] A really quick way to estimate compounding effects is to use the Rule of 72.[5] The rule of 72 allows you to estimate how long it takes for an amount to double given its growth rate by dividing 72 by the

---

[3]Report prepared for the United Kingdom's Department of International Development by The Nature Conservancy, WWF, and the University of Manchester, "Improving Hydropower Outcomes through System Scale Planning, An Example from Myanmar," 2016.

[4]Warren Buffett, "My Philanthropic Pledge," *Fortune*, June 16, 2010.

[5]Our friend Barry Nalebuff of Yale points out that the actual rule is 69.3, but is usually rounded up to 72 because it is easier to do the division in your head.

rate of growth. So, if the growth rate is 5% an amount will double in about 14 years (72/5 = 14.4 years). If the growth rate is 15%, doubling occurs in four to five years. In a team meeting, Rob asked our research team what a $1000 investment in Amazon would be if you invested at the time of the initial stock offering in 1997. Charles thought about it for about 90 seconds: He tried a low rate of compounding of 5%, where doubling occurs every 14 years, then a high rate of 50% where doubling occurs every 18 months, before settling on $100k. The actual answer is $83k based on a 36% compounding rate, doubling every 2 years. Pretty good with no facts, just the Rule of 72! Where do errors occur with the rule of 72? When there is a change in the growth rate, which of course is often the case over longer periods. This makes sense, as few things continue to compound forever (try the old trick of putting a grain of rice on the first square of a chessboard and double the number on each successive square).

A useful heuristic if you are involved in estimating the adoption rate for a new innovation is the *S-curve*, which shows a common pattern of sales with a new product or a new market. S-curves are drawn with the percent of full adoption potential on the Y-axis and the years since adoption on the X-axis. The shape of the S will vary a lot depending on the reference class you select and particular reasons for faster or slower take up in your case. Charles led a successful start-up in the early days of Internet adoption. At that time, many forecasters overestimated the impact of Internet penetration in the short term (think of Webvan or Pets.com), but underestimated adoption in the longer term of 10 to 15 years. It looks in hindsight very clearly to be a classic S-curve. In 1995 fewer than 10% of Americans had access to the Internet. By 2014 it reached 87%. The S-curve can take many specific profiles as Exhibit 5.2 shows. Like any heuristic, you don't want to apply this rigidly or blindly, but rather use it as a frame for scoping a problem. The challenge is to get behind sweeping statements like "the world has speeded up," to understand why a particular technology will have adoption at a certain rate.

HISTORIC ADOPTION CURVES FOR TECHNOLOGICAL INNOVATIONS
ADOPTION TREND BY TECHNOLOGY

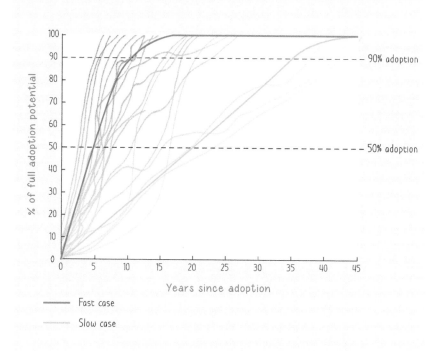

EXHIBIT 5.2

Source: McKinsey Global Institute, *A Future that Works: Automation, Employment, and Productivity*, McKinsey Global Institute, January 2017.

Expected value is simply the value of an outcome multiplied by its probability of occurring. That is called a single point expected value, but it is usually more useful (depending on the shape of the distribution) to take the sum of all probabilities of possible outcomes multiplied by their values. Expected value is a powerful first-cut analytic tool to set priorities and reach conclusions on whether to take a bet in an uncertain environment. As an example, in venture capital the goal could be expressed as the desire to create a unicorn—a billion-dollar company. The probability of reaching unicorn status calculated for Silicon Valley in recent years turns out to be 1.28%.[6] The single point expected value is $1 billion times 1.28% or $12.8 million. No wonder many 22 year olds enter risky entrepreneurial ventures against the odds when their next best alternative could be $50k a year working in a call center! But be careful: Single point expected value calculations are most useful when the underlying distribution is normal rather than skewed or long tailed. You check that by looking at the range, and whether the median and mean of the distribution are very different from each other.

When the Australian government research organization CSIRO defended its WiFi intellectual property, it used a simple expected value calculation—but with a difference: It worked backward to the break-even probability of success, given its estimates of the costs of court action ($10m) and what they would receive if they prevailed ($100m). The decision was made to pursue action in the courts because the board felt the chances of success were greater than an indifference probability of 10% ($100 million expected value of a successful court action divided by legal costs of $10 million). We will see this example more fully in the next chapter.

Much has been made of *Bayesian thinking* in recent years with books like *The Signal and the Noise*.[7] Bayesian thinking is really about conditional probability, which is the probability of an event *given* another event took place which also has a probability, called a *prior probability*. As a simple example, look at the probability of it raining given that it is cloudy (the prior probability), versus the probability of it raining if it is currently sunny. Rain can happen in either case, but is more likely when the prior condition is cloudy. Bayesian analysis can be challenging to employ formally (as a calculation), because it is difficult to precisely estimate prior probabilities. But we often use Bayesian thinking when we think

---

[6]CB Insights, May 25, 2015, www.cbinsights.com.
[7]Nate Silver, *The Signal and the Noise* (Penguin, 2012).

conditional probabilities are at work in the problem. In Chapter 6 we look at the *Challenger* space shuttle disaster in the way a Bayesian statistician would approach the problem of a launch at a temperature not experienced before.

Reasoning by analogy is an important heuristic for quick problem solving. An analogy is when you have seen a particular problem structure and solution before that you think may apply to your current problem. Analogies are powerful when you have the right reference class (that is, have correctly identified the structure type), but dangerous when you don't. To check this, we typically line up all the assumptions that underpin a reference class and test the current case for fit with each. For example, our colleague Professor Dan Lovallo has looked at how you can use reference classes to predict movie revenues.[8] He takes a genre like drama, the presence of well known or little-known stars, and the budget, and then creates a model based on the reference class of movies to compare with the one to be made. This can be surprisingly accurate and produce results better than a more complex regression model.

There are limits to reasoning by analogy. For example:

- When traditional business models in retailing, book publishing, and real estate were first challenged by disruptive Internet models, there weren't useful prior analogies to draw on, to explain how the competitive dynamics would play out.
- In the liquor market in Australia, a beer company acquired a wine company, reasoning that they were in the alcoholic beverages market and had common customers and distribution requirements. The differences in product range, brand management, customer segments, and working capital requirements meant in practice they had few success factors in common.

[8]Dan Lovallo, Carmina Clarke, and Colin Camerer, "Robust Analogizing and the Outside View: Two Empirical Tests of Case Based Decision Making," *Strategic Management Journal* 33, no. 5 (2012): 496–512.

- Halo effects follow executives who have led turnarounds, assuming that their success will be replicated in new settings. "Chainsaw" Al Dunlap had such a reputation based on a turn-around at Scott Paper, but was fired in his new role at Sunbeam less than two years into the role.[9]

Break-even point. Every start-up company Charles and Rob see likes to talk about their cash runway—the months before cash runs out and they need a new equity infusion. Not enough of them really know their break-even point, the level of sales where revenue covers cash costs. It's a simple bit of arithmetic to calculate, but requires knowledge of marginal and fixed costs, and particularly how these change with increased sales volume. The break-even point in sales dollars or units equals fixed costs/unit price less unit variable costs. Typically, the unit price is known. You can fairly quickly calculate the costs associated with each sale, the variable costs. The tricky part is how fixed costs will behave as you scale a business. You may face what are called *step-fixed costs*, where to double volume involves significant investment in machinery, IT infrastructure, or sales channels. Knowing the break-even point and cost behavior brings insight about many aspects of a business, as we saw with the Truckgear pricing example in Chapter 1.

As a real-world example of this, Charles used to ask McKinsey job applicants why car rental firms don't charge your credit card if you don't show up within the 24-hour window, but hotels do? This is a good example of rule of thumb thinking with high and low fixed cost businesses. It turns out that rental car firms have lower fixed costs and a much higher variable cost percentage than hotels, partly because they pay insurance and a number of other costs in a variable way (unlike regular consumers). Hotels, by contrast, have relatively low variable costs (room cleaning) per customer and large fixed costs. Rental car agencies also face many more substitutes (buses, trains, Uber, taxis) than hotels (Airbnb nowadays, but in the past really just a friend's couch), and experience greater spatial competition in airports (they are much easier to price shop). By using some simple heuristics to understand these differences, you can relatively quickly understand why hotel companies both

---

[9] "'Chainsaw Al' Axed," *CNN Money*, June 15, 1998.

need to charge for no-shows, and why they have the market power to do so relative to rental car firms.

Marginal analysis is a related concept that is useful when you are thinking about the economics of producing more, consuming more, or investing more in an environment of scarce resources. Rather than just looking at the total costs and benefits, marginal analysis involves examining the cost or benefit of the next unit. In production problems with fixed costs of machinery and plant, marginal costs (again, the cost of producing one more unit) often fall very quickly—favoring more production—up to the point at which incremental machinery is needed. We add units until the marginal benefit of a unit sale is equal to the marginal cost.

We can apply this idea to our hotel problem above. Imagine that the total fixed costs (mortgage, core staff, real estate taxes) of a 200-room hotel are $10,000 per night, or $50 per room. If a potential guest shows up at 6 p.m. and there is a free room, should the hotel accept his offer of $30 for the night? We know the average cost is $50, but the marginal cost to take one more customer is tiny (probably close to zero, given even cleaning staff are already on duty), so they should take her offer. These economics are what has encouraged new internet businesses in last minute hotels and flights.

Similarly, imagine a business that covers employee healthcare costs is considering subsidizing gym membership, which costs $400 per person.[10] They believe that employees who go to the gym can save the company as much as $1000 per person in healthcare costs, and assume that if they pay a membership the team member will go. Should they do it? You are guessing the answer already: It depends on what percentage of staff members is already paying for their own gym memberships. In this case the marginal analysis tells us the company indifference point is 60% already paying their own way. If fewer make regular use of the gym without subsidy, it makes sense to offer the program (assuming the assumption of use and health benefits holds), but if more are already paying their own way (and getting the company a free benefit from lower health costs), they should spend their benefit budget on something else.

---

[10]This problem was suggested by Barry Nalebuff of Yale University.

As a final heuristic, consider the *distribution of outcomes*. Companies planning large projects often add contingencies of 10% or more for cost overruns, which can run into millions of dollars. Recently we saw data that for infrastructure megaprojects costing $1 billion or more, some 90% go over budget by 20% in the case of roads, and 45% in the case of rail projects.[11] In these cases the expected overspending is not in line with the contingency of 10%, but closer to 30%, almost a full standard deviation higher for cost overruns. These errors are large enough to wipe out the profitability of the projects. Take a look at the distributions shown in Exhibit 5.3.

WHAT DISTRIBUTION OF OUTCOMES IS LIKELY?
PROJECT COST DISTRIBUTION

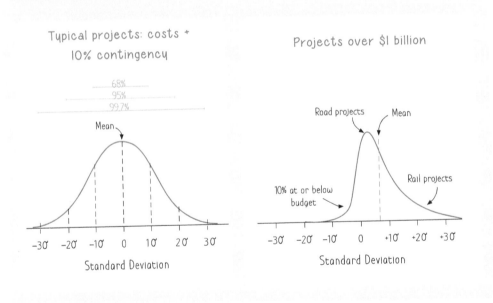

EXHIBIT 5.3

[11]Nicklas Garemo, Stefan Matzinger, and Robert Palter, "Megaprojects: The Good, the Bad, and the Better," *McKinsey Quarterly*, July 2015 (quoting Bent Flyvberg, Oxford Saïd Business School).

We see many common errors that relate to the distribution of outcomes. These include placing too much emphasis on the mean outcome, typically called the base case, and insufficient weight on outcomes that are one or even two standard deviations from the mean in a normal distribution. In the case of large projects, asking "Is the worst case bad enough?," (as Kahneman and his co-authors put it) when it can turn out to be the true expected case![12] You have to bring history, analysis, your own experience, and sometimes the experience of others through reference classes, together with judgment to estimate the shape of the project cost distribution. Simulations become a valuable tool to highlight the range of outcomes possible. They are discussed in Chapter 6.

Question-Based Problem Solving

Once you have roughed out the scale and direction of your problem levers by using heuristics, it is time to dig deeper into the analysis. But not all the analysis you will do requires huge number crunching. Often you can get to good understanding and preliminary solutions with a straightforward Sherlock Holmes framework.

We have found that the Sherlock Holmes approach of painting a picture of the problem by asking **who, what, where, when, how, and why** is a powerful root-cause tool to quickly focus problem solving. We touched on the powerful role of questions in problem solving in the previous chapter, not simply to clarify the problem under scrutiny but in defining choices and how they are to be evaluated.

As we'll show below, we can often get to rough-cut solutions in as few as three questions. These examples illustrate the utility of posing simple questions to advance good problem solving. For example, when we were discussing Charles's vote for the school levy in Chapter 1, he asked *who* were the best performing schools, *what* explained their better student outcomes, and *why* teaching quality was so important. Three question shortcuts can be represented in

[12]Daniel Kahneman, Dan Lovallo, and Olivier Sibony, "Before You Make that Big Decision," *Harvard Business Review*, June 2011.

a decision-tree format; we show two examples in healthcare, one at the institution level and one at the individual level. The institution example is how hospitals classify heart-attack patients. The individual example is whether or not to have a knee arthroscopy.

Example: How to classify heart attack patients

Hospitals have to make quick decisions to help suspected heart attack victims. What the hospital staff needs to decide is into what category to put incoming heart-attack patients, whether they are high risk or low risk. High risk requires much closer monitoring and allocation of staff. In a prior study, it was found that hospitals can segregate risk levels by asking three questions: whether the minimum systolic blood pressure over the initial 24 hours is greater than 91, whether the age of the patient is greater than 62.5 years, and whether a condition known as sinus tachycardia is present.[13] The data confirmed this categorization and can be represented in the decision tree structure of Exhibit 5.4

INCOMING HEART ATTACK PATIENT CLASSIFICATION

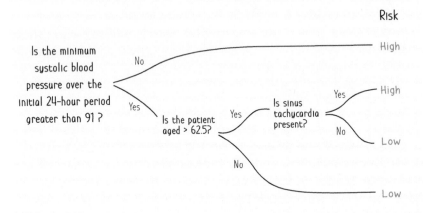

EXHIBIT 5.4

---

[13]Gerd Gigerenzer, Peter M. Todd, and the ABC Research Group, *Simple Heuristics That Make Us Smart* (Oxford University Press, 1999) (drawing on a medical study at the University of California, San Diego Medical Center by Breiman et al., 1993).

What we especially like about this example is how you start with hypotheses, test them with analysis, and then arrive at an inductive logic conclusion. It does a really nice job of helping decide how to quickly segregate high- and low-risk patients suspected of heart attacks. We note that this isn't a new finding and may have been overtaken by newer approaches such as machine learning algorithms that are increasingly important in patient classification.

Example: Rob's bad knee

SHOULD I HAVE A KNEE ARTHROSCOPY?

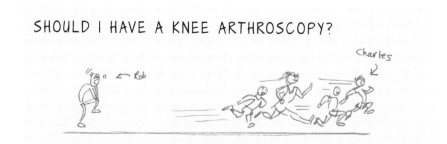

Rob had a successful arthroscopy on his left knee 20 years ago and was able to compete in 10k and half marathon races each year. When he started to get inflammation in his right knee recently, which restricted his training schedule, he unsuccessfully tried icing and rest, and then had a meeting with a sports medicine professional.

Every runner's knees are a focal point and the subject of important decisions following injury. The authoritative *New England Journal of Medicine* (NEJM) noted that over 700,000 APM (arthroscopic partial meniscectomies) knee procedures are carried out in the United States each year.[14] When the diagnosis is meniscus tear, the runner is often presented with a recommendation to have an APM as the next step.

---

[14]R. Sihvonen et al., "Arthroscopic Partial Meniscectomy versus Sham Surgery for a Degenerative Meniscal Tear," *New England Journal of Medicine* 369, no. 26 (December 26, 2013): 2515–2524.

What should Rob do? He had four options:

1. Have an APM surgery performed by a sports medicine professional.

2. Gather more information on probability of success for APM surgery in his particular case, planning a go/no-go decision after.

3. Wait for new technologies in combination with physiotherapy and rehabilitation.

4. Receive physiotherapy and rehabilitation.

In Rob's case the sports-medicine professional assessed his condition as being low discomfort, and degenerative with age and years of running. The sports medicine professional proposed a conservative treatment approach, one that didn't involve APM surgery. On the other hand, he learned from the sports medicine specialist of cases of football players with an average age of 22 with knee injuries who were going in for surgery immediately. He had also heard of research suggesting that APMs led to no better outcome than physiotherapy, and that he might be better waiting for stem cell treatments or printable hydrogel menisci, new technologies in development.

How would you make this decision faced with so many disparate pieces of information? As in most problem solving you need to gather some facts. In Rob's case, he read a Finnish study in *The New England Journal of Medicine* that indicated that when there is low discomfort and age-degenerative meniscal tear, there is no significant improvement from APM compared to physical therapy. The research method involved a particular kind of randomized control trial termed a sham control, where participants weren't aware of whether they had the procedure or not. The conclusions of the 12-month follow-up were that the outcomes for the APM surgery were no better than for the sham APM surgery, notwithstanding that "both groups had significant improvement in primary outcomes."[15]

[15]R. Sihvonen et al., "Arthroscopic Partial Meniscectomy versus Sham Surgery for a Degenerative Meniscal Tear," *New England Journal of Medicine* 369, no. 26 (December 26, 2013): 2515–2524.

Rob also wanted to assess whether he should wait for a new technology solution to develop, such as stem-cell treatment or a printable hydrogel meniscus. It turns out that clinical trials are getting underway for articular cartilage but not meniscal repair, so a reasonable conclusion can be drawn that any alternative to an arthroscopy is more than five years away.[16] 3D printable hydrogel menisci are now getting a lot of interest but he couldn't estimate when they might be an option.[17]

With the best facts and estimates in hand, things now started to fall into place. Rob decided the best option was to wait and see if a technology solution emerges while continuing to manage activity levels and the resulting inflammation in his right knee. The logic tree in Exhibit 5.5 shows both Rob's choices, and those faced by others with more discomfort. Of course they need individual opinions from specialists on the likelihood of APM surgery being successful given their circumstances. Finally, there are a lot of people who have a degenerative condition, who experience low discomfort, are not athletes, and are happy to adopt exercise regimes and physiotherapy as their path forward.

The approach Rob developed is a three-question rule. In his case the answers led him to a course of action—to wait for new technology while continuing with physiotherapy and rehabilitation (see Exhibit 5.5).

In summary, we believe smart analysis starts with heuristics and summary statistics to assess the magnitude and direction of the key problem levers. When we have a good sense of these underlying relationships, we often turn to questions like the examples above. This allows us to further refine our understanding and either make a decision based on available evidence, or to select more detailed answers.

---

[16]Cartilage repair via stem cells, Herbert Kim interview, UCSF, 2015.
[17]David Nield, "New Hydrogel That Mimics Cartilage Could Make Knee Repairs Easier," *Science Alert*, April 25, 2017.

THREE QUESTION HEURISTICS

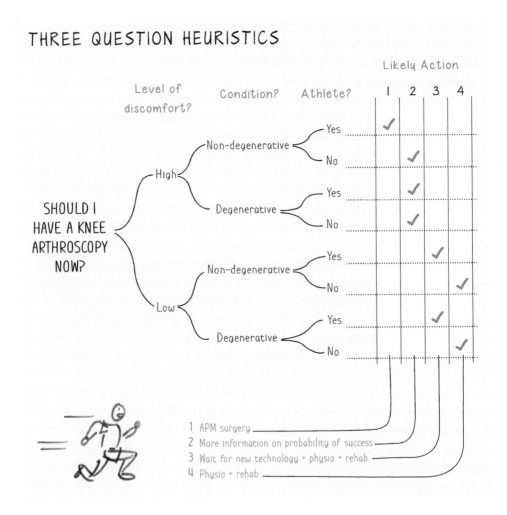

EXHIBIT 5.5

Root cause analysis is a problem solving tool that also uses questions in a clever way. The technique of asking 5 Whys to get to the bottom of a problem was developed at the Toyota Motor Corporation.[18] What is often termed a fishbone diagram is laid out to visualize contributing factors to a problem (see Exhibit 5.6).

---

[18]Taichi Ohno, "Ask 'Why' Five Times about Every Matter," Toyota Traditions, March 2006.

ROOT CAUSE ANALYSIS

Root cause analysis (RCA) is a useful problem solving toolkit for some kinds of problems—and as a mindset or way of approaching problems. Most RCA tools were developed in complex industrial settings, and in the safety and accident investigation fields. The core idea is to dig deeper than the superficial or proximate causes of manufacturing faults or aviation accidents to uncover the source or root causes. You know you have a root cause when addressing that source removes the later problem.

There are a number of specialist tools and processes employed in RCA, but three of them have good general problem solving utility: fishbone diagrams, 5-Whys, and Pareto Thinking (80-20 thinking, already covered above). When you have really complex processes, such as those we encounter in high tech manufacturing, it can be really difficult to isolate the sources of product defects and related problems. Fishbone diagrams, sometimes called by their Japanese name Ishikawa diagrams, can give you a comprehensive perspective on the potential sources of proximate and root causes. Good RCA processes use clear problem definition, careful disaggregation by time and stage of production, and team brainstorming on each potential source of error to tease out root causes.

ROOT CAUSE FISHBONE OR ISHIKAWA DIAGRAM

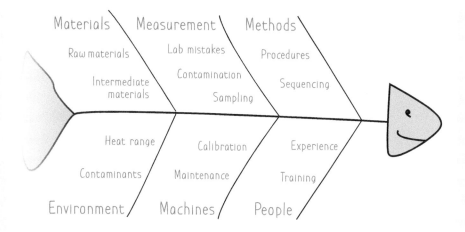

EXHIBIT 5.6

The 5 Whys are often used as above in production and operations problems where the technique was developed, and in developing safety cases. But the technique can be useful in other kinds of business problems too. The example in Exhibit 5.7 looks at a diagnosis of market-share loss, looking at superficial causes until the deeper source of the problem is found.

Root cause analysis can also be applied to social problems such as homelessness. A recent *Harvard Business Review* article on how philanthropy is addressing deep-seated social problems made the remark that "donors don't want to fund homeless shelters and food pantries. They want to end homelessness and hunger."[19] To do so means you first need to understand the homelessness problem and its various manifestations. Using the same technique as the example above we need to explore root causes by answering questions like these:

- Is homelessness an issue mainly for men or women as well?
- For women is it younger or older women who are disproportionately represented?
- Are homelessness events for younger women episodic or long term in nature? If they are episodic, are they related to domestic violence or financial factors?
- Are there adequate women's shelters and support services in a particular community?
- Are there programs in communities where domestic violence has been significantly reduced?

The same train of questions applies to other parts of the homelessness logic tree, and most likely will produce different outcomes, including where the problems' origins lie in mental health or drug or alcohol addiction, rather than financial distress or domestic violence. We will revisit homelessness in Chapter 9, where we talk about how to tackle wicked problems.

---

[19]Susan Wolf Ditkoff and Abe Grindle, "Audacious Philanthropy," *Harvard Business Review*, September–October 2017.

The 5 Whys approach, famous for use in Toyota's automotive production lines, is a powerful brainstorming tool for problem solving teams. It forces us to push beyond the local or contributory causes of problems toward root causes by asking 'why' until there is no further possible 'why'. Here is an example from a company that is losing market share but doesn't know the source of the problem. By forcing greater and greater specificity, the ultimate source of customer loss is found in inadequate training of phone customer service agents.

ROOT CAUSE OF MARKET SHARE LOSS

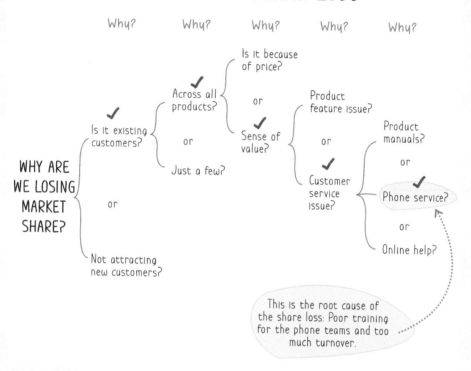

While RCA tools were developed to find the sources of problems retrospectively, a root cause mentality can also be a forward-looking tool for your problem solving.

EXHIBIT 5.7

Chapter 5 Takeaways

- Start all analytic work with simple summary statistics and heuristics that help you see the size and shape of your problem levers.
- Don't gather huge data sets or build complicated models before you have done this scoping reconnaissance with rules of thumb.
- Be careful to know the limitations of heuristics, particularly the potential for reinforcing availability and confirmation biases.
- Question-based, rough-cut problem solving can help you uncover powerful algorithms for making good decisions and direct your empirical work (when required).
- Root cause and 5-Whys analytics can help you push through proximate drivers to fundamental causes in a variety of problems, and not just limited to production and operations environments.

Problems to Try on Your Own

1. How would you go about preparing estimates for whether Sydney Airport has a capacity shortage from the case in Chapter 1?

2. What is the break-even point for Truckgear from Chapter 1? Should they focus on margin or market share?

3. Try reasoning by analogy about the next new thing in mobile devices. What are the biases you might be bringing into this? How can you avoid the Walkman problem (not seeing something that didn't exist before)?

4. Make a forecast of something you're interested in. It could be the economy, fashion, sports, or entertainment. Set out what you have to believe for the forecast to be true. Then ask whether it's likely to happen. Check out fivethirtyeight.com, where they do this for a living.

5. The blockchain is now 10 years old and a promising technology for smart contracts and governance. Draw out the diffusion curve for blockchain and explain how you validated your assumptions.

6. Take a business plan in a tech venture or social enterprise you have seen and do a knock-out analysis, followed by a set of questions to the entrepreneur about what you have to believe for success.

7. What are the three questions that will help you decide whether to buy an electric car in the next two years?

8. Can you think of an example from your work where you have a problem you can interrogate with 5 Whys? Lay out the tree and sequence of questions.

9. How would you take the root cause case of homeless women to the next stage of inquiry? What are the second- and third-order questions to be asked? What analysis would you want to see undertaken before you felt comfortable with policies to address the issue?

Big Guns of Analysis

ANALYZE

In Chapter 5 we introduced a set of first-cut heuristics and root cause thinking to make the initial analysis phase of problem solving simpler and faster. We showed that you can often get good-enough analytic results quickly for many types of problems with little mathematics or model building. But what should you do when faced with a complex problem that really does require a robustly quantified solution? When is it time to call in the big guns—Bayesian statistics, regression analysis, Monte Carlo simulation, randomized controlled experiments, machine learning, game theory, or crowd-sourced solutions? This is certainly an arsenal of analytic weaponry that many of us would find daunting to consider employing. Even though your team may not have the expertise to use these more complex problem solving tools, it is important for the workforce of today to have an understanding of how they can be applied to challenging problems. In some cases you may need to draw on outside experts, in other instances you can learn to master these techniques yourself.

The critical first step is to ask this question: *Have you adequately framed the problem you face, and the hypothesis you want to test, so that it's clear you do need more firepower?* If you decide your problem does fall into the genuinely complex range, you then need to consider other questions. Is there data available to support using an advanced analytic tool? Which tool is the right one for your problem? Is there user-friendly software available to help your team use some of these tools? Can you outsource this aspect of the problem solving work?

Firepower Availability

It used to be that larger problems involved specialist-managed, time-intensive, and costly analytic processes. With the rapid rise in available computing power and the decline in data storage costs, more of these tools are now accessible. Software packages that allow you to run sophisticated analyses with only a few command lines are becoming more common, and have become substantially more straightforward for the everyday user. For example, regression analysis is available in Excel by loading the Analysis ToolPak, and Monte Carlo simulation and other tools are available from the R-Project, a free analytic software resource.

Given greater accessibility, we are seeing increased use of sophisticated modeling tools, such as machine learning, earlier in the problem solving process in businesses, consulting firms, and government institutions. Sometimes this is warranted, but often the use of high-powered tools seems to be premature or misplaced. As we saw in Chapter 5, before embarking on complex analyses, we believe you are better off refining your thinking about the problem structure and the hypotheses you're testing by doing some initial order-of-magnitude analysis. Why? First-cut data analysis often points to direction of causality and size of impact, which are critical to evaluating the results of complex models later. Showing model correlations in the absence of clear explanation doesn't prove anything. And knowing that one configuration or algorithm explains slightly more variance in a multivariable model often brings you no closer to understanding root causes. Data-fishing expeditions or unfocused analysis that "boil the ocean" are likely to result in inefficient problem solving.

Professor Stephen Roberts, a machine-learning expert at Oxford, emphasizes the need to rigorously frame a question or hypothesis before embarking on complex analysis. He advises students not to commence machine-learning analysis until such time as they have developed a clear idea of the structure of the model and testable hypotheses, the essence of the scientific method.[1]

In this chapter, we explain where and how to apply advanced analytical approaches, as well as some of their limitations. Even if you don't personally employ the analytic big guns, you are likely to be presented with analysis that comes from these approaches.

Sequence Your Thinking

The process we recommend for deciding when to use the big guns is a sequential one. Our preferred sequence, not surprisingly, is to start with clearly defining the problem and forming initial hypotheses. Then get to know your data by looking at the mean, median, and mode, as well as other summary statistics. Plotting the distributions of key variables will point to the skew (difference from

---

[1]Personal communication with Professor Stephen Roberts, Oxford University.

a normal distribution), if any, in the data. Experiment with visualizing the data and correlations with scatter plots or hot-spot diagrams (Exhibit 6.2, which shows the air quality and asthma in London, is a good example of this). Of course this assumes you have data—we'll show some approaches to dealing with limited data environments below.

Which Big Gun to Choose?

We worked with Oxford academics and our research team with experience in data analytics to design a decision tree that can help guide you to using the right analysis tool. The most important defining question at the outset is to understand the nature of your problem: Are you primarily trying to *understand* the drivers of causation of your problem (how much each element contributes and in what direction), or are you primarily trying to *predict* a state of the world in order to make a decision? The first question leads you mostly down the left-hand branch into various statistical analyses, including creating or discovering experiments. The second question leads you mostly down the right-hand side of the tree into forecasting models, the family of machine or deep learning algorithms, and game theory. Some problems have elements of both sides, and require combining tools from both branches of the decision tree. And simulations and forecasting models can be found on both sides of the tree (see Exhibit 6.1).

When you are focused on *understanding* the complex causes of your problem, so that you can develop strategies for intervention, you are usually in the world of statistics. Here the quality and extent of your data is critical to knowing which tool you can use. If you have good data, you can use correlation and regression tools, many of which are available in quite easy-to-use software packages. There are more and more externally available data sets, many of which are low cost or free. Sometimes external data doesn't exist for your problem, but you can design an experiment to develop your own data. Experiments have long been so important in safety-critical fields like medicine, for instance, where robustly inferring whether

SELECTING AN ANALYSIS APPROACH

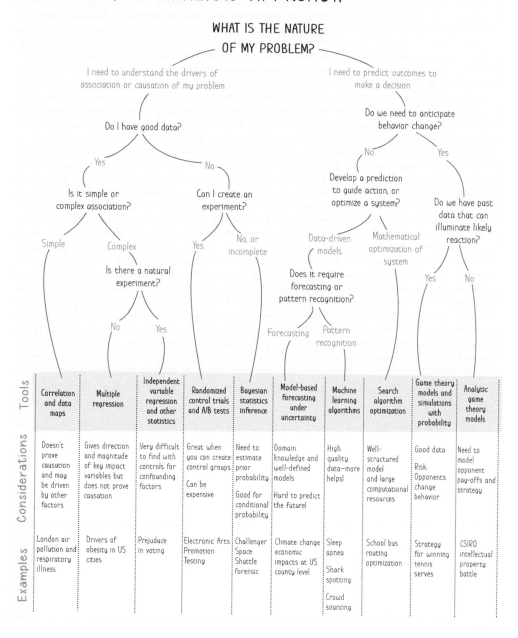

EXHIBIT 6.1

drugs cause intended effects and side effects is essential. Experiments have become ubiquitous in business and economics as methodologies improve and costs to run experiments have declined, particularly in online settings. In lots of cases, however, there are costs, complexity, and ethical hurdles to experimentation (which involve treating two similar groups differently). If you are clever (and lucky) you may be able to find a natural experiment where the structure of some real-world situation provides its own control group. You may also find yourself in a situation where you have only partial data and no potential for experiment. Here Bayesian (conditional) statistics can be helpful.

When you are mainly focused on *predicting outcomes* or potential states of the world to plan decisions, you first have to determine if it is important to anticipate and model the reaction of other players or competitors. If you do, you will probably be employing game theory, perhaps enhanced with statistical knowledge. If you are not focused on competitor strategies, you are probably optimizing some kind of system or forecasting uncertain outcomes. If the first of these, you may be learning how to employ tools from machine learning (where understanding is less important that accurate prediction). Particular problems around image recognition and language processing may be best suited to the sub-field of neural networks. If the second, you will likely be employing forecasting models or simulations.

Case Studies for Employing the Big Guns

We know this is a complicated decision tree. To illustrate each of these analytic tools in action, we provide case examples of how they are used in problem solving. We start with simple data analysis and then move on to multiple regression, Bayesian statistics, simulations, constructed experiments, natural experiments, machine learning, crowd-sourced problem solving, and finish up with another big gun for competitive settings, game theory. Of course each of these tools could warrant a textbook on their own, so this is necessarily only an introduction to the power and applications of each technique.

Summary of Case Studies

1. Data visualization: London air quality

2. Multivariate regression: Understanding obesity

3. Bayesian statistics: Space Shuttle *Challenger* disaster

4. Constructed experiments: RCTs and A|B testing

5. Natural experiments: Voter prejudice

6. Simulations: Climate change example

7. Machine learning: Sleep apnea, bus routing, and shark spotting

8. Crowd-sourcing algorithms

9. Game theory: Intellectual property and serving in tennis

It is a reasonable amount of effort to work through these, but bear with us—these case studies will give you a solid sense of which advanced tool to use in a variety of problem settings.

Data Visualization: Clusters and Hotspots—London Air Quality Example

Publicly available data sets are becoming more widely accessible. To illustrate the power of relatively simple analysis on public data sets, we take the case of air quality in London (Exhibit 6.2). We know that one of the major factors affecting air quality is small particulate matter, PM 2.5 and PM 10. You don't want to live in places where PM 2.5 levels are frequently high because of respiratory and cardiovascular impact. We looked at London using air quality data and asthma hospital admissions by postcode for the year 2015. The heat map that results shows the neighborhoods with the highest level of risk. As a first cut, it suggests exploring the issue further is warranted, even though the correlations aren't especially high between particulate matter and hospital admissions for year-long data. And as we know, correlations do not prove causation; there could be an underlying factor causing both PM 2.5 hotspots and asthma hospital admissions. Experiments, more granular data analysis, and large-scale models are the next step for this work.

WHERE TO LIVE: PART II
ZEROING IN ON AIR QUALITY

The air that we breathe is key to our health. It was a factor in Charles's analysis of where to live. In this case we zero in on air quality and what it implies for where to live in London.

Rob had noticed a Public Health England report a few years ago concluding that 3000 people in London died in 2010 as a result of PM_{25} particles in the air that affect respiratory health including asthma and is correlated to heart and lung disease. A number of studies have concluded that there is really no safe level of exposure to PM_{25}.[1]

We asked William Rathje, a Rhodes scholar on our team with data analysis and machine learning skills, to spend an hour on the question of whether we could identify 'hotspots' for asthma and PM_{25} levels. William produced these remarkable pictures below, based on 2015 data, that show where the asthma hotspots are. The left image is measured by accident and emergency admissions, and the right is measured by PM_{25} hotspots. The visual representation shows a significant overlap.

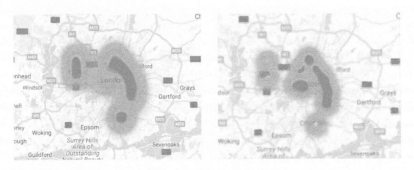

The analysis shows what you can learn about things like air quality from modest commitments of time and data analysis skills. We'd argue that this is a non-trivial consideration when making a decision on where to live.

EXHIBIT 6.2

Source: Q. Di et al., "Air Pollution and Mortality in the Medicare Population," *New England Journal of Medicine* 376 (June 29, 2017), 2513–2522.

Regression Models to Understand Obesity

Obesity is a genuinely wicked problem to which we will return in Chapter 9. There are multiple explanations for its prevalence and increase, wide differences between communities, and complex behavioral and policy factors at work. Moreover, there are no success stories that we are aware of for communities of any scale reversing the trend. In this example we want to highlight regression analysis as a powerful analytic tool to understand underlying drivers of the problem of obesity. It doesn't solve the obesity conundrum, but it shows us where to look for solutions.

We asked one of our research assistants, Bogdan Knezevic, a Rhodes scholar doing a PhD in genomics and big data analytics, to test several hypotheses related to obesity at the city level using regression analysis. The hypotheses were developed from the comprehensive McKinsey Global Institute (MGI) study on obesity.[2] Bogdan gathered data on 68 US cities, including obesity prevalence,[3] educational attainment, median household income, city walkability,[4] and climate comfort score.[5] The climate comfort score is the suitability of weather to physical activity. It is calculated as the sum of temperature and relative humidity divided by four. Comfort scores are like Goldilocks's porridge: You don't want it too hot or too cold but just right with temperature and humidity. The data showed that education, income, walkability, and comfort score are all negatively correlated with obesity. Bogdan found that all the variables except walkability were individually correlated with obesity. Perhaps, surprisingly, the comfort index and walkability had almost no correlation with each other. Other variables, especially income and education, are highly correlated with each other

---

[2]MGI Obesity Study, 2013.

[3]American Fact Finder, https://factfinder.census.gov/faces/nav/jsf/pages/index .xhtml.

[4]Tim Althoff, Rok Sosic, Jennifer L. Hicks, Abby C. King, Scott L. Delp, and Jure Leskovec, "Large-Scale Physical Activity Data Reveal Worldwide Activity Inequality," *Nature* 547 (July 20, 2017): 336–339.

[5]Sperling's Best Places, www.bestplaces.net.

(68%), which can make sorting out relative influence in causation more difficult.[6]

In Exhibit 6.3, individual cities are compared for obesity prevalence measured by BMI (body mass index) and household income, with comfort scores shown as circles. The correlation between obesity and income is clear and large: Income accounts for 71% of the variance in obesity between cities. The line of best-fit shows that having household income at $80,000 versus $60,000 is associated with a seven-percentage-point reduction in obesity, over 30% percent.

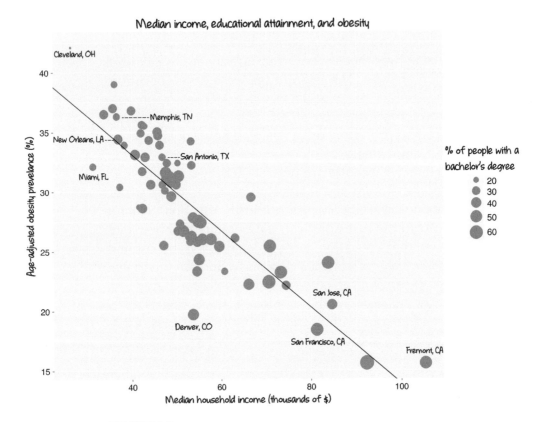

EXHIBIT 6.3

_____

[6]The test for multicollinearity, the extent to which one independent variable could be linearly predicted from another independent variable, were positive for income and education, while others returned negative correlations between the two; both variables were retained.

The best model for capturing obesity differences between cities depended on a combination of income, education, comfort, walkability, and an income/education interaction term that accounts for the relationship between those two variables. All the variables were statistically significant and negatively correlated with obesity. Some 82% of the variance in obesity can be explained when all four variables are included, a level of explanatory power that is relatively high in our experience. Nonprofits, such as the Robert Wood Johnson Foundation, have noted how significant income and education factors are in explaining obesity differences in the United States.

Multiple regression analysis allows us to combine and control for variables as we explore our understanding of the underlying relationships. For instance, running a linear regression on our data using only walkability leads us to conclude that there is no significant correlation between city walkability and obesity rates. However, when we put both walkability and a comfort score together using multivariable regression, we see that walkability is significantly correlated with obesity after controlling for weather.

This example is just a simple one to show how regression analysis can help you begin to understand the drivers of your problem, and perhaps to craft strategies for positive intervention at the city level.

As useful as regression is in exploring our understanding, there are some pitfalls to consider:

- Be careful with correlation and causation. Walkable cities seem to almost always have far lower obesity rates than less walkable cities. However, we have no way of knowing from statistics alone whether city walkability is the true *cause* of lower obesity. Perhaps walkable cities are more expensive to live in and the real driver is higher socioeconomic status. Or perhaps healthier people move to more walkable communities.
- Regression models can be misleading if there are variables that we may not have accounted for in our model but that may be very important. This model is configured at the city level, and so is blind to individual level behavioral or cultural factors.

- Adding more variables may improve the performance of the regression analysis—but adding more variables may then be *overfitting* the data. This problem is a consequence of the underlying mathematics—and a reminder to always use the simplest model that sufficiently explains your phenomenon.

Bayesian Statistics and the Space Shuttle *Challenger Disaster*

For those who lived through the Space Shuttle *Challenger* disaster, it is remembered as an engineering failure. It was that of course, but more importantly it was a problem solving failure. It involved risk assessment relating to O-ring damage that we now know is best assessed with Bayesian statistics. Bayesian statistics are useful in incomplete data environments, and especially as a way of assessing conditional probability in complex situations. Conditional probability occurs in situations where a set of probable outcomes depends in turn on another set of conditions that are also probabilistic. For example the probability of it raining will vary depending on whether there are clouds in the sky, which itself is probabilistic.

Lets look at our *Challenger* space shuttle example from the Introduction again to see how this analytic approach can help you assess risk. O-ring failure under low temperatures was the probable cause of the *Challenger* space shuttle erupting shortly after lift-off.[7] Rubber O-rings were used on the *Challenger* to prevent hot gases from leaking and were designed to compress and expand with temperature. However questions were raised about the resiliency of cold O-rings given the unusually low temperature at launch of 31 degrees Fahrenheit, some 22 degrees below the minimum on previous launches, coupled with the finding by incident investigators that a compressed O-ring is five times more responsive at 75 degrees than at 30 degrees Fahrenheit. In this case the probability of O-ring failure is (partially) conditional on the probability of experiencing a particular temperature range.

---

[7]Presidential Commission on the Space Shuttle Challenger Accident, 1986.

Researchers have relooked at the circumstances of the O-ring failure and reached conclusions that substantiate the focus on O-rings but relate specifically to the data analysis and problem solving undertaken prior to launch on January 28, 1986.[8] They argue that if Bayesian statistics had been employed, and correct sampling done, this near inescapable conclusion would have been reached: that the probability of failure, given a predicted launch temperature of 31 degrees Fahrenheit, was a near certainty.

What made the analysis difficult for engineers at the time was that the data they had was for flights where the temperature at launch was in the range of 53 to 81 degrees Fahrenheit, when in this instance the launch of *Challenger* was to occur at an unusually cold 31 degrees Fahrenheit. They looked at the temperature when O-ring damage occurred and noted the level of O-ring thermal distress that occurred between 53 degrees and 75 degrees. They did look at limited data below this temperature range, but couldn't see a clear pattern (Exhibit 6.4). The engineering team reported this conclusion to NASA prior to the launch to address concerns that a low launch temperature could affect O-rings.

FLIGHTS WITH DAMAGED O-RINGS & TEMPERATURE

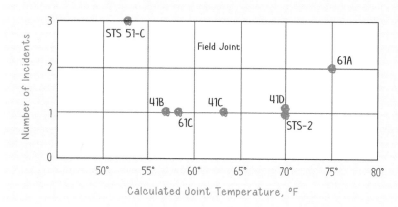

EXHIBIT 6.4

---

[8]C. J. Maranzano and R. Krzystztofowicz, "Bayesian Re-Analysis of the Challenger O-ring Data," *Risk Analysis* 28, no. 4 (2008): 1053–1067.

The data they should have been looking at, however, was the data on *all* flights in relation to temperature and O-ring damage. What becomes clear from the data below, when you include all flights with no O-ring damage incidents, is a different picture: For temperatures below 65 degrees, all 4 flights had incidents, or 100%! Above 65 degrees only 3 of 20 flights, or 15%, had damage incidents. With all the data, the relationship between temperature and O-ring performance becomes a lot clearer to see (Exhibit 6.5).

FLIGHTS WITH DAMAGED O-RINGS & TEMPERATURE

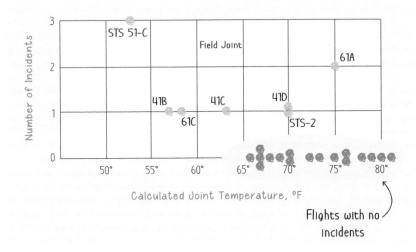

EXHIBIT 6.5

Bayesian statistician Professor Sally Cripps of the University of Sydney, a former colleague of Rob's at the Australian Graduate School of Management, has taken this data and combined it with a prior probability of failure of 30% (the failure of seven O-rings in 23 flights). The resulting posterior probability of failure given launch at 31F is a staggering 99.8%, almost identical to the estimate of another research team who also used Bayesian analysis.

Several lessons emerge for the use of big guns in data analysis from the Challenger disaster. First is that the choice of model, in this case Bayesian statistics, can have an impact on conclusions about risks, in this case catastrophic risks. Second is that it takes careful thinking to arrive at the correct conditional probability. Finally, how you handle extreme values like launch temperature at 31F, when the data is incomplete, requires a probabilistic approach where a distribution is fitted to available data. Bayesian statistics may be the right tool to test your hypothesis when the opportunity exists to do updating of a prior probability with new evidence, in this case exploring the full experience of success and failure at a temperature not previously experienced. Even where actual Bayesian calculations aren't employed, a Bayesian thinking approach (taking account of conditional probabilities) can be very useful.

Constructed Experiments: RCTs and A|B Testing

Often data we would love to have to shed light on our problem just doesn't exist. Experiments give us a way to make our own data. There are lots of advantages to this—in particular, your competitors are sure not to have your data. Let's take a look at two types of experiments that have become popular in the corporate world.

Randomized controlled experiments allow us to test a change in one variable while controlling for all other variables. As we saw in the obesity example above, maybe it's not a feature of walkable cities themselves that makes people less obese. Maybe people who are already healthy tend to move to cities that are walkable because they like to walk. Experiments avoid this kind of potential mistake in understanding causality. But they're often hard to execute in practice. We can't easily make a city more pedestrian friendly and compare it to another city. But when we can set up a good experiment, they can have great explanatory power.

Experiments can be useful for evaluating different types of interventions. For example, a randomized-controlled experiment can help you test whether a specific new program offering individuals incentives to walk five miles per day reduces obesity better than an existing program, controlling for all other factors. Randomized controlled trials (RCTs) require you to recruit a pool of participants, and randomly allocate participants into two or more treatment groups and a control group. In this case, the treatment is the new exercise incentive program. They work particularly well when you want evidence that a *specific intervention* is the likely cause of a change in outcome. By randomly allocating the treatment and control groups, you ensure that all other characteristics of this group—like demographics, general health status, baseline exercise rates, and diet—vary only at random. When your sample size is large enough, no one group should be unbalanced compared to the general population. For example, when assigned randomly, your exercise-treatment group won't have more women than men compared to your control group. If your treatment group improved more than the control, by a statistically significant amount, you know that your exercise program, not gender or any other variable, is a strong candidate for explaining the improvement. It doesn't entirely remove so-called confounding factors, but it's a good start.[9]

Special types of experiments are variations on randomized controlled trials. Market trials are one such special case of experimental methods, where a new product is tried on a small test market before a full roll out. One of the most frequently used experimental techniques in business today is A/B testing. A/B testing is used to make adjustments to product offers in real time. For instance, you may want to test the effect of changing the background color of your website homepage on the length of time visitors stay on your website. An experiment is quick and easy to perform and provides evidence for one design over another. An A/B test would involve randomly selecting two groups of visitors to your website and showing one group (group A) your webpage with the new design while the other group (group B) of users, the control group,

---

[9] *The Book of Why* by Judea Pearl and Dana Mackenzie (Allen Lane, 2018) has a good example of confounding factors with the example of the correlation between Nobel Prize winners and per capita chocolate consumption of the country they come from. Wealthy countries invest more in education *and* eat more chocolate, so the wealth and location of prizewinners are confounders.

sees your old design. You track each group's usage pattern, and in some cases follow up with a survey after they visit the site. You can then choose your website homepage color using real data about how the design, color, or other variations affect user retention times or e-commerce uptake. And because you ran a randomized experiment, you know that it's more likely the design—not other variables—influencing user experience.

A/B Testing

Electronic Arts (EA) recently used an A/B test to explore the impact of sales and promotions on the sale of new game releases.[10] Driven by revenue targets coincident with the release of the next version of SimCity, SimCity 5, EA was surprised when the initial advertising layout of the website with a promotional offer in a headline banner were not generating rising pre-orders. Could it be that the pre-order call to action was incorrectly placed? Their team constructed several additional variations on the pre-order page and randomly exposed the site visitors to the different options, say A/B/C/D. Option A, without any promotion at all, and Option B with a promotional banner, are shown in Exhibit 6.6.

The team concluded that the site with no promotional offer led to 43.4% more purchases of the new game edition, a significant increase. Here A/B testing allowed them to experimentally explore their customers' responses to sales and advertising. In the process they learned that SimCity customers' decision to purchase was not contingent on a promotion. This kind of testing is particularly easy to do in online environments, but can also be employed in different cities or at the retail store level to generate similar results. Real-world experiments are harder when large numbers are required to create controls for confounding factors, as is often true in healthcare examples, or where it is unethical to expose people to experimental choices without their consent. This might lead us to look at so-called natural experiments.

---

[10]https://blog.optimizely.com/2013/06/14/ea_simcity_optimizely_casestudy/.

A/B TESTING

EXHIBIT 6.6

Natural Experiments: Voter Prejudice

Even if a question could be answered by a constructed experiment, sometimes you can't run one. Your turnaround time or budget might be too limited, or ethical considerations might rule out experimentation. Governments, for example, often want to understand the effects of changing a tax or benefit program. But it is difficult (and often illegal) to adjust taxes or social benefits for some groups but not for others (the control groups) in a way that would shed light on the best course for public policy. How can you collect convincing evidence under such constraints?

One answer is the natural experiment, also called a quasi-experiment: If you can't run an experiment yourself, look to see if the world has already run it—or something like it—for you. Institutions often make choices that, by accident, create environments that can be much like an experiment. Many government programs rely on essentially arbitrary cutoffs or, by some combination of history and happenstance, treat some geographic areas differently from other similar areas. This creates natural affected groups and control groups. In the United States, for instance, the national minimum drinking age of 21 creates a sharp change in the legal status of drinking between people aged 20 years and 364 days and 21 years and 0 days. When we can safely compare people just on one side of a policy's cutoff to those on the other side, or areas that were heavily affected by a given intervention to areas that were less affected, then we have a natural experiment that can tell us many of the same things an actual experiment could.

Natural experiments can be powerful tools, giving us high-quality evidence in environments unsuitable for experimentation. But because they are, by definition, not actual experiments, natural experiments require more attention to context and potential confounding factors that might damage the experimental character of the environment. To see how you might use a natural experiment to answer a question where actual experiments can't go and that would stump our other problem solving tools, let's consider one example from Evan Soltas, a Rhodes Scholar, and David Broockman, a political scientist at Stanford University (now published as a Stanford GSB Working Paper). Evan and David's question was: *Do voters discriminate against minority candidates in elections?*

It's important, first, to see what methods *won't* work to answer this question. We can't simply gather data on white and nonwhite candidates for office, calculate the average difference in the number of votes they receive, and declare whatever difference exists to be "discrimination." There are potentially many differences between white and nonwhite candidates other than race; for instance, whites and nonwhites may run for different offices or campaign on different platforms. Without an experiment—or something very close to one—untying this knot, and distinguishing the independent effect of discrimination, is hopeless.

Evan and David found their natural experiment in an obscure, unusual procedure in the Illinois Republican presidential primary.

In it, voters cast multiple ballots for delegates selected to represent presidential candidates at the Republican convention, where a candidate is formally nominated. An Illinois voter who supported Donald Trump, for instance, couldn't vote for him in the primary, but rather would vote for three delegates who are legally bound to attend the convention and support this candidate. The twists that create the natural experiment in this case are: first, that these delegates' names appear on the ballot, even though their identities are nearly entirely irrelevant. Most delegates are political unknowns— so unnoteworthy that many aren't discoverable on Google, and certainly are not known to most voters. Second, voters don't have to vote for all of their favored presidential candidate's delegates, and so delegates for the same candidate need not receive the same number of votes to effectively represent the candidate at the convention.

Imagine a candidate nominated two presumably-white delegates, Tom and Dick, and a presumably-nonwhite delegate, Jose. To support their candidate fully, his voters should cast ballots for Tom, Dick, and Jose. Some voters might subtly discriminate, however, by voting for Tom and Dick but not for Jose. If enough voters discriminate, then minority delegates like Jose will receive significantly fewer votes than non-minority delegates like Tom and Dick; that is, relative to delegates who are perfectly comparable in the sense that they face exactly the same pool of voters at the same time, and are bound to support the same presidential candidate, and differ only in their identity as indicated by their name on the ballot. This is a great natural experiment!

In the terminology of natural experiments, one delegate is "treated" with a likely minority name and is compared against the control of two delegates without likely minority names. Evan and David's Illinois election data, in fact, contained over 800 such experiments. What they found was revealing about the extent of prejudice among American voters: The delegates with names that suggested they were nonwhite received about 10% fewer votes as compared to their respective white control delegates.

NATURAL EXPERIMENT:
TESTING FOR PREJUDICE IN VOTING PATTERNS

Natural Experiment Design

Evaluation*

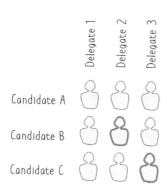

Candidate A

Candidate B

Candidate C

Delegate 1

Delegate 2

Delegate 3

🧑 Minority Delegate (Treated Unit)

🧑 Non-minority Delegate (Control Unit)

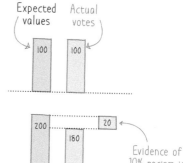

Expected values   Actual votes

100   100

200   180   20

Evidence of 10% racism in voter choice

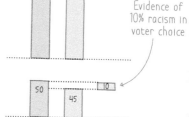

50   45   10

Note: Actual evidence done with independent variable regression analysis in the form of:

$$\log \text{Votes}_i = a_c + b \text{ Nonwhite}_i + c X_i + e_i$$

Where:

$\log \text{Votes}_i$	= logarithm of the number of votes for delegate i
a_c	= fixed effect for each candidate c
Nonwhite_i	= delegate i has a likely-nonwhite name
b	= causal effect of being nonwhite on votes
X_i	= control variables (e.g., officeholding)
e_i	= error term

EXHIBIT 6.7

Exhibit 6.7 shows how Evan and David went from research design—that is, the idea of their natural experiment—to their statistical analysis. While we could, by simple arithmetic, calculate the percentage gap between the nonwhite and white delegates in each of Evan and David's experiments, a properly specified independent variable regression analysis will do such a calculation for us. Standard statistical software, such as R, Stata, or various Python packages, can easily support regression analyses similar to Evan and David's.

In this analysis, the crucial independent variable was the perceived race of delegates. To get the data, Evan and David were entrepreneurial: They matched delegates' last names to a dataset from the US Census that provides, for each last name, a share of Americans with a last name who are nonwhite. They also paid online workers on Amazon's Mechanical Turk (mTurk) marketplace to guess, without further information, the racial background of delegates from their names alone, replicating their view of what voters might be doing in the privacy of the voting booth. This is a form of crowdsourcing, which we'll discuss more below. The actual vote counts, their dependent variable, came from the Illinois State Board of Elections. Knowing where and how to find data, whether from administrative releases from the Census or from mTurk surveys, is itself a vital tool in your analytical arsenal.

What can go wrong in natural experiments like Evan and David's? Natural experiments rely upon the assumption that treatment and control groups are comparable—whereas, in an actual experiment, this would be guaranteed by randomizing treatment. Evan and David had to rule out differences within groups of delegates like Tom, Dick, and Jose other than Jose's minority status. One potential confound of this kind would be if minority delegates were less likely to hold other public offices than nonminority delegates. Then some voters might support Tom or Dick, but not Jose, because Tom is their mayor or Dick is their councilman, not because Jose's minority background makes them uncomfortable. A large part of the work Evan and David put into their project, Evan said, was in addressing such comparability concerns.

It doesn't mean that you can extrapolate from this analysis to other regions or voters; you only know that it's true and present for the precise setting where the data was collected.

Simulations: Climate Change Example

Simulations are computer imitations of what is expected to happen in the real world. They are powerful because they allow you to see many potential states of the world with different input assumptions. All you need is a model, some initial conditions, and a software program, such as Microsoft Excel, to implement a simulation. Simulations are often fast and low cost; if you have a well-configured model—and that is the hard part—they can allow you to test parameter changes without expensive real-world data collection. They can be useful in both branches of our analytical tools selection tree.

Simulations are particularly helpful for forecasting the impact of policy or parameter change on an outcome of interest, for example of climate change or economic outcomes. Given your known model (and the source of uncertainty if you have it), changing the value of different independent inputs in the model can change the distribution of your results. This is called *sensitivity analysis* and could allow you to use simulations to test the effects of climate change on global mean temperatures, and then on economic outcomes at the county level, as recently highlighted in *The Economist*.[11] The authors of the underlying paper, Hsiang et al, combined a range of temperature and other weather outcomes from climate models,

---

[11] The *Economist* article referenced the work of Hsiang, Kopp, et al. ("Estimating Economic Damage from Climate Change in the United States," *Science* 2017) that with each 1 degree Fahrenheit increase the cost of climate change for the United States would be an aggregate reduction of .7% of GDP. http://science .sciencemag.org/content/356/6345/1362.full?ref=finzine.com%20; "Climate Change and Inequality," *The Economist*, July 13, 2017, https://www.economist.com/ news/finance-and-economics/21725009-rich-pollute-poor-suffer-climate-change-and-inequality; http://news.berkeley.edu/2017/06/29/new-study-maps-out-dramatic-costs-of-unmitigated-climate-change-in-u-s/.

with a set of economic models that predict outcomes at the county level under different climate scenarios, in a large-scale simulation of future impacts of climate change.

The simulation model used by the authors incorporated 44 separate climate change models, rainfall and temperature weather predictions, and uncertainty. They mapped their projections onto joint distributions of possible economic outcomes, exploring the impacts on labor, violent crime, mortality, rainfall, electricity consumption, temperature, and CO_2 at the county level in the United States (Exhibit 6.8). To calculate economic costs in terms of GDP, they monetized non-market impacts and then aggregated each county prediction to the country level. This analysis showed that

TOTAL DIRECT DAMAGES (% COUNTY GDP)

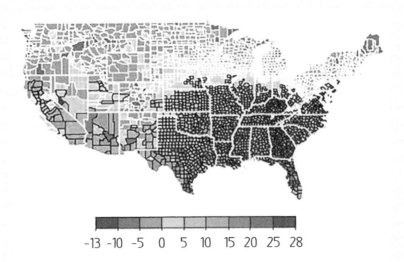

-13 -10 -5   0   5   10   15   20   25   28

EXHIBIT 6.8

the negative impacts of climate change are likely to be disproportionately felt by counties that are already poor. Climate-change analysis, like this one, exhibits one of the main strengths of simulations rather than actual experiments. In the case of climate, we cannot wait for global temperatures to increase to explore the effects, rather we want to simulate possible future effects reliably now in an effort to mitigate and prevent irreversible damage. Simulations work best when you have well configured and tested underlying models, and where your simulations are testing projected ranges in line with the underlying ranges of the original data.

Machine Learning Solutions

Machine learning techniques are at heart very similar in concept to traditional statistical tools like multiple regression. They often perform much better than these traditional techniques when there is a large amount of data in the right format, and when there are more complex patterns and interactions in the data. These tools have caught on, particularly in the past several years, because computing power has grown and is available at reasonable cost to manage large datasets and sophisticated learning algorithms. Learning a simple scripting language such as Python or R allows you to begin using state-of-the-art machine learning tools, and it is within the capabilities of many teams.

Let's look at the problem of classifying whether an individual is at high or low risk of becoming obese. If you have large amounts of data—perhaps walking records from individuals' mobile phones, demographics, and health information—and information about what profiles in this population went on to develop obesity, you allow the machine learning algorithm to *learn* how to identify hallmark signs of obesity risk from the data. Unlike with linear regression, you're less concerned here about identifying and measuring the specific variables that indicate disease risk (although you can often infer these using machine learning) as you are about building a learning model that can make accurate *predictions*. With these techniques you're often less involved in the learning process: Instead of selecting which variables to use, you often allow the computer algorithm to select the correct combination of features. With the right amount of data, machine learning can often outperform traditional statistical techniques for prediction.

We now turn to examples of machine learning that are producing outcomes that save lives and resources. We have selected one in the field of medicine, one that relates to education, and one in the field of drone technology to illustrate the diversity of machine-learning applications in problem solving.

Can a Computer Predict the Onset of Sleep Apnea Better Than Doctors Can?

One of the reasons machine learning has gained so much traction is because of its demonstrated ability to make predictions that are better than human judgment in particular domains. Oxford doctoral students Logan Graham and Brody Foy, cofounders of the Rhodes Artificial Intelligence Lab, a student-led organization dedicated to solving social problems with machine learning, spearheaded the development of a machine-learning model that outperformed expert doctors at predicting whether children would go on to develop sleep apnea within 6 to 12 months from clinical examination. The tool used data from a simple questionnaire containing information on demographics, patient BMI, and co-morbid diseases like asthma and acid reflux to make predictions that consistently outperformed clinicians by upwards of 20% in accuracy. Logan speculates that the model might succeed by shortcutting biases in doctors' decision-making processes or by considering relevant combinations of predictive features that medical practitioners might overlook. The model they developed takes into account the general population while practitioners work patient by patient. The algorithm showed marked success even on a relatively small sample of just over 400 patient records. Conventional diagnosis of sleep apnea requires patients to undergo costly and invasive sleep studies. A predictive model that reduces false positive screens could save patients and doctors considerable time and money.

Logan notes that machine learning works very well for problems that involve predicting future outcomes. However, he also cautions that prediction problems require a dataset that matches the general population distribution. The sleep apnea data was drawn from patients who had already been flagged by their clinicians as being at risk of a sleep disorder. Because of this, a different and larger dataset would be required to make robust predictions if the tool were to be used on the general public. The important point here is that machine learning is predicting an outcome, not understanding the solution or how a decision is being made.

Routing School Buses with Computers

A group of MIT researchers developed an algorithm that saved the Boston Public School System $5 million by optimizing school bus routes for 30,000 students. Previously, school administrators designed bus routes by hand, a laborious process that took weeks every year. The MIT algorithm runs in minutes and eliminated a number of routes to 230 different schools, which used to be serviced by 650 school buses.

Bus routing is an example of a problem where investing in the creation of a computational tool upfront can save time and money in the long run. The algorithm automates the process of bus routing, a process that humans can do with their own intuition, but is so computationally intensive that it can be better served by relying on a mathematical process. It's a problem well suited to automation. The routing system will need to be run year after year, but the underlying decision-making engine need not change each time it is used. There's no real need for human decision making here, and, if anything, human oversight would hamper the decision process. We have objective external criteria that we can use to assess the effectiveness of the algorithm.

Shark Spotting from Drones

Shark attacks are a real and perceived danger on many beaches around the world. Netting is often put in place to reduce the risk of shark attacks but at considerable financial cost and species loss due to entanglement. A solution is emerging on Australian beaches by a company called the Ripper Company that Rob is involved with, a company we shall discuss in more detail in Chapter 8. The solution involves the combination of camera-carrying drones and machine learning. The inspiration for shark spotting via machine learning came from Australian publisher Kevin Weldon, who was the first president of International Surf Life Saving, and Paul Scully Power, Australia's first astronaut.

Here's how it works. Drones patrol the beach and transmit video to the operations center. Together with machine learning experts at the University of Technology Sydney (UTS), the Ripper Company developed a shape-interpreting algorithm, the first of its kind, which predicts the presence of a shark, as distinct from porpoises or humans. When a shark is detected by the algorithm and confirmed by an operator, the beach patrols alert swimmers and clear the water until such time as the drone surveillance confirms no further sightings on the beach.

The algorithm has a mean average precision (MAP) of 90.4% detection, using true-positives and false-positives for the calculation. Precision here relates to how many correct images of sharks are identified from the total images (Exhibit 6.9). This is an impressive result. But it leaves open the question of false negatives—how many sharks aren't spotted (which seems important!)—but the ability to detect with high precision other species like dolphins is thought to minimize the number of false negatives. Like other deep-learning algorithms, the expectation is that results will improve further with additional data.[12] In addition, trialing technology, such as multi-spectral cameras, is expected to provide better ocean penetration, particularly for cloudy days.

---

[12]Communication with Paul Scully Power AM, CTO, The Ripper Company.

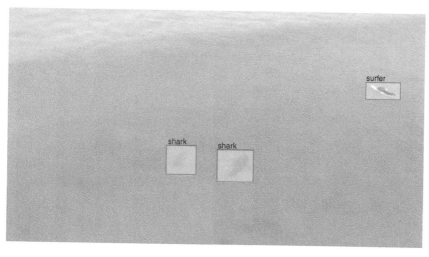

EXHIBIT 6.9

The beach of the future, as The Ripper team pictures it, will incorporate three technologies:

1. A drone tethering system that allows the drone to be powered and sit atop a cable with full view of the beach, able to operate 24/7, but most likely for the hours the beach has lifeguards on duty.

2. A machine learning algorithm linked to the drone video to provide an alert that a shark is within proximity of surfers.

3. A drone payload called a shark shield® that can be dropped to a surfer close to a shark. The shark shield® emits electronic pulses that cause the shark to experience temporary muscle spasms and turn away from the electronic field.

As you can see from these examples, machine learning works well when you want to produce a very accurate model or optimization path, and when you care less about understanding key variables that influence the decision-making process. This tends to be most useful when you already have an understanding of the decision-making mechanism, but it's complex, and you have lots of diverse data examples. Machine learning neural networks can produce impressive results by automating complex processes like human vision for pattern recognition. But many business decisions lack the sheer amounts of high-quality data required to employ learning algorithms.[13] Some business and life decisions require subjective intuitions about past events and future issues unavailable in data, or involve guessing the responses of other players. Could you imagine delegating your decision to a machine about which city to move to, an algorithm that made the decision based on carefully weighing the preferences of thousands of other individuals and considering your situation? Clearly not—though you might be interested in seeing the results.

Crowdsourcing Algorithms

Besides doing sophisticated analysis within your own team, we now have the ability to go outside the organization to harness more analytic power. Enter *crowdsourcing* as a way to pair enterprises searching for solutions with teams of individuals that have ideas for implementation. Participants often compete for a prize to solve challenging problems, which previously required the contracting of consultants and experts. Often problem solving competitions are presented at hackathons, daylong events where programmers and analysts compete for the best solution given the data available to solve the problem at hand.

Kaggle is one such platform that hosts competitions. The range of prizes, challenges, and entrants is quite remarkable. Here are some recent ones.[14]

1. A challenge by the US Department of Homeland Security to generate a passenger-screening algorithm for a $1.5 million prize attracted 518 teams.

---

[13]Machine learning is as powerful and weak as the data used. If a model has significant errors—and we have seen examples of 10% or more errors in data sets—it inherently embeds all the biases of that data into its predictive efforts.
[14]Kaggle website.

2. Real estate company Zillow requested a model that would predict home value, rewarding $1.2 million to the winning team from a field of 3779 teams.

3. Predicting borrower default: 924 teams competed for a $5,000 prize to assess data on 250,000 borrowers and come up with the best predictive algorithm for the probability that a person will experience financial distress in the next two years.

4. Identifying fish species from cameras on fishing boats to estimate fish catch and fish stocks, in a contest format set up by The Nature Conservancy, where Rob is an Asia Pacific trustee. The prize of $150,000 attracted 293 teams around the world.

5. Predicting survival on the *Titanic* using machine learning: Over 10,000 teams entered the competition and were provided data on ship manifests, passengers, and survivors.

The Good Judgment Project is an example of applying crowdsourcing to decision making at a large scale.[15] Philip Tetlock, its founder, developed the project and website around the principle of the *wisdom of the crowd*. If enough people weigh in on a particular forecast, they'll cancel out any individual contributor's biases and come to more accurate conclusions than a single forecaster would. This is a lot like when a crowd of people guess the number of marbles in a jar: A single guess may be very far from correct, but when enough people's guesses are pooled, deviations are canceled out and the crowd usually comes to the right conclusion. Forecasts were surprisingly accurate for major and sometimes very specific world events, including predicting military invasions. The best contributors are dubbed superforecasters, and the entire process is described in the book *Superforecasting*.[16]

Exhibit 6.10 shows a decision tree to help determine whether to use a crowdsourcing competition over other methods (such as an expert contract). It takes into account whether there is an achievable

---

[15]Philip E. Tetlock and Don Gardner, *Superforecasting: The Art and Science of Prediction* (Crown Publishing, 2015).
[16]Tetlock and Gardner, *Superforecasting*.

goal, whether there are few or many resources available, and the willingness to take risks and incur costs. Not surprisingly, there have been entries on Kaggle, including finding a cure for malaria, with a large prize that wasn't collected. You can see how it turned out not to be an achievable goal in the short term as few were in a position to believe they could win and the risks and costs were deemed to be large.

WHEN TO CROWDSOURCE PROBLEM SOLVING
USING COMPETITIONS AND PRIZES

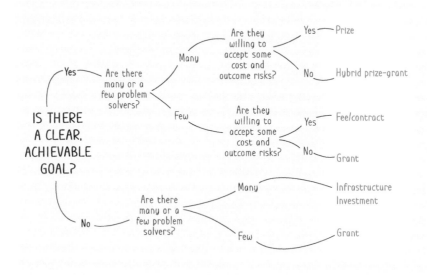

EXHIBIT 6.10

Source: Jonathan Bays, Tony Goland, and Joe Newsum, "Using Prizes to Spur Innovation," *McKinsey Quarterly*, July 2009.

Elon Musk's Hyperloop project is an attempt to rapidly advance transportation technology. The Hyperloop is a pod transportation system currently under development, designed to transport people over long distances at astonishing, near supersonic speeds. Given its clear, well-defined goal, and a large, diverse population of problem solvers, many of whom are students willing to accept the risk and hungry for the experience, the SpaceX Hyperloop competition is a great example to test the power of crowdsourcing. With an available testing track at its disposal, SpaceX ran its Hyperloop Pod Competition in January 2017. By hosting a competition they were able to increase the quantity of prototypes being simultaneously explored. The jury is still out on Hyperloop as a viable concept, but the process is harnessing resources in a way not seen even a decade ago.

Game Theory Thinking

The analytic big guns we have discussed so far are based largely on statistical techniques. One of the other powerful tools in your toolbox for complex problems is game theory. Competitive situations in business and life mean that your actions influence and are influenced by another player, for these purposes called an adversary or opponent. For instance, your strategy has to consider your choices to compete aggressively or collaborate (where that is allowed under competition law). These strategic moves are sometimes played out over hours, days, or years. We employ game theory thinking to work through our own choices and competitor choices, set out in a logic tree. To assess how we should respond to an opponent's moves, we typically create a simulation in which we break the team into an attack team and a defense team, and make a series of moves that the other team has to respond to. We may cover as much as 18 months of moves in a one-day workshop. Then we reconvene and have the business-unit leader reflect on the moves and countermoves, and the likely payoffs from each pursuing their best strategies. Game theorists use terms like *minmax* and *maxmin* to describe strategies where you choose an outcome that maximizes your minimum gain or conversely minimizes your maximum loss. These are constructs for formal games that go beyond the scope of what we are able to share in this book, which involve putting yourself in an opponent's shoes and crafting competitor responses. This is the right tool to use in difficult competitive and adversarial problem solving settings.

We illustrate game-theory thinking with two different examples, an example from business (should you go to court?), and an individual one: Where should I serve in tennis?

Should We Go to Court? CSIRO Wifi Example

If you ask a businessperson the question, "Should we go to court?" the answer is typically "no." Going to court involves uncertainties about outcomes, lengthy periods of executive time in court, and substantial costs. But there are times when it makes sense, and game-theory thinking is a useful framework to help make this decision. Let's consider the case of a successful defense of a wifi patent by a small Australian government research organization called CSIRO against the world's largest technology companies, including Microsoft, Intel, Dell, and HP. It's a story that played out over more than decade in a series of passive and then increasingly aggressive moves by the parties. This strategy resulted in $400m of payments to CSIRO, which was used to fund additional research in the Australian national interest.

CSIRO believed that its wifi technology was valuable, that its patent was being infringed, and that it was entitled to receive a reasonable fee for use. The giant tech companies who were using this technology, on the other hand, believed the right transfer price was zero for many reasons, including that CSIRO was a publicly funded research agency. In a CSIRO briefing to the US government, it was reported this way: "CSIRO tried to license this product. In 2003 and 2004, it became aware of products that it believed infringed on its patent, and sent letters to 28 companies asking them to please discuss terms for a license from CSIRO. The companies did not accept CSIRO's offer."[17]

CSIRO had to decide whether to pursue its case in the courts or not. Doing so, it faced formidable companies in computing and networking with deep pockets and deep experience in patent fights. Besides the cost of legal action and uncertainty of a favorable outcome, CSIRO faced potential costs from being countersued by the tech companies. On the other hand, not defending its patent set a precedent for any future licensing deals it might seek to do in the United States.

[17]CSIRO briefing to US government, December 5, 2006, https://wikileaks.org/plusd/cables/07CANBERRA1721_a.html.

Here's how they reached the decision to go to court. The executive director of Business Development and Commercialization for CSIRO at the time of the decision, Mehrdad Baghai, a former colleague of Charles and Rob, put it this way: "Going back to the beginning, we first of all had to satisfy ourselves that we had a claim that we could pursue. That involved spending about $1 million to get some preliminary expert advice. Then we estimated what we could expect to receive if our claim succeeded in court. I felt it was upwards of $100 million and possibly over $1 billion. To get there meant we needed to commit $10 million to the initial court action. As a back of the envelope calculation, we needed a 10% probability of winning. I felt we had that, easily. I also felt we had a fallback option in the event of costs blowing out, that was an abandonment option, the option to sell all or part of the claim to a group that specializes in intellectual property litigation."[18] Having got to the point of being prepared to go to court, here's how they used game theory thinking to win.

In competitive strategy for business, the cleaving lines are often around *where and how* to compete. Strategies are often depicted contrasting competitor choices about market segments, and whether they compete on cost or value. CSIRO's defense of its patent for wifi provides an example of how strategy plays out over time, in a series of moves designed to learn more about competitor intentions, and to position their own moves for the highest level of success.

CSIRO's strategy for how to compete went from an unsuccessful passive approach of letter writing to ask for voluntary licensing of its technologies, to suing the big tech giants. Even more dramatic was their strategy about *where* to compete. CSIRO had to decide which players it should target initially (Exhibit 6.11). It chose to sue a small to medium networking company called Buffalo Technology for patent infringement in what has been described as a test case. Buffalo was a Japanese company rather than a US giant, with less experience in US patent cases, and at that time it had an almost complete reliance on networking technology that was transitioning

---

[18]Private communication with Mehrdad Baghai.

DAVID VERSUS GOLIATH
WIFI PATENT INFRINGEMENT

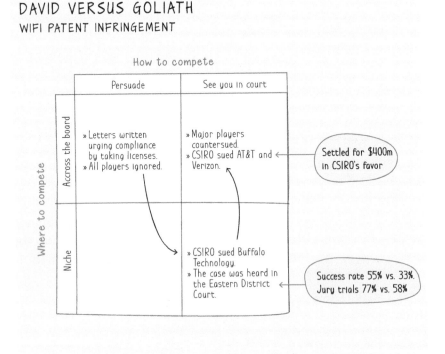

EXHIBIT 6.11

rapidly to wifi. CSIRO's advisers reviewed the record of patent litigation in the US to assess their chances of success. They noted that the Federal Court for the Eastern District of Texas had a much higher success rate for patent holders, and that the time to court for plaintiffs was much faster than for other jurisdictions. For the period 1995–2014, which includes the wifi case, the success rate for plaintiffs in Texas Eastern was 55% compared to 33% overall. They also took note of the fact that trial success rates for plaintiffs with juries were higher than for the judicial bench; for the period 2005–2009 they were 77% compared to 58% for the bench.[19]

Following CSIRO lodging the suit against Buffalo Technology, countersuits were lodged by other patent infringers, including Intel, HP,

[19]PriceWaterhouse Coopers, *Patent Litigation Study: A Change in Patentee Fortunes*, 2015.

Microsoft and Dell. CSIRO had to decide what to do in response to this aggressive action. CSIRO responded the following year by adding another eight companies to its infringement list. Soon CSIRO was facing 14 companies in a jury trial. Their nerve lasted and HP settled first, followed by the 13 others for $205 million. The action CSIRO brought in 2009 against ATT, Verizon, and T Mobile was settled before trial in 2012 for an additional $220 million, a year before the patent was due to expire!

Decisions to go to court require a problem solving approach that takes into account how an adversary will respond. In this case CSIRO was smart to pick a weak adversary in a favorable court to demonstrate its patent, and then it chose to fight larger players from a stronger position. Furthermore, CSIRO had decided they could afford to lose $10 million to put themselves in the game.

Where to Serve in Tennis: Game Theory Example

Many of us play tennis and, as a result, engage in competitive strategy. Barry Nalebuff, a game theorist at Yale Management School, has analyzed where to serve in tennis with fellow strategist Avinash Dixit.[20] Their answers are simple and powerful. The recommendations are to remove predictability by making each serve appear random, and to place your serves to your opponent's forehand 40% of the time and to their backhand 60% of the time. The analysis was described for two types of serve, to the opponent's forehand, and to their backhand, and where the receiver anticipated one serve or the other. The likelihood that your opponent successfully returns serve is highest if you serve to their forehand and he or she anticipates this by moving to the right place. Nalebuff and Dixit prepared a payoff table to reach this conclusion that we show below (Exhibit 6.12). You read it as follows:

- If you serve to your opponent's forehand and they anticipate it, they will return the serve 90% of the time.

- If you serve to their forehand and they do not anticipate it, they will only return successfully 30% of the time.

---

[20]Avinash K. Dixit and Barry J. Nalebuff, *Thinking Strategically* (W.W. Norton, 1991).

PROBABILITY THAT RECEIVER
SUCCESSFULLY RETURNS SERVE

Server's Aim

	Forehand	Backhand
Forehand	90%	20%
Backhand	30%	60%

Receiver's Anticipation

EXHIBIT 6.12

Source: Avinash K. Dixit and Barry J. Nalebuff, *Thinking* Strategically (W.W. Norton, 1991).

- If you serve to their backhand and your opponent anticipates it, they will return the serve 60% of the time (assuming their backhand side is weaker, as it is for most amateur players).
- If you serve to their backhand and they do not anticipate it, they will only return 20% of the time.

Rob took these findings to heart and tried to apply them to his own game, where he is an amateur lefthander who plays mostly on grass or synthetic grass.

Since Nalebuff and Dixit's *Thinking Strategically* was published in 1991, there has been a big change in tennis racket technology and as a result, serving power. Commentators now talk about three types of serve: wide, to the body, and down the T (see Exhibit 6.13). When you watch top players receiving serve today they position themselves in a 45-degree line to the server and don't do much anticipating, just find a position that gives the best chance of returning a serve from all three places. Does this invalidate Nalebuff and Dixit's conclusion that the server needs genuine unpredictability of each serve, and that the serves should be in a 40/60 mix? Rob wanted to know.

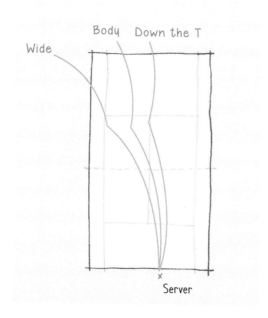

EXHIBIT 6.13

Data analytics comes in to help us with this question. Since the use of Hawkeye technology for line calls, we can analyze what servers actually do in serving and measure predictability. We can also link it to what analysts call important points or clutch points—that is at 30–40 and Advantage out, which are always served to the Ad court. GameSet MAP reviewed the 2012 Olympics final between Andy Murray and Roger Federer using GIS technology. This was a match Murray won. They noted that Murray served with more spatial variation (less predictability) on clutch points than Federer, and that he directed seven of eight serves wide to Federer's backhand.[21] That doesn't sound unpredictable, but he was serving to Federer's backhand, his weaker side. The unpredictability came from mixing one serve in another direction to sow a seed of doubt. On clutch points left handers will serve to the Ad court predominantly because they have the advantage in serving the big carving wide serve to the backhand of a right hander. It's a weapon, so you use it. Rafael Nadal will go wide probably two-thirds of the time on the advantage side, but mix up body and T-serves with the rest.

Game-theory problems can be set out as decision trees as well as payoff matrices. We have put the factors described above into a tree to help Rob think about what he should do in deciding where to serve. We start with whether the server is left or right handed, whether the opponent is left or right handed, whether the opponent is stronger on the forehand than backhand and whether the serve is to the Deuce court or the Ad court. We stopped the tree there as it captures the essence of the game. (We could have added two other branches for completeness: whether it is a clutch point or a regular point, and whether it is a first or second serve). The mix that results is shown in Exhibit 6.14. We show only two cases: a right hander serving to a right hander, like Federer versus Murray, and a left hander serving to a right hander, like Nadal versus Federer. The percentages are in effect conditional probabilities. They show considerable variation depending on the opponent and whether you're serving on the deuce court or ad court. This analysis concludes that it is no longer a simple 40/60 mix as per the two-serve place example, but one with a richer mix.

---

[21]GameSet Map, February 19, 2013.

WHERE TO SERVE THE BALL DURING A TENNIS GAME

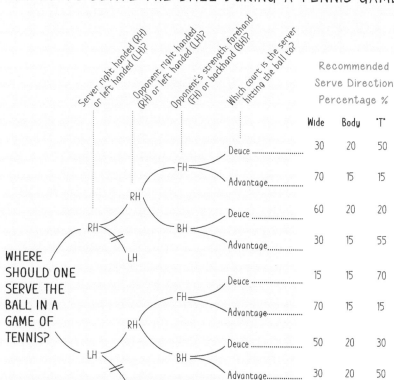

				Recommended Serve Direction Percentage %		
				Wide	Body	'T'
			Deuce	30	20	50
		FH				
			Advantage	70	15	15
	RH					
			Deuce	60	20	20
		BH				
RH			Advantage	30	15	55
	LH					
			Deuce	15	15	70
		FH				
			Advantage	70	15	15
	RH					
			Deuce	50	20	30
LH		BH				
	LH		Advantage	30	20	50

WHERE SHOULD ONE SERVE THE BALL IN A GAME OF TENNIS?

EXHIBIT 6.14

So the tennis greats are lined up at the baseline ready to serve with their own algorithm based on these factors, plus the importance of the point, and whether it's first or second serve. The conclusion of *Thinking Strategically*, to make each serve appear random remains a sound one, albeit with lesser unpredictably to take advantage of your strengths and opponents weaknesses. This is the key aim of every game theorist. The conclusion we reach about serve direction is conditional on three to five questions. When you're standing at the service line, you have to quickly take these factors into consideration. The result is a mixing strategy as the authors of *Thinking Strategically* argued, but clear preference in the left-hander's case for the backhand side on clutch points and first serves. Take the tree and place yourself on it and figure out how you should serve on important points to a regular opponent in singles.

Complex problems often require the big analysis guns we have described. We have examined the sophisticated tools now available to problem solvers. We expect them to be employed more in the future as more large data sets become available, as experiments become cheaper, and as software packages and scripting languages become more widely used. Remember to start your analysis with time-tested heuristic short cuts, simple statistics, and root-cause analysis before taking on sophisticated tools. This initial step may lead you to the decision that these more sophisticated tools aren't needed for your problem situation, and will in any case give you important information on advanced tools to employ.

Takeaways

- Getting to a solution for many complex problems means you will need to be aware of and know how to use sophisticated analytic tools.
- The starting point is always to get a thorough understanding of your data through graphing, visualization, and summary statistics.
- Which advanced tool you use is often dictated by whether you are seeking to understand drivers and develop an intervention strategy, or predict outcomes and plan accordingly.
- Experiments are a powerful and often overlooked tool in the big gun arsenal; if you can't make one, sometimes you can find a natural experiment.
- Machine learning is emerging as a powerful tool in many problem spheres; we argue to understand problem structure and develop hypotheses before employing deep learning algorithms (huge mistakes can come from bad data and bad structuring, and these models offer little transparency).

- You can outsource problem solving, including deep learning, through crowdsourcing on platforms such as Kaggle.
- Where there is an adversary whose behavior many change in reaction to your choices, you can look to game theory approaches with logic trees to work out the best course of action.

Problems to Try on Your Own

1. What big gun would you select for understanding causes of mental-health problems using the framework in Exhibit 6.1?

2. Set out how you would predict Olympic games medals for the top five countries at the next Olympics.

3. How would you test effectiveness of social media campaigns using experiments in your business or nonprofit?

4. How would you set out the logic tree to decide whether to take a competitor to court where you believe they have appropriated your IP?

Chapter Seven

Synthesize Results and Tell a Great Story

Introduction

The final elements in the seven steps process, synthesizing your findings and telling a compelling story, can be the most fun. It is the culmination of all your hard work, and, with luck, answers the difficult question you set out to solve. Done right, your conclusions are an engaging story, supported with facts, analyses, and arguments that convince your audience of the merits of your recommended path. This can attract volunteers to your social causes, funding for your social organization or start-up company, build harmony in your family, or boost confidence in your own career path. Good problem solving and the story telling that goes along with it make our lives better—for problem solving done well translates into action that improves our circumstances.

Of course it doesn't always work out like this. Most readers will have experienced a project at work or in a volunteer organization that got through the analysis stage, and then fizzled. Failures at the later stages of problem solving have a number of causes: where giant models are not quite finished, reams of data produced without a clear point of view, conflicting interview or market survey data, or team members at odds over the right way forward. As young consultants, we dreaded the nervous presentation of detailed results that never jelled into a real story; in McKinsey this was called the *anxious parade of knowledge*, or APK.

If you follow the straightforward seven-steps process we have described, you should never succumb to deadlocked teams, confused findings, or empty APK. You will have been driving your logic trees from component disaggregation to strong and testable hypotheses, you will have followed good team processes to surface alternative hypotheses early on and avoid confirmation bias and other problem solving mistakes, and you will have practiced one-day answers that summarize your best understanding at any point in the process, supported with synthesis of your best evidence at that juncture.

This chapter addresses the transition from one-day answers to more complete story telling. It addresses approaches to synthesis of data and analysis, using pyramid structuring of your overall case, inductive and deductive support for your argument, and compelling story telling, including to challenging audiences.

Synthesis of Findings

The quality of your synthesis will determine the quality of your decision making. This is why it pays to triangulate your views with people who you know synthesize well.

—Ray Dalio[1]

The first step toward compelling story telling is to synthesize the findings from your data gathering, interviews, analysis, and modeling. If you have been following the seven-steps approach we outlined in Chapter 1, this should be relatively straightforward. Charles learned the power of this approach on his first McKinsey project. He got on a plane to Calgary for the first meeting with the client and found himself sitting next to the senior partner on the project, who nodded a greeting and went back to his work. He was furiously scribbling on a pad of paper and ripping off the sheets. When Charles worked up the courage to ask what he was doing, his colleague answered, "I am writing the final presentation." Final presentation? How could that be? They hadn't even met the client. He answered, "Look, I know my hypotheses are early stage and some will be wrong, but if I guess at the answers now, I'll know what questions to ask the client when we meet their team." And he was right. Imagining a set of hypotheses allowed the team to begin focused data gathering from the first meeting.

Our recommended process is iterative at each stage and driven by the interaction of the strong hypotheses of your one-day answers with the analyses of your workplan. Alternative hypotheses should already have been tested and embraced or rejected, and dead-end analyses pruned off. Regular team meetings (even if you have to press family and neighbors into service in makeshift teams) should have already begun to link analysis and emerging findings in a convincing way.

---

[1]Ray Dalio, *Principles: Life and Work* (Simon & Schuster, 2017) (referenced in Shane Parrish's blog Brain Food #233).

As you move to final synthesis, you draw together the individual findings of the work on each branch and twig of your logic tree into an overall picture. Humans are mostly visual learners, so it is often useful to represent each of your findings in the form of pictures or graphics that highlight the insights that emerged from your work. Where possible, the most powerful visualization is to show each graphic as branches on your revised tree structure. Exhibit 7.1 is an example from the battle of the hardware company giants we introduced in Chapter 1.

This kind of visualization of findings illuminates the overall problem. It allows for insights to emerge that cut across and combine the different branches of analysis. We can see the overall story begin to emerge from individual branches on revenue, costs, and asset productivity. Looking at the relative sales growth curves, we know that one business (Home Depot) far outstripped the other (Hechinger); examining the selling price data, purchasing costs, logistics expenses, overheads, store design, and inventory turns starts to paint a fuller picture of what drove the different revenue growth results. Lower prices drove higher sales growth; sales volume, along with better store design and logistics systems, allowed higher asset and inventory turnover and lower costs per unit sold in every part of the business. The synthesis in pictures in Exhibit 7.1 begins to tell a visual narrative of competing business models.

We encourage you to draw pictures from the analysis that synthesize your findings. There are good primers on how to do this from the methods we learned at McKinsey such as Gene Zelazny's *Say It with Charts* to Cole Nussbaumer Knaflic's *Storytelling with Data.*[2] As a young consultant in New York, Rob would take his pack of findings to Gene Zelazny, only to have Gene say, "Now what are you saying here Rob? These charts don't really support what you just told me you've concluded so let's ditch them. I'm really interested in that point you made about declining market share of the client

---

[2]Gene Zelazny, *Say It with Charts: The Executive's Guide to Visual Communications* (McGraw-Hill, 2001), and Cole Nussbaumer Knaflic, *Storytelling with Data: A Data Visualization Guide for Business Professionals* (Wiley, 2015).

RETURN ON INVESTED CAPITAL ANALYSIS
HECHINGER VS. HOME DEPOT

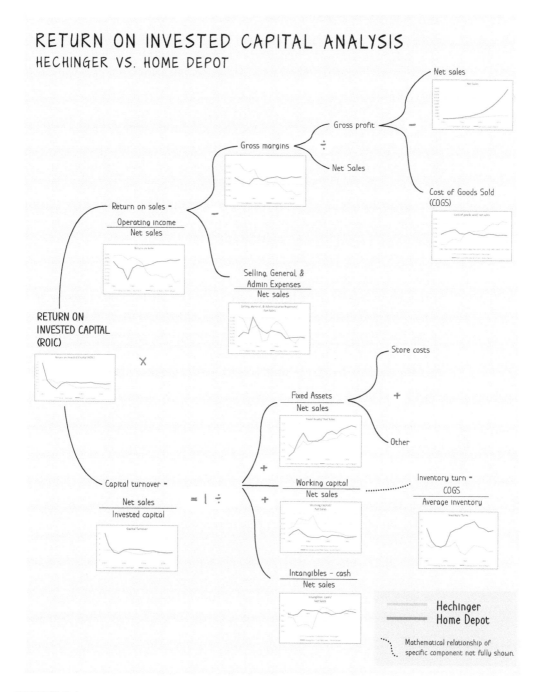

EXHIBIT 7.1

but you don't have a chart on that. Let's get that in the pack to support your findings." This sometimes bruising process, despite Gene's positive and encouraging style, became the boot camp for consultants to learn how to synthesize findings and support them with graphics.

Good team process is important here as in the other steps. We like to bring the whole team together for synthesis sessions and have each team member present their analyses and results to the assembled group. This gives another checkpoint to pressure test alternative hypotheses, and it provides the foundation for moving from the simple situation-observation-resolution story summary to a more complete and supported argument.

This is often the stage where a big insight emerges that wasn't obvious in the branch-level analysis. In our BHP mining example in Chapter 8 the analysis of the viability of the single mineral deposit absorbed the team right up to the point that synthesis showed the huge potential value in other nearby deposits that were unlocked by the transportation infrastructure required to develop the first mineral deposit.

From One-Day Answers to Pyramid Structure

As we move from the early days of problem definition to work planning and completing analyses, our reasoning is sharpened. Here is a graphical way of showing this (Exhibit 7.2).

In the early stages, our porpoising into data with well-designed analyses is a process of *reasoning toward implications*. We hypothesize a one-day answer using a situation-observation-resolution structure and we constantly pressure test this with our analyses under the structure of our workplan and team processes. As we discussed in Chapter 3, these one-day answers are critical to the process. Summarizing the situation allows us to update our best

EVOLUTION OF MODE OF REASONING

EXHIBIT 7.2

understanding of the problem; observation or complication provides the tension in the problem, what isn't working, and our best insights into ways to unpick it; resolution is your best understanding of the solution path that moves us toward the answer.

As the workplan is executed and our critical path analyses begin to yield fruit, our reasoning mode shifts from understanding toward marshaling *reasons to drive action*. We move from simply stating the implications of analyses toward how those results can motivate a plan for change. The seven steps approach is always oriented toward evidence-based action—it aims to answer "What should we do and how should we do it"?

Telling Compelling Stories

Once you have synthesized your findings into a series of pressure-tested and convincing graphics, you can move to the final step of structuring a compelling communication for your audience.

The starting point for this is to return to your problem definition worksheet and remind yourself:

- What problem are we trying to solve? How has this evolved?
- What are the key criteria for success that our decision maker (which may be yourself) set out in advance? It is important to reflect these explicitly in your story.
- Did you honor the boundaries of the problem set by the decision maker? If not—which may be for good reasons around creativity or deciding to relax a constraint to open up new possibilities— you need to make the case here.

The visual structure we use to represent our story structure is traditionally a pyramid—which is really just one of our logic trees turned on its side (Exhibit 7.3). This is the standard organizing structure taught to journalists and consultants, and was popularized in the problem solving literature by our former McKinsey colleague Barbara Minto.[3] This visual helps show clearly how each element of our argument is supported by data, interviews, and analyses.

BASIC PYRAMID STRUCTURE

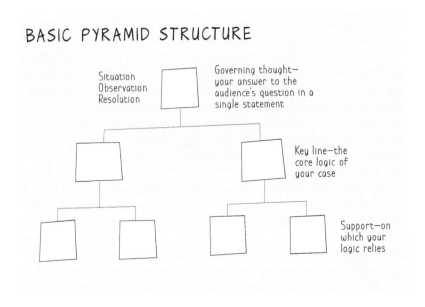

Situation
Observation
Resolution

Governing thought— your answer to the audience's question in a single statement

Key line—the core logic of your case

Support—on which your logic relies

EXHIBIT 7.3

---

[3]Barbara Minto, *The Pyramid Principle*, 3rd ed. (Prentice Hall, 2009).

At the very top level is our lead or governing statement of the problem. Not surprisingly, your latest situation–observation–resolution statement is usually the best governing statement. Depending on the audience, you can vary the order of these three statement elements. As we will show below, sometimes it is best to carefully lead the audience from situation to observation to resolution, which are your recommended actions. But our bias in most circumstances is to lead by answering the question "What Should I Do?" and then summarize the situation and key observations that support action.

Using the insights from your synthesis stage, you then begin to fill in supporting arguments that back up your top-level answer. There are a number of different ways to do this depending on the nature of your answer and your audience. Exhibit 7.4 shows two structures that we often use.

STRUCTURING YOUR ARGUMENTS

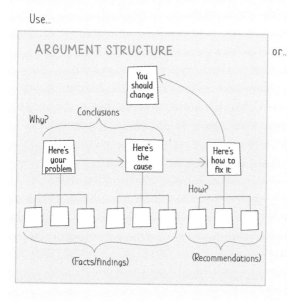 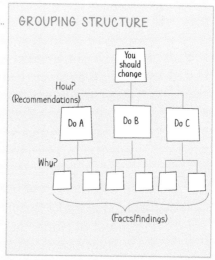

EXHIBIT 7.4

As you have likely already recognized, our basic deductive logic (from general principles to individual cases) and inductive logic (from individual observation to general conclusions) approaches to generating answers introduced back in Chapter 3 underpin these two structures (Exhibit 7.5). You can use both inductive and deductive structures in the same tree.

ARGUMENT TYPES

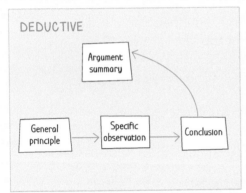 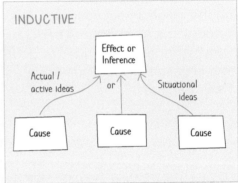

EXHIBIT 7.5

There is no general preference for inductive or deductive reasoning in your pyramid structure, though Minto argues that constant reference to deductive arguments can feel labored or pedantic.

To complete this section, let's look at the complete narrative of our battle of the hardware companies case in Exhibit 7.6. This draws together the evidence from our analysis phase into a synthesis of the findings, and then tells the story: Hechinger needed to change its business model quickly to address the competitive threat of Home Depot.

HECHINGER DRAFT STORYLINE

RESOLUTION: Hechinger must work to develop and implement a lower cost, higher volume hardware retail store model to compete in markets which Home Depot is in or planning to enter.

SITUATION: A new warehouse superstore model has emerged and is planning expansion concurrent with Hechinger's expansion and into Hechinger's markets.

OBSERVATION: Home Depot is able to price 15% lower, has higher asset turns and is growing revenue very quickly.

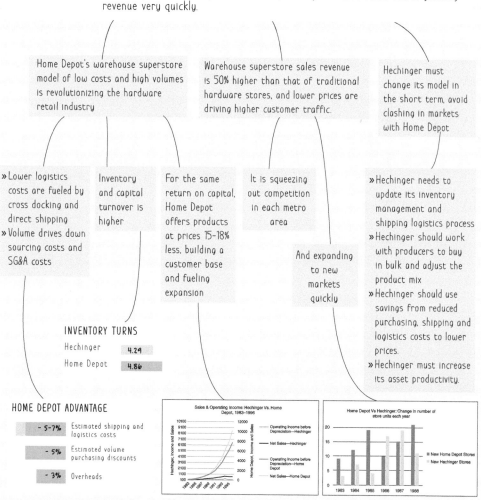

Home Depot's warehouse superstore model of low costs and high volumes is revolutionizing the hardware retail industry

Warehouse superstore sales revenue is 50% higher than that of traditional hardware stores, and lower prices are driving higher customer traffic.

Hechinger must change its model in the short term, avoid clashing in markets with Home Depot

» Lower logistics costs are fueled by cross docking and direct shipping
» Volume drives down sourcing costs and SG&A costs

Inventory and capital turnover is higher

For the same return on capital, Home Depot offers products at prices 15-18% less, building a customer base and fueling expansion

It is squeezing out competition in each metro area

And expanding to new markets quickly

» Hechinger needs to update its inventory management and shipping logistics process
» Hechinger should work with producers to buy in bulk and adjust the product mix
» Hechinger should use savings from reduced purchasing, shipping and logistics costs to lower prices.
» Hechinger must increase its asset productivity.

INVENTORY TURNS
Hechinger — 4.29
Home Depot — 4.86

HOME DEPOT ADVANTAGE
- 5-7% Estimated shipping and logistics costs
- 5% Estimated volume purchasing discounts
- 3% Overheads

EXHIBIT 7.6

Here you can see the whole story on one page, with the governing thought and call to action at the top (provided by our concise situation–observation–resolution structure), the three major arguments made that underpin the governing thought, and supporting arguments and data that provide the proof for the need for action and the formula for change. The next stage from this storyline summary is to storyboard out your entire presentation. We usually divide our paper into nine boxes and cartoon or dummy each exhibit, with the storyline leads across the top of each cell. This is what Cole Nussbaumer Knaflic calls developing and checking the horizontal logic of the narrative.[4] Humans are storytelling creatures, not logical robots. Remember that as you craft your messages.

How to Deal with Difficult Audiences

A number of years ago Rob and Charles were working with a refinery company in a remote island location, owned by a larger company based in Australia. It was a difficult situation. The local management team resented the foreign owner meddling in their business, and they were resistant to change. The consulting team worked as best we could, employing the problem solving process we have introduced here, and came up with a final answer that looked like Exhibit 7.7.

As you can see, the recommendation was for the refinery business to cut costs substantially and become a modest growth, niche operator. While this conclusion, based on comparative analysis of competitors, was rock solid, it was not one that the local management team wanted to hear. In circumstances like this, it can make sense to use a revealed approach to your arguments, employing a decision tree structure rather than the traditional pyramid. Exhibit 7.8 is an example of what that might look like.

With a decision tree final storyline structure, you provide evidence for each yes/no branch in your tree, slowly working the

---

[4]Cole Nussbaumer Knaflic, *Storytelling with Data* (Wiley, 2015), 181.

OILCO STORYLINE

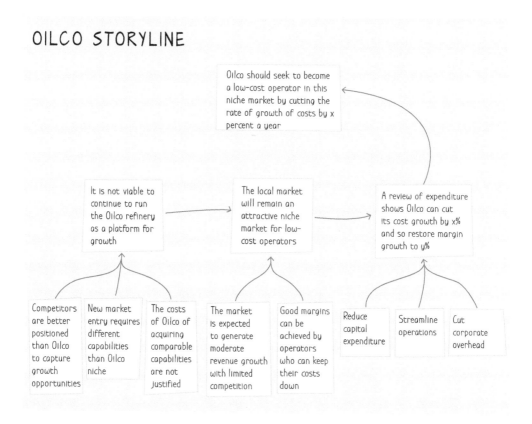

EXHIBIT 7.7

decision maker toward your conclusion. You *reveal* the answer rather than leading with it. In the Oilco case the team carefully revealed compelling competitor data, layer by layer, that helped the local management team get comfortable with the difficult conclusions.

In summary, the final stages of good problem solving are to synthesize the findings of your analysis in a way that highlights your insights. You are then prepared to revisit your original problem definition and answer your decision maker's question, "What should I do?" in compelling way that motivates action. The pyramid structure helps to structure arguments and support into a powerful story.

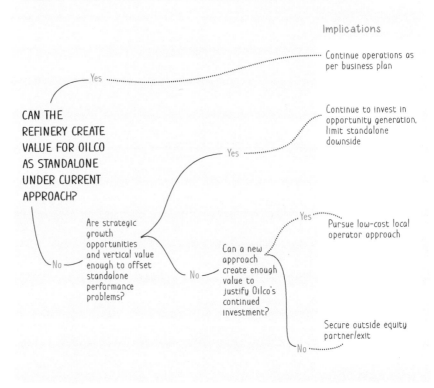

OILCO DECISION TREE ARGUMENT STRUCTURE

EXHIBIT 7.8

Chapter 7 Takeaways

- Synthesis brings together all the separate pieces of your analytic work and often yields new insights you didn't notice when you were in the weeds of analysis.

- To avoid the dreaded anxious parade of knowledge, use your logic tree structure pyramid to organize a compelling story.

- Your one-day answer structure of situation–observation–resolution, kept up to date for your findings, is usually the starting place for the governing thought of your narrative.

- Try several storyline structures to see which are most clear and compelling; sometimes a decision tree format that reveals the answer step-by-step is useful with difficult conclusions and audiences.
- Use a storyboard to plan out your deck of slides and have your leads be the argument of the story (not boring titles); read across the slides to check horizontal logic and coherency.

Problems to Try on Your Own

1. Do a storyline pyramid for Rob's solar panel problem in Chapter 1.

2. Take any good newspaper story and put the arguments in pyramid structure.

3. Look at Lincoln's Gettysburg address or Marc Antony's speech in Shakespeare's play *Julius Caesar*—what narrative structure do they use to be so compelling?

Chapter Eight

Problem Solving with Long Time Frames and High Uncertainty

As problem solvers, we shuffle through a deck of strategies when we face high uncertainty. We edge into risk, looking for the opportunities to learn before acting precipitously, hedging our bets where we can, and taking steps that build capabilities and future resilience. We know there is value in being systematic and working through a range of potential strategies when faced with uncertainty and long time frames.

As we have seen, the seven-steps framework is robust and adaptable in addressing a wide range of personal, work, and societal problems. Many of the examples to date exhibit low to moderate uncertainty, where the cost of error is relatively low, and where time frames are relatively short. But there is a class of problems where time periods are long, complexity and uncertainty are high, and the consequences of error are substantial. The case of protecting Pacific salmon that we have looked at in previous chapters is a good example. Outcomes for salmon depend on many variables, including inherently uncertain ones like climate change. Species success plays out over decades rather than months, and the consequences of bad outcomes are broadly felt in human incomes and ecosystem losses. We believe the seven-steps model is useful for complex problems with high uncertainty, particularly the emphasis on an iterative approach, but we will add some frameworks to our problem solving kit to manage these more difficult, long-term problems, some of which involve putting the analytic tools of Chapter 6 into practice.

In this chapter we define levels of uncertainty and the implications for problem solving. We provide a problem solving toolkit with escalating actions to address different levels of uncertainty. We demonstrate the tools via a number of cases where we have employed these approaches, from long-term capital investment in resources, to making career choices, to determining whether you risk outliving your savings, and to developing strategies comprising a portfolio of initiatives.

Levels of Uncertainty

There are many ways to understand and evaluate uncertainty, including statistical measures of variability and conditional probability. Previously, we lacked a way to describe and respond to different levels of uncertainty, without having to make spot predictions that could dangerously underestimate the range of uncertainty. Several of our former McKinsey colleagues addressed this need with a five-level schema for assessing uncertainty.[1] They brought new language into play in tailoring actions to uncertainty, such as "big bets" and "no regrets" moves that are now in widespread use. In this model, uncertainty levels range from level 1, what is a reasonably predictable future, to level 5, the unknown unknowns (Exhibit 8.1). Level 1 uncertainty, such as simple predictions and short-term forecasts, is discussed in earlier chapters and can be addressed with good team processes. More challenging settings are where the level of uncertainty rises to levels 2, 3, and 4.

WHAT IS THE LEVEL OF UNCERTAINTY?

UNCERTAINTY LEVEL		HOW UNCERTAINTY IS DEFINED	EXAMPLE
Unknown unknowns	5	Unexpected or unforeseen conditions	Meteorite hits Earth
	4	True ambiguity—impossible to predict	Manhattan sea level 2050
	3	A range of futures	Energy balance 2025
	2	Alternative futures	Brexit
Known unknowns	1	Reasonably predictable futures	Mobile phone sales

EXHIBIT 8.1

- Level 2 are situations in which there are alternative futures that could follow from a legislative change or technology change, where the results will be binary in the sense of who wins/loses. The Brexit decision in the UK is an example. Another is how should auto insurers prepare for driverless cars on the road, where the time frame for adoption is uncertain, and the role of carmakers in providing the insurance is unclear. Both of these examples are likely to have uncertainty resolved in a 5- to 10-year time period.

---

[1]Hugh Courtney et al., "Strategy Under Uncertainty," *McKinsey Quarterly*, 2000.

- Level 3 is where there is a range of futures that are possible but where it isn't clear which one is more likely. Where fossil fuels fit in the energy mix in 15 years is an example. Scenarios range from similar to today all the way to a very diminished role. Another frequently discussed topic is what jobs will we have in the future with advances in artificial intelligence/machine learning and robotics. This will be clearer in a 10- to 20-year time frame.
- Level 4 describes true ambiguity, where it is not possible to conceive of all the potential outcomes or to predict them with confidence. You could put the issue of sea levels in Manhattan in 2050 into that category, although some climate scientists will have different views. In an update of "Strategy Under Uncertainty," author Hugh Courtney gave the example of early-stage biotech investments having Level 4 uncertainty.[2]
- Level 5 is the nearly absolute uncertainty of events that are unpredictable with current knowledge and technology, sometimes called unknown unknowns.

Uncertainty levels 1 through 4 are colorfully called "the known unknowns," in contrast to level 5. We don't put them in a too-hard basket. Instead we approach them recognizing and quantifying the level and type of uncertainty, and then develop approaches to move toward our desired outcomes by managing the levers that we control. The next and harder step is to identify what actions you can take to deal with a particular level of uncertainty.

It is important to remember this as we dive in to this topic: Uncertainty can be a good thing for strategic problem solvers! Hedge fund and other clever investors hope for uncertain and volatile markets—provided they have an analytic edge. If your problem solving is right you can earn good returns and guard your downside while others are floundering.

---

[2]Hugh Courtney, "A Fresh Look at Strategy Under Uncertainty: An Interview," *McKinsey Quarterly*, December 2008.

Logic Trees to Deal with Uncertainty

The spectrum of actions you can take when faced with level 2 to level 4 uncertainty range from buying time (which you can also call do nothing, wait for more information), all the way through to taking big bets and no regrets moves (Exhibit 8.2). You will typically see actions linked to the level of uncertainty as follows.

- **Buying information,** which may involve data gathering and analysis of underlying processes, to clarifying the sources of uncertainty and the motives of protagonists.[3] The information for level 3 and 4 uncertainty may be modeling for distant events

WHAT YOU CAN DO TO ADDRESS UNCERTAINTY

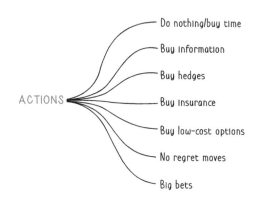

ACTIONS
- Do nothing/buy time
- Buy information
- Buy hedges
- Buy insurance
- Buy low-cost options
- No regret moves
- Big bets

EXHIBIT 8.2

Source: Albert Madansky, "Uncertainty," in *Systems Analysis and Policy Planning*, edited by Edward S. Quade and Wayne I. Boucher (American Elsevier Publishing, 1968); and Hugh Courtney, Jane Kirkland, and S. Patrick Viguerie, "Strategy Under Uncertainty," *McKinsey Quarterly*, June 2000.

---

[3]*Uncertainty*, Chapter 5 by Albert Madansky in *Systems Analysis*, Quade and Boucher, RAND Corporation, 1968.

rather than fact gathering of observable things. There is likely to be a high cost of moving toward perfect information and a point at which it is too costly to acquire more information.[4]

- **Hedges** are a way of dealing with uncertainty that involves making a reasonable cost move or investment that will counter downside events. An example is fossil fuel companies investing in renewable energy. Other examples of hedges involve buying water rights in areas expected to have lower rainfall with climate change. Sometimes these can involve options, futures contracts, or other financial instruments—although few financial hedging mechanisms are as long-lasting as many difficult problems require.

- Acquiring **low-cost strategic options** through a portfolio of initiatives, or betting on multiple horses in the race, is another way we deal with uncertainty. Major financial institutions are investing relatively small equity stakes in financial technology (fintech) start-up companies to be in a position where they can first understand and then capitalize on innovation that challenges established players. We saw how important information gathering is in times of disruptive technologies in our newspaper versus new media example in Chapter 2. These are typically low-cost options, and often involve bets on competing technologies. How IBM lost the PC business is put down to a failure to exercise the low-cost options it held in its key suppliers. "Early on IBM had the financial resources to take a large equity position in both Intel and Microsoft. It did make an investment in Intel in 1982, getting a 20% equity stake and warrants to purchase another 10%. But, ironically, IBM sold out in 1986 and 1987 for $625 million. Ten years later that 20% stake would have been worth $25 billion. As for Microsoft, IBM had an opportunity to buy 30% of Microsoft for under $300 million in mid-1986. By the end of 1996 that $300 million investment would have been worth $33 billion."[5] That is just the financial investment loss—the loss in learning value is incalculable.

---

[4]James C. Morgan and Joan O'C. Hamilton, *Applied Wisdom: Bad News Is Good News and Other Insights That Can Help Any Anyone Be a Better Manager* (Chandler Jordan Publishing, November 2016).

[5]Adam Brandenberger and Barry Nalebuff, *Co-Opetition* (Currency Doubleday, 1996), 156.

- **Buying insurance.** The threat of global warming is sometimes framed as an insurance problem, with estimates that a little over 1% of global GDP has to be committed to paying the annual premium to keep CO_2 levels below a 2-degree centigrade increase. That hasn't happened to date but there is some progress toward international agreements that would move toward this. There are also insurance products for a range of uncertain situations, known as cat bonds or catastrophe bonds, that cover events like typhoons or hurricanes.

- **No regrets moves** come into play when you are comfortable with the level of uncertainty, or can edge out into a competitive space with incremental learning moves; this often involves the capability building you'll need no matter what the outcome.

- **Big bets** are taken when you have a level of confidence about an outcome not shared by others. *The Big Short* book and film, describing the investments in shorting subprime mortgage credit default swaps in the US, is a great example of a big bet when uncertainty remained high.[6] The investors spotlighted in the book felt the mortgage securities were mispriced and took big bets when others weren't prepared to. Of course, big bets can also go bad when uncertainty resolves itself in ways that leave an asset investment stranded. For example the generous feed in tariffs for Spanish solar investment a decade ago looked to be too good to be true. In this case the assumptions made about the behavior of host governments turned out to be incorrect. Where uncertainty sits at level 2 or greater, most decision makers will seek to defer irreversible commitments. That can work in the absence of competition but becomes a more difficult equation where there is the possibility of preemption. Big bets are open only to a few, as Hugh Courtney pointed out—those with business models that generate a lot of cash and have low debt. They can be shaping winning strategies, as a recent book by some of our former colleagues demonstrates.[7]

---

[6]Michael Lewis, *The Big Short* (W. W. Norton, March 2010).
[7]Chris Bradley, Martin Hirt, and Sven Smit, *Strategy Beyond the Hockey Stick: People, Probabilities, and Big Moves to Beat the Odds* (Wiley, 2018).

When we can estimate the parameters of uncertainty, mathematics can help us calculate what is a fair bet and estimate the value of different options. We can estimate conditional probabilities through experiments and sampling, and we can use joint probabilities to estimate complex risks involved in a decision. All this requires *thinking probabilistically*, a term a statistics colleague of Rob's uses. In her view, our inherent biases in decision making make us reasonably bad at this without systems and good mathematical discipline. She calls humans "the unintuitive statistician."[8] As we know from Chapter 5, we can fight these biases with good processes and team norms.

Case Examples of Long Time Frames and Uncertainty

Now that we have a framework for assessing uncertainty levels and some actions for addressing risky situations, let's look at a range of individual, business, and societal level cases to see how strategies under uncertainty come together. The cases we cover are as follows:

1. **How to make education and career choices when the jobs available in 20 to 30 years' time are uncertain in nature and scope**. The impact of automation and advances in human level machine intelligence (HLMI) will have an impact on jobs, both positively and negatively. Some forecasts will prove to be right and others horribly wrong. How do you navigate your way through educational investment and career decisions now to avoid a high cost of error and have a good chance of realizing your career goals? Our team of young Oxford researchers encouraged us to tackle this problem. Career choice has elements of level 3 and even level 4 uncertainty.

---

[8]Professor Sally Cripps, Professor of Statistics, University of Sydney.

2. **How to plan for far horizon events: Will I outlive my savings?** This is one of the highest uncertainty events we face as individuals. It's a relatively recent problem as people used to retire at 65 and have a life expectancy of 72. Now they often retire at 60 and live to 85 or more. Probability assessment is a key part of tackling this level 2 issue.

3. **How you make really long-term investments with growth options.** Long time frames for investments like infrastructure call for particular attention to uncertainty and the role of development options. We take a resource company investment example at a level 3 uncertainty to illustrate how our tools are put to work. This is one where Rob can look back and see how it played out over more than two decades.

4. **How you build new businesses with a staircase strategy approach.** Where you set out to build new businesses in rapidly changing environments, there is a need for a step-by-step approach that simultaneously buys information to reduce uncertainty and builds new capabilities to reduce risk. Charles and Rob developed this approach with colleagues at McKinsey.[9] It has proved valuable to large businesses and start-ups. It features level 2 uncertainty.

5. **How a complex portfolio of strategies in a highly uncertain environment are constructed.** High uncertainty settings often require selecting multiple paths to a long-term goal and making trade-offs among strategies as the real world unfolds. Charles used these techniques at the Moore Foundation when managing a large portfolio of grants that employed often-competing strategies to preserve Pacific salmon. The issues here were mostly level 3 and 4 uncertainty.

Let's look at each of these case studies.

---

[9]Mehrdad Baghai, Stephen C. Coley, and David White with Charles Conn and Robert McLean, "Staircases to Growth," *McKinsey Quarterly* 4 (November 1996).

Case Study: How Should I Choose My Career?

As automation's and artificial intelligence's roles in the workplace expand at ever increasing rates, predictions for the labor market have many facets of uncertainty compared to 25 or 50 years ago.[10] The tailwinds are around mostly non-routine, cognitive jobs that didn't exist 10 years ago—you may have seen the World Economic Forum new jobs list: app developer, social media manager, driverless car engineer, cloud-computing specialist, big-data analyst, sustainability manager, YouTube content creator, drone operator, millennial generation expert. In 10 years the list will be different again.

So as a young person choosing a career, how would you best position yourself in this changing labor landscape? First, we build a tree to capture the economic labor landscape (Exhibit 8.3). It shows clearly that the employment share of non-routine cognitive jobs is growing, as are non-routine manual jobs, while routine cognitive and routine manual job shares are shrinking in share of employment.

You can use your inside knowledge about your personal level of ability, interests, and risk tolerance to guide your education and career choice decisions. Jeff Wald, the cofounder and president of WorkMarket asks, "What are you passionate about? Does that map to what skill sets are needed?"[11] To do this, we begin with a simple chart to fill in. Each horizontal row in the chart represents a broad potential field or sector in which you may end up working; there are four vertical columns: The first is the current economic predictions for the field, the next are your personal assessments of your ability, interest, and ability to take risks. The first column can be completed and updated using economic predictions.

---

[10]McKinsey Executive Briefing. Technology, Jobs, and the Future of Work. www .mckinsey.com/global-themes/employment-and-growth/technology-jobs-and-the-future-of-work.

[11]"The Digital Future of Work," McKinsey Global Institute, July 2017, https://www .mckinsey.com/featured-insights/future-of-work/the-digital-future-of-work-what-skills-will-be-needed.

DATA ABOUT CURRENT LABOR MARKET

		Skills	Existing Job Titles	$\triangle$ in the employment share	Pay
Non-routine	Cognitive	Problem solving / Creativity and design / System thinking / Abstract thinking / Collaboration	Management / Professional / Research	Large, growing + 9.2%	High
	Manual	Planning / Caring / Execution	Service / Construction	Medium, growing + 16.1%	Low–medium
Routine	Cognitive	Analysis / Application of knowledge	Back Office Administration / Some professions	Medium, shrinking − 11%	Low–medium
	Manual	Dependability / Communication / Craftsmanship	Manufacturing	Medium, shrinking − 11%	Low

OCCUPATIONAL GROUP TYPES

EXHIBIT 8.3

Source: St. Louis Fed, Jobs Involving Routine Tasks Aren't Growing (2016); Jaimovich & Siu, The Trend Is the Cycle: Job Polarization + Jobless Recoveries.

For each potential field, subject area, or employment sector, you fill in your self-assessed strength, interest, and risk-tolerance levels in the second, third, and fourth columns. You can choose low, medium, or high, to rank your preferences. Exhibit 8.4 shows a filled-in matrix for one of our research team members.

CAREER CHOICE

Sector/Skill area	Economic projection for this sector (time horizon and error) (L, M, H)	My strength level (L, M, H)	My interest level (L, M, H)	My ability to take risks (L, M, H)
Art/Design	M	H	H	L
Business/Finance	M	L	L	L
Health/Human services	H	L	L	L
Math/Science	H	L	L	L
Social Science	L	H	M	L
People/ Interpersonal	M	M	M	L
Trades/Technical	L	L	L	L

EXHIBIT 8.4

Now how does this information help lead you to a decision? You can start by eliminating or pruning sectors in which you have low strength or abilities and low interest. Beginning with the most promising sector, the sectors for which you have the highest interest and ability, you can use this tree to guide your next step or action. We define three potential strategies or actions:

- Make a **big bet** and embark on a path with considerable risk.
- Make a **no regrets move** and gain a base level of education or training in a safe field that safeguards you from risk.
- **Hedge your bet** by investing time and energy in education or training for two or more fields or positions.

NOW, TAKE ACTION...

Beginning with highest-ranked field with respect to individual strengths and interests

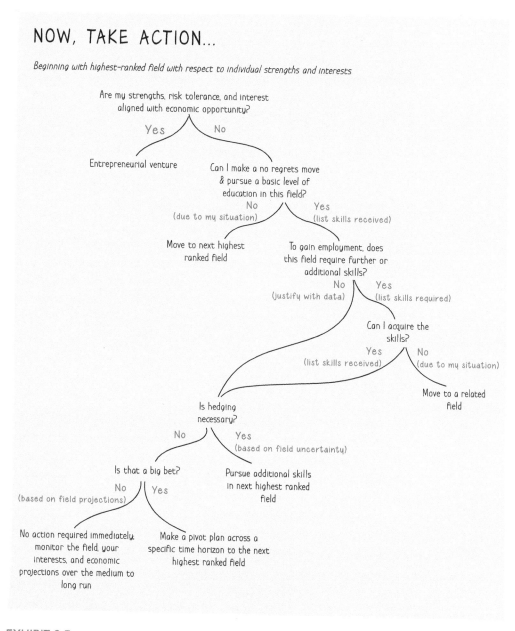

Are my strengths, risk tolerance, and interest
aligned with economic opportunity?

Yes / No

Entrepreneurial venture

Can I make a no regrets move
& pursue a basic level of
education in this field?

No
(due to my situation)

Yes
(list skills received)

Move to next highest
ranked field

To gain employment, does
this field require further or
additional skills?

No
(justify with data)

Yes
(list skills required)

Can I acquire the
skills?

Yes
(list skills received)

No
(due to my situation)

Move to a related
field

Is hedging
necessary?

No

Yes
(based on field uncertainty)

Is that a big bet?

No
(based on field projections)

Yes

Pursue additional skills
in next highest ranked
field

No action required immediately;
monitor the field, your
interests, and economic
projections over the medium to
long run

Make a pivot plan across a
specific time horizon to the next
highest ranked field

EXHIBIT 8.5

Within these strategies you can see two broad paths: one entre-preneurial and the other educational. When faced with high ability, high interest, high risk tolerance, and high economic opportunity, entrepreneurship may be calling out your name. However, it is often more likely that all your stars may not be in perfect alignment; in this case, you may need to make a no regrets move and obtain a base of education, or choose to hedge your bets across two fields with strategies such as double majoring or continued education while working.

Exhibit 8.5 illustrates these strategic choices.

The tree, table, and series of action trees shown in Exhibit 8.5 can easily be applied and iterated upon by an individual while they are in the process of making their education or career choice, making decisions appropriate to their passions, skills, and risk tolerance.

Case Study: Will My Retirement Savings Last?

At the other end of life planning, we also find uncertainty. In the past, retirement savings typically only needed to last 10–15 years. Now the need for retirement income is often stretching out to 25–35 years, where early retirement is taken and longevity is improving. Many retirees now face the question "Will my retire-ment savings last?" The answer to this question depends on the longevity runway you're on *and* the income pool you can gen-erate, as well as your risk preferences (see Exhibit 8.6). As life expectancy increases, and returns on conventional savings remain modest, an increasing number of people risk outliving their sav-ings. On the minds of people approaching retirement are these questions:

- How should I plan for this uncertainty?
- Are there actions to take now to mitigate this risk?

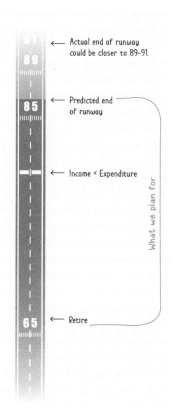

EXHIBIT 8.6

- Are there decisions that can be deferred to a later point in time?
- Do I need to go beyond my financial planner or accountant for advice?

We admit this isn't the kind of issue you want to deal with every day, but there is a way to do it simply and comprehensively. It requires you to estimate your longevity runway, adjust for bias, and take a view on your risk preferences in investment strategy.

We start with a first-cut calculation to solve this problem. In order to work out whether you face a risk, you can simply calculate how far your retirement nest egg will go, measured in years of target income, and compare that to how long you can expect to live given your age. This can be as simple as dividing your retirement savings by your target retirement income less expenses, adjusting for any defined benefit pensions. That is your years of retirement runway.[12]

This heuristic is a good starting point to understanding your situation but doesn't provide the whole answer. Why? By definition, not everyone is going to reach average life expectancy and individuals have different risk tolerance. Also, your nest egg can be invested in different assets that earn more or less, and that have more or less volatility. The analysis needs to be taken further than the heuristic in order to account for these factors.

Sketch Out Your Longevity Runway

Let's look at your longevity runway more closely. If you are a healthy 35-year-old, your life expectancy is 80 years, but if you make it to 60, the average life expectancy increases to 82.8 years.[13]

At age 60, there is a 50% chance of:

- A male exceeding 85
- A female exceeding 88
- At least one of a male and female couple together exceeding 91[14]

---

[12]Personal assets and savings are an important part of retirement income in developed countries. Government practices vary widely in allowing personal assets to be held in addition to a pension. Some countries require assets to be included in pension calculations; others, like Australia, permit them to be retained outside pension calculations. As a result, your calculations will be different depending on the rules that apply where you live.

[13]www.helpage.org/global-agewatch

[14]Australian Bureau of Statistics.

Planning is typically done for couples, and what is relevant is the age at death of the surviving partner. It is another case where the *joint probability* is the relevant calculation, and you can find tables online for this joint-longevity question. In this case, the likelihood of one or the other living to over 90 is 50%, a 30-year planning runway, almost as long as a working life that starts at 22 and finishes at 60! The irony is that people tend to underestimate their life expectancy by upward of 4 years.[15] If you have grandparents who are in their 90s, your life expectancy increases. If you have a healthy lifestyle, it is higher again. If you live in a town with high environmental quality, it reduces respiratory and cardiovascular illnesses and other diseases. If your runway has all the positives, you need to be planning to live longer.

Consider Your Risk Tolerance

Volatility around investment returns for your retirement account movements creates income uncertainty. Different individuals will have different risk tolerance for how to handle this uncertainty. If you believe you will have high longevity and you have low risk tolerance for depleting your savings, then you could consider buying an annuity that covers your lifetime and making adjustments to your budget to balance spending to income. Buying an annuity is a classic insurance policy to handle uncertainty. You get peace of mind around having savings that last a lifetime with an annuity, but trade that certainty off with lower returns. On the other hand, if you anticipate living a long life and have a tolerance for risk, you should consider holding a growth portfolio for investing, rather than what is termed a balanced fund.

Decide What Actions to Take

The possible actions you might take are shown in the decision tree in Exhibit 8.7.

---

[15]International Longevity Council UK, 2015.

NOW, DECIDE WHAT ACTION TO TAKE...

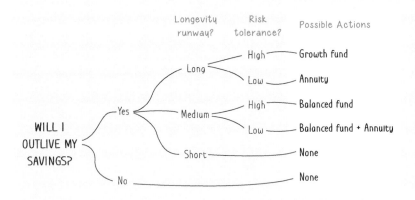

EXHIBIT 8.7

There is a surprising conclusion here that we need to explain. It has to do with longevity and compounding. Most financial planners we know recommend balanced funds for clients approaching retirement that provide a measure of safety against stock market volatility to provide stable current income, typically for investors with a 10- to 20-year investment horizon. But what if that investment horizon at age 60 is 25 years or even 35 years? The simple table below helps to show why the duration period of an investment and the power of compounding returns are so important.

The returns from a growth fund are 34% higher for the 25-year period and a staggering 51% higher if the investment period is 35 years (Exhibit 8.8). But you have to have some tolerance for greater annual variability in income after retirement. The point is we have uncovered a different way to think about the problem of the adequacy of retirement savings, one that may feel counterintuitive. Moreover, starting down this problem solving path allows a retiree at 60 to switch funds if their circumstances change, such as having a need for income earlier. On the other hand, you're unlikely to make

INVESTMENT OF $100K AT AGE 60

Life expectancy	85	95
Balanced Fund (40% stocks, 60% equities) Weighted return 7.73%	$0.64m	$1.35m
Growth Fund (60% stocks, 40% equities) Weighted return 9.0%	$0.86m	$2.04m

EXHIBIT 8.8

Source: Thomas Kenny, thebalance.com, June 23, 2017, for long-term returns (1928–2013) on stocks of 11.5% p.a. and T bonds 5.21% p.a.

a switch from a balanced fund at 80+, when the longevity runway is shortening.

We have reached a conclusion here that you won't hear from many financial planners, to consider investing for growth as you enter retirement if you expect a long life for yourself or your partner. When we add risk tolerance, a different strategy emerges than hedging by buying annuities. Heuristics like a longevity runway and compound growth get us to a rich solution set to an all too real problem. There is also the need for many to increase their savings rate to extend the runway. That should be addressed along with asset allocation to avoid outliving your savings.

Case Study: How to Make Really Long-Term Investments

Investments like bridges, mines, roads, and infrastructure have long lives. There is uncertainty over the future operating environment that has to be factored in to the problem solving up front. There is the need to deal with a range of possible outcomes, which often requires flexibility to address the value of future development options that are either enabled or blocked by the decision today (another kind of conditional probability). We have chosen to illustrate how to address these issues with a real example of how the giant Australian company BHP approached making a long-term investment in a mining venture in the past.

Resource companies seek to find or acquire reserves that are low on the cost curve (a tool we introduced in Chapter 3 with the climate change abatement cost curve), high quality, and have long lives. This is easy to say but hard to do in practice. Low-cost suppliers like BHP expect to be able to sell their output in good times and bad. And they usually have to plan on real prices declining, as they have for the past century. Rob led a team advising BHP on the acquisition of a major mining asset that was low cost, high grade, and that had more than 50 years of life. The problem solving approach had two distinctive features to deal with long time frames and the associated uncertainty. One was to define the key uncertainties related to drivers of value of the mine, such as price and volume. The other involved the use of scenarios to model the range of possibilities.

Value Including Development Options

The team developed a typical valuation tree for BHP by estimating net cash flows from the existing mine and discounting them at the cost of capital.[16] You will note that this tree is similar to the return on investment trees we developed for Truckgear and Hechinger in earlier chapters. The math is straightforward and you can find online net present value (NPV) spreadsheets in Excel and other software tools. The cost of capital was based on the risk profile of the project, the cost of raising capital for BHP, and assumptions made about terminal value for a declining resource.

---

[16]Tim Koller, Marc Goedhart, and David Wessels, *Valuation: Measuring and Managing the Value of Companies*, 5th ed. (Wiley, 2010).

BHP VALUE

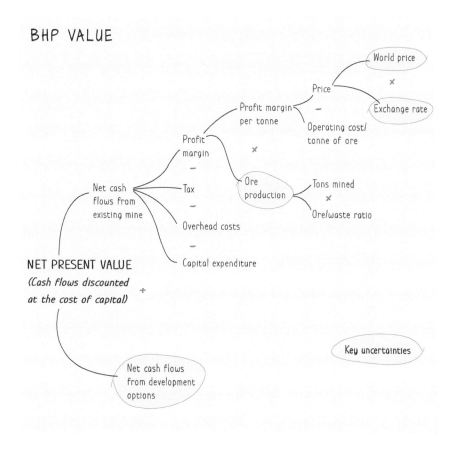

EXHIBIT 8.9

The tree Rob's team used for this analysis has an additional branch that we termed the *value of development options* (Exhibit 8.9). We added it because we cleaved the problem around existing assets *and* future growth or development options. What made the development options so important in this instance was that they could be brought "into the money" at a relatively low exercise price. Why was this the case? It was because they were able to piggyback the infrastructure of rail and port facilities already in place for the existing mine. Whenever you are valuing long-lived assets in uncertain situations, think about what future projects are made easier or harder by the moves you make today—sometimes these can have more value than the immediate decision at hand.

Four major uncertainties had to be addressed to estimate the net present value in this case: the world price for the mineral, the Australian exchange rate versus the US dollar, the volume of ore production, and the value of development options. The volume of ore is in a much smaller range of variation than the other factors, so received less attention in the analysis. There is a range of future outcomes that make it level 3 uncertainty.

Scenarios for Major Uncertainties

The use of scenarios in commodity forecasting and resource investment has a long history and predates the study Rob led. Nowadays large-scale computing has made it easier to run large Monte Carlo simulations, and to more accurately measure the value of options using Black–Scholes and other valuation approaches.

Our approach was simpler. We had time pressure from the competitive auction for the asset, and we were confident we could address the uncertainties without the need for a large-scale simulation model. We looked at the demand/supply balance on the world ore market 10 years out in order to generate a range of price forecasts. These were based on how the industry cost curve (supply curve) would look in the future based on current and expected cost positions, reserves coming on stream, and opportunities to reduce costs. A range of demand estimates for the commodity 10 years forward was overlaid against the cost curve to generate a likely pricing band. We also considered extreme cases, such as a price level two standard deviations lower and two standard deviations higher, cases that have 95% confidence intervals.[17] We overlaid a range of foreign exchange rate assumptions, as financial hedging wasn't possible 10 years out. We were then able to put together a matrix of net present value calculations for the price, volume, and exchange rate assumptions (see Exhibit 8.10).

---

[17]Confidence intervals for events we don't know are often way too low, a point made in M. H. Bazerman and D. A. Moore, *Judgment in Managerial Decision Making* (Wiley, 1986); This can be a big issue for level 3 and 4 uncertainty settings.

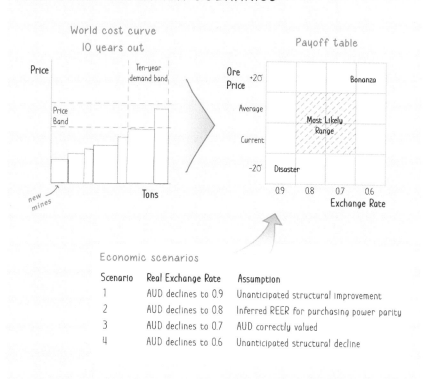

BHP MINE: VALUATION SCENARIOS

Economic scenarios

Scenario	Real Exchange Rate	Assumption
1	AUD declines to 0.9	Unanticipated structural improvement
2	AUD declines to 0.8	Inferred REER for purchasing power parity
3	AUD declines to 0.7	AUD correctly valued
4	AUD declines to 0.6	Unanticipated structural decline

EXHIBIT 8.10

Displaying the results of our analysis in the payoff table allowed discussion with the client of how they felt about the assumptions, particularly where we ended up in the best-guess range. Importantly, it put on the table for consideration the possibility that there was a truly worst-case disaster, where price fell precipitously and the real exchange rate appreciated strongly. This combination was considered highly unlikely but not impossible. The disaster case is another joint probability instance—what is the likelihood of prices plummeting *and* the exchange rate being extremely unfavorable. If each has a 10% chance of occurring, the joint probability of both events is only 1%. The same is true of what we called the bonanza case. This is a case where the price is two standard deviations above the mean and where the exchange rate is highly competitive.

You might say why only look at 10 years out with a 50+ year life asset? We felt it was a conservative approach to valuation in an uncertain and cash-constrained environment. We incorporated a terminal-value estimate by discounting the cash flows after year 10 at a much higher cost of capital (20%), compared to 10% for the first 10 years. We ended up being comfortable in recommending the acquisition, as the NPV of the initial asset purchase was higher than the purchase price under all likely scenarios.

We have discussed biases to good problem solving at length. Large-scale investments, such as company or major asset acquisition, are ones where biases can creep in, particularly confirmation bias. People get excited in auction situations and want to win the bidding contest. Besides the analytic efforts to use scenarios, good problem structuring, and sensitivity analysis, we had a team environment where the client was genuinely seeking a dispassionate external view as input to a board of directors' decision. On the team, we had analytical strength with proponents, and a divergent view from one team member who took the antithesis perspective. These were our efforts to address confirmation bias and realistic worst cases, similar to what we suggest in Chapter 4.

Look backs are a tool corporations use to assess how robust their capital-investment processes are. Our team did an informal look back on this proposal 20 years later from public sources and concluded that Rob's original team had been very conservative. We didn't anticipate the China resource boom that came 20 years later. The resource boom changed both the price and volume received for the commodity dramatically. This made the value of the development options attached to the acquisition of enormous value, such that something close to a bonanza scenario was the actual outcome.

In this case, the value of further development options is an important way to ameliorate the risks of uncertainty. In BHP's case, the development options were estimated to be 22% of the NPV of the acquisition, an important component but one that our look back showed was far too conservative (Exhibit 8.11). In hindsight, we estimate the value created was in the order of billions of dollars above the value of the core mining asset BHP acquired.

DEVELOPMENT OPTIONS

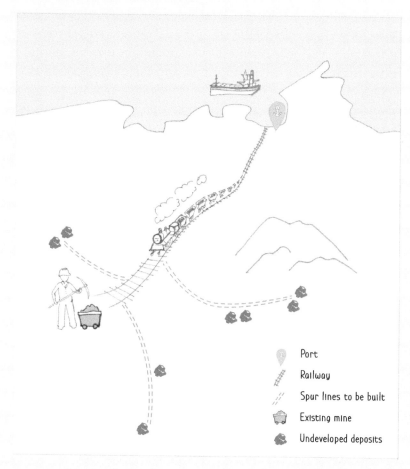

Port
Railway
Spur lines to be built
Existing mine
Undeveloped deposits

EXHIBIT 8.11

Case Study: Building New Businesses with Strategic Staircases

There are many ways to develop company strategies, depending on the industry context and company characteristics. Michael Porter's 5-Forces map or the McKinsey Structure-Conduct-Performance model looks at industry dynamics to evaluate entry.[18] Dixit and Nalebuff focus on mapping competitive game evolution,[19] like our CSIRO example from Chapter 6. The framework we introduce here, which we call *growth staircases* (or *horizons*, in some publications), is directed at determining the steps that allow successful companies to edge out into new businesses in uncertain environments, and emphasizes learning, buying options, and building capabilities.

The origins of the staircases and horizons framework were when Charles, Rob, and McKinsey colleagues were trying to come to grips with a new business growth aspiration for an energy client.[20] We marshaled a number of cases of how companies had built valuable new businesses in a little over a decade. We started drawing out the initiatives they took to enter markets, hire skilled people in unfamiliar areas, and make acquisitions, as steps on a staircase. We analyzed what steps were taken in what order to build capabilities, add assets, and reduce uncertainty. The staircase approach we visually set out involves:

- Working backward from a planned outcome, thinking through the capabilities, assets, and business learning required to be successful.
- Taking a step-by-step approach to strategic moves, allied to the uncertainty level, expanding commitment as uncertainty is reduced.
- Framing in time the staircase steps, knowledge captured, and capabilities that are being built.

---

[18]M. E. Porter, *Competitive Advantage: Creating and Sustaining Superior Performance* (New York: Free Press, 1998).

[19]Avinash Dixit and Barry Nalebuff, *Thinking Strategically* (Norton, 1991).

[20]Our Australian office colleagues David White and Mehrdad Baghai, co-authors of *The Alchemy of Growth* (Perseus, 2000), were important partners in this work.

To illustrate, one of our favorite examples of staircase strategies is the way J&J built a global contact lens business in a little over a decade. This was done in a series of initially small steps, then larger and more expansive moves. The staircase and associated capability platform are shown in Exhibit 8.12.

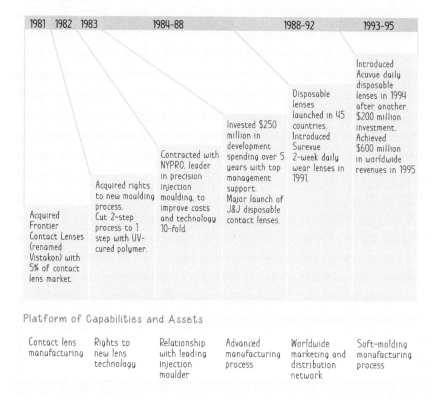

JOHNSON & JOHNSON CONTACT LENSES
STAIRCASE

1981 1982 1983	1984-88	1988-92	1993-95

Acquired Frontier Contact Lenses (renamed Vistakon) with 5% of contact lens market.

Acquired rights to new moulding process. Cut 2-step process to 1 step with UV-cured polymer.

Contracted with NYPRO, leader in precision injection moulding, to improve costs and technology 10-fold.

Invested $250 million in development spending over 5 years with top management support. Major launch of J&J disposable contact lenses.

Disposable lenses launched in 45 countries. Introduced Surevue 2-week daily wear lenses in 1991.

Introduced Acuvue daily disposable lenses in 1994 after another $200 million investment. Achieved $600 million in worldwide revenues in 1995.

Platform of Capabilities and Assets

Contact lens manufacturing	Rights to new lens technology	Relationship with leading injection moulder	Advanced manufacturing process	Worldwide marketing and distribution network	Soft-molding manufacturing process

EXHIBIT 8.12

Source: Mehrdad Baghai, Stephen Coley, and David White, *The Alchemy of Growth* (Perseus, 1999).

It's one thing to see a staircase in hindsight like J&J's, but how do you go about building one from scratch? How do you deal with uncertainty about the success of staircase steps and competitor action?

We outline the approach with a discussion of staircase architecture and an example of a staircase under construction.

Staircase Architecture

There are three considerations in staircase architecture:

1. **Stretch:** The distance of the step-out from the established platform, the complexity of new capabilities targeted by a step-out including the degree of integration required. Whether the stretch is too great is a balance between the ability to absorb new skills and the competitive demand for speed to establish market presence.

2. **Momentum:** The positive effect of early success, often based on small moves, on the learning and confidence of the organization. Momentum becomes a critical factor in markets that feature increasing returns to scale, involve de facto standard setting, or where winners take all.

3. **Flexibility:** Maintaining fluidity in the face of uncertainty has several features, including picking step-outs that generate the greatest option value for follow-on initiatives and being prepared to run more than one horse in the race, as we discussed in the Pacific salmon strategy example. Part of maintaining flexibility is avoiding creating sunk assets that could later become stranded. This can be achieved by variable cost structures like contracting and outsourcing.

Staircase architecture involves bringing these three considerations together to work through choices about staircase steps and how they are sequenced (Exhibit 8.13). Teams have to debate the trade-offs between smaller versus larger steps, option-laden moves versus focused commitments (that may be better at blocking competitors), and the speed of moves that can create momentum—but may be challenging to integrate with the existing business. The usual techniques of role-playing and competitor assignment enrich the team discussion of the planning of staircase steps to be taken. Google has investments in hundreds of new ventures.

That's an approach where they place many small and medium bets in interesting spaces, and often multiple horses in the same race. By contrast, a start-up may have one route to market with no more than a couple of options, a focused commitment necessitated by available venture funding.

STAIRCASE ARCHITECTURE: 3 KEY DRIVERS

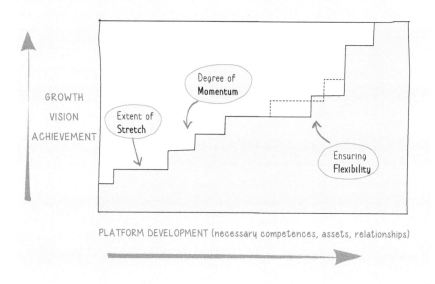

EXHIBIT 8.13

Staircase Under Construction: Ripper Group Example

Staircases can be used by start-ups to map the business goals and to show the desired strategic path to get there with learning steps and capability building. The value of working backward then forward is to gain agreement on what capabilities need to be built, and in what order. Consistent with having one-day answers and iterating in the seven steps the aim is to agree in detail on the staircase steps for the next 12–18 months, take stock, and then plan the next 12–18 months as new information on the market and the capability trajectory come to hand. The end goal or its timing is then altered to reflect the market and competitive realities. Agile development, failing fast, and sprints are the hallmarks of this approach to strategic problem solving.

The Ripper Group shark-spotting algorithm was discussed in Chapter 6. Ripper is an Australia-based company started by Kevin Weldon, who was president of International Surf Life Saving, and Paul Scully-Power, the first Australian to journey into space. Ripper's goal is to be a global leader in emergency services employing unmanned aerial vehicles (UAVs) or drones, building from their current competence in beach life saving toward flood rescue and damage assessment, and bushfire fire detection and response. National security events and other natural disasters fall within their scope.

Their initial staircase steps for Ripper are similar to those faced by most new ventures—start with a paying customer and seek to bootstrap its way to building operational capability (see Exhibit 8.14). Make some early judgments about the ecosystem you are in and how you plan to compete. In this case they chose to have a customer focus around emergency services, based on having distinctive operational capability, and to have a software rather than hardware focus.

The Ripper Group views itself as a player in an ecosystem of early-stage customers, regulators, hardware suppliers, and software and data analytics. This has taken them down a path of collaboration with the principal regulator to address issues of safety and performance, such as operating beyond visual line of sight (BVLOS) and night flights. In order to fulfill their mission of saving lives on beaches, they collaborated with machine-learning scientists to develop the world's first shark-spotter algorithm, software that distinguishes drone data streaming between a person, a dolphin, and a shark, a visual of which we showed in Chapter 6.

Their staircase shows the foundations and capabilities they have built in a couple of years and the major moves they plan to reach

RIPPER GROUP
STAIRCASE

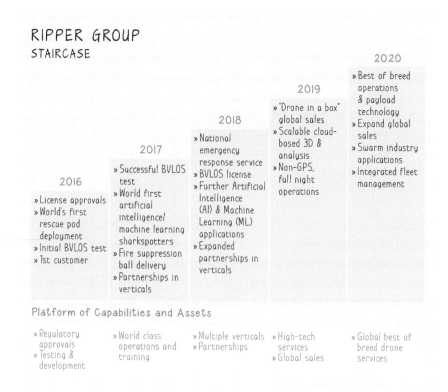

2016
- » License approvals
- » World's first rescue pod deployment
- » Initial BVLOS test
- » 1st customer

2017
- » Successful BVLOS test
- » World first artificial intelligence/machine learning sharkspotters
- » Fire suppression ball delivery
- » Partnerships in verticals

2018
- » National emergency response service
- » BVLOS license
- » Further Artificial Intelligence (AI) & Machine Learning (ML) applications
- » Expanded partnerships in verticals

2019
- » "Drone in a box" global sales
- » Scalable cloud-based 3D & analysis
- » Non-GPS, full night operations

2020
- » Best of breed operations & payload technology
- » Expand global sales
- » Swarm industry applications
- » Integrated fleet management

Platform of Capabilities and Assets

- » Regulatory approvals
- » Testing & development

- » World class operations and training

- » Multiple verticals
- » Partnerships

- » High-tech services
- » Global sales

- » Global best of breed drone services

EXHIBIT 8.14

the goal set by 2020. In an arena where entry barriers are currently low, they are focused on building a reputation as trusted operators who are able to take on the most difficult assignments. This requires that they continue to build capabilities related to flight operations, payloads, and data analytics. They are responding to opportunities in related vertical markets such as the risks mines face with tailings dams, asset inspections for utilities where flood or fire damage has occurred, and agriculture use of drones for weed control. Uncertainty is level 2 or 3, as regulation on drone use could encourage or curtail market potential.

Further out on the Ripper Group staircase are measured steps, incomplete at this point as you might expect, to achieve global sales and distribution. Other steps are to deepen cloud and analytics skills so they have distinctive technology capabilities. The Ripper

Group is invited regularly to go to other countries and replicate what they are doing in Australia. At this point they have neither the resources nor the time to do that without local partners. One idea is to follow the lead of other software suppliers and provide a package of software and operational capability that they call *drone in a box* for emergency services. International customers have the opportunity to visit their training academy to test out payloads for different applications and be trained in innovations such as BVLOS, LIDAR, non-GPS flights, and the use of ML algorithms in emergency services.

Staircases allow visualization of a growth plan, with active debate about the size and scope of staircase steps. They are planned in line with reducing uncertainty over time of the market evolution and regulatory environment so that the enterprise doesn't get ahead of itself. Flexibility is built-in: As new information comes to light, for example, on regulation like BVLOS or night flights, the staircase is redrawn. Similarly, early success with international sales may lead to accelerating global rollout of products like the beach of the future we described in Chapter 6.

Case Study: Managing a Long-Term Strategy Portfolio, Pacific Salmon Example

The longest term and most uncertain problems to solve are those in the social and environmental space. Our Pacific salmon case, which Charles worked on for a dozen years, is a great example. The scale of the problem was literally oceanic (covering four countries and the entire North Pacific ocean) and multidecadal, and affected whole ecosystems—for which Pacific salmon are an apex or foundational species—and huge numbers of people, both in livelihoods and culture. This is a big one!

The tools we introduced in earlier chapters are entirely applicable here, and the team made frequent iterative use of them over the fifteen-year project. But some other tools, particularly related to managing portfolios of strategies, were also important to cracking a problem of this scale. Let's take a look at them.

Theory of Change Map

For large, multiyear problems it is important to have an overall theory of change (TOC)—the strategic map for visualizing social or environmental change at this scale. In the case of the Pacific salmon team Charles worked with, that TOC map was an evolved variant of the logic tree introduced in Chapter 3.

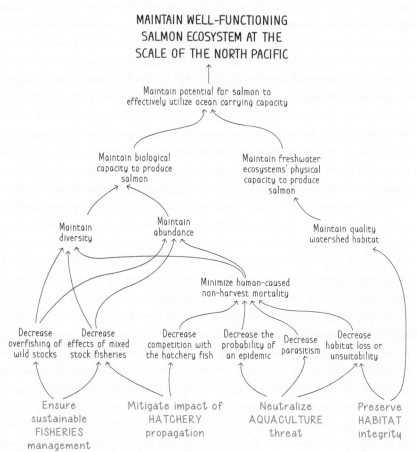

THEORY OF CHANGE EXAMPLE: PACIFIC SALMON
INITIATIVE LEVEL

EXHIBIT 8.15

As you can see in Exhibit 8.15, this map summarized the team's overall strategy for preserving salmon and salmon ecosystem function at the North Pacific scale. This included strategies for (1) preserving habitat integrity, (2) neutralizing the threat from open-net pen aquaculture, (3) mitigating the impact of hatchery propagation, and (4) ensuring sustainable fisheries management. Those high-level strategies led to more than 300 grants to nearly 100 organizations over a decade and a half—a lot of detail to manage.

Portfolio of Strategies Map

One of the ways the team managed and communicated about the large portfolio of strategies and investments was to visualize them in a matrix that captures both the stage of investment and the level of aspiration, expressed as incremental or transformational change (see Exhibit 8.16).

The team wanted to balance the investments it was making in Pacific salmon ecosystems across the logical stages of change:

1. **Seed:** Those strategies designed to create early conditions for change, which included some fundamental science investments to build understanding among government management agencies, early-stage habitat protection investments based on land planning and First Nations' ownership rights, and mobilizing a base of support for other long-term change efforts.

2. **Cultivation:** Those strategies where interest groups had come to the table and were willing to work together on solutions for both ecosystems and economic users. These are mostly investments in multi-stakeholder negotiations to change older status quo resource harvest regimes.

3. **Harvest:** Those investments to cement conservation gains and solidify institutional support for new conservation centered resource management processes.

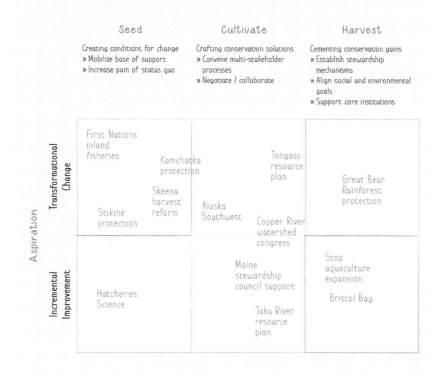

SALMON STRATEGY PORTFOLIO

Seed	Cultivate	Harvest

Creating conditions for change
» Mobilize base of support
» Increase pain of status quo
	Crafting conservation solutions
	» Convene multi-stakeholder
	  processes
	» Negotiate / collaborate
		Cementing conservation gains
		» Establish stewardship
		  mechanisms
		» Align social and environmental
		  goals
		» Support core institutions

EXHIBIT 8.16

And the team wanted balance between those initiatives that had transformational aspirations—expensive and risky—and those that aimed for incremental but important change.

This visualization of a complex portfolio made it easy to see if the balance was off relative to the Foundation's values, which would have been true for a set of only high-investment, high-risk strategies, on the one hand, or a set of sensible workaday approaches that would only lead to incremental change, on the other. It was an effective picture for trading off the risks of individual strategies against others, and for communicating the overall risk and return profile to the Foundation's trustees and senior decision makers.

Managing Regional and Topical Strategies

With a problem at this large scale, each of the individual regional or topical strategies required its own logical disaggregation, prioritization, and strategy mapping. To give a concrete example, one of the regional Pacific salmon strategies that Charles worked on was in Northern British Columbia, centered on the massive Skeena River watershed.

The Skeena has a very long history of sustainable aboriginal fisheries before European fishers turned up—and a very contested one since then, with different types of fishers fighting for share, and also conflict between federal and provincial fisheries management agencies. In recent decades, this conflict has been set against a backdrop of declining salmon runs and difficult economic conditions for resource users. The federal government had developed a science-based management policy for salmon fisheries, but failed to implement it. Conflict grew as access to salmon and the salmon economy was constrained for fishers, and as environmental groups ramped up pressure on managers. No one liked the status quo, but finding incremental pathways to change was challenging.

In complex situations of this nature, where many things are broken but stakeholders don't agree on fixes, it can help to set out a vision for change that nearly everyone can agree on. This helps warring parties to see what element of a vision they have in common, which can lead to collaborative problem solving. Exhibit 8.17 shows the vision for change in the Skeena watershed that was developed by a number of the groups involved.

While this vision didn't lead to an immediate détente, it did help bridge the parties to an agreement to conduct an independent science review (ISRP) of conditions in the Skeena watershed. The findings of that ISRP helped generate stronger, science-based management plans and multi-stakeholder governance conversations that led to improvements that are ongoing.

SETTING A VISION FOR CHANGE: SKEENA WATERSHED EXAMPLE

	From ⟶ To	
	Conventional Contested Mixed-Stock Fishery	Community-Based Ecosystem Management under Wild Salmon Policy
External perception	Maximize commercial harvest with minimal conflict with other interests and ecosystem	Long-term fish and ecosystem resilience and sustainability with appropriate harvest levels
Decision making	Top-down control with few official and many informal influence channels	Multiple stakeholder consensus + science in best interest of long-term sustainability
Use of science	Modest: non-peer reviewed abundance model and few monitoring points; not consistent with Wild Salmon Policy	Complete map of Conservation Units/sub-stocks, destination, and timing, including real-time monitoring at many points and genetic data
Allocation	Unpredictable, potentially dangerous, commercial derby system; First Nations and others feel they come second; uncontrolled expansion of some recreational segments	Some form of share system with First Nations first; recreational fishery equitable with commercial fishery
Economics	Highly tenuous, barely covers commercial variable cost; food fishery comes up short	Solid for commercial, First Nation, and recreational fishery operators
Product	Low-value commodity product	High-value, locally processed, branded commercial products
Gear & capture point	Mostly marginally selective locations, timing and gear; capture mostly at sea or estuary	Optimally located, selectivity and lower costs optimized
Enforcement	Modest	More comprehensive, like ground fish fishery
"Feel"	"Fight to get mine now"	Collaborative effort to ensure long-term sustainability of resource with fair allocation of surplus

EXHIBIT 8.17

For the Foundation team Charles worked with and its allies in the Skeena region, it was useful to visualize the map toward change as a set of strategies, some of which were competing (that is, one or the other was likely to succeed, but not both) and some of which were mutually supportive. Exhibit 8.18 is what that picture looked like.

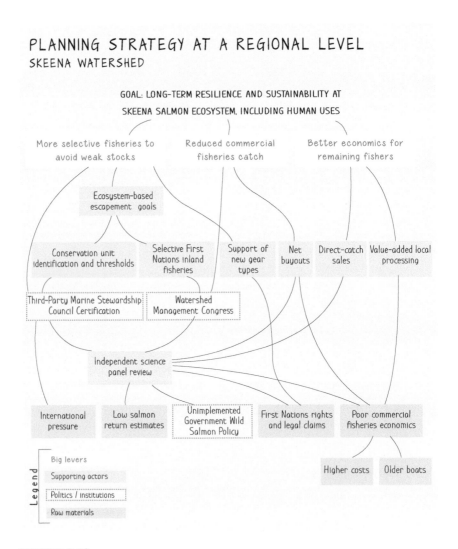

PLANNING STRATEGY AT A REGIONAL LEVEL
SKEENA WATERSHED

GOAL: LONG-TERM RESILIENCE AND SUSTAINABILITY AT
SKEENA SALMON ECOSYSTEM, INCLUDING HUMAN USES

More selective fisheries to avoid weak stocks

Reduced commercial fisheries catch

Better economics for remaining fishers

Ecosystem-based escapement goals

Conservation unit identification and thresholds

Selective First Nations inland fisheries

Support of new gear types

Net buyouts

Direct-catch sales

Value-added local processing

Third-Party Marine Stewardship Council Certification

Watershed Management Congress

Independent science panel review

International pressure

Low salmon return estimates

Unimplemented Government Wild Salmon Policy

First Nations rights and legal claims

Poor commercial fisheries economics

Higher costs

Older boats

Legend
- Big levers
- Supporting actors
- Politics / institutions
- Raw materials

EXHIBIT 8.18

As you can see, the map is based on a logic-tree disaggregation of the big levers for change in the watershed, but it shows the different supporting actions and policies and institutions that were critical to drive change. With complex social problems, it is helpful to develop detailed strategic maps that help you manage problem solving on multiple levels. Game theory trees are also useful here.

Uncertainty will remain one of problem solving's biggest challenges. But there is a toolkit for working through your own long time frame and complex problems: Frame the uncertainty and then iterate through the analysis to decide which actions to take to address the uncertainty. Uncertainty is about probability, subjective and objective, that brings into play how you pursue options, take fair bets, take out insurance policies and hedges and make no regrets moves.

Chapter 8 Takeaways

- Uncertainty is a feature of most difficult problems.
- Understanding the type and level of uncertainty—and your risk tolerance—is the first step to problem solving under uncertainty.
- There is a suite of actions to build into your strategy development to deal with uncertainty and risk: buying information, acquiring low-cost options, paying for insurance, and taking low-regrets moves that build capabilities and knowledge.
- The value of long-term options gained or blocked by strategic moves in uncertain environments may be a key element of your calculations.
- A staircase approach can help companies step-out into new and uncertain markets, managing stretch, maintaining flexibility, and driving momentum as new capabilities and assets are built.
- Really long term and uncertain strategies require an overall theory of change map and a portfolio of strategies matrix to visualize and manage families of strategies.

Problems to Try on Your Own

1. Place the long-term issues your business or nonprofit faces into the five-level schema.

2. What uncertainty reducing mechanism are you taking for each level?

3. Take a personal long-term problem and develop the approach you might take to resolving it.

4. For a growth plan you are developing, lay out the staircase for the next five years.

5. For a long-term societal issue you're interested in, try developing a theory of change and portfolio of strategies.

Chapter Nine

Wicked Problems

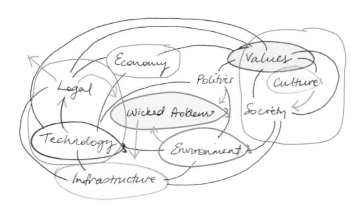

"Wicked problems" is the name given to describe a class of problems that seem to defy problem definition and solution because
they are impossibly linked to complex systems.[1] These problems
typically involve multiple causes, major values disagreements

---

[1]Horst W. J. Rittel and Melvin M. Webber, "Planning Problems Are Wicked
Problems," *Polity* (1973).

among stakeholders, unintended consequences, or substantial behavior change in order for the problem to be solved. Terrorism, environmental degradation, and poverty are often proffered as examples of wicked problems. Wicked problems *are* different, and we won't pretend they are easy to crack. But we believe the seven-steps approach sheds light on even these most difficult conundrums. As citizens, we have to have tools to help us understand and evaluate the solutions proposed by politicians and policy makers.

In this chapter we explore the range of problems that have been termed wicked problems. These are typically at a societal or even global scale. In particular, we take on the "wickedness" involved in two case examples, obesity and overfishing of the commons.

Obesity as a Wicked Problem

Obesity is a global phenomenon with huge economic, social, and personal costs. The McKinsey Global Institute (MGI) estimated obesity to have a similar social burden ($2 trillion) as smoking, armed violence, and terrorism. As the authors put it, "Obesity is a complex, systemic issue with no single or simple solution. The global discord surrounding how to move forward on this growing problem underscores the need for integrated assessments of potential solutions."[2] Obesity has dozens of contributing causes and has all the elements of a wicked problem with its complexity and interdependencies.[3] There are genetic, environmental, behavioral, cultural, societal, and income and education dimensions involved. How then do you look to solve such a problem?

The MGI report allows us to see how the McKinsey team approached the obesity problem in a way similar to the way we have outlined through the book, by defining the problem scope and constraints on solutions, disaggregating the problem along familiar demand/

[2]Richard Dobbs et al., *Overcoming Obesity: An Initial Economic Analysis*, McKinsey Global Institute (November 2014).
[3]Bryony Butland et al., *Foresight:Tackling Obesities: Future Choices – Project Report*, 2nd ed. (UK Government Office for Science, 2007).

supply lines, undertaking comprehensive analysis of intervention options using a well-known public health framework, and concluding with a synthesis and call to action. We explore these elements of problem solving in more detail to illustrate how you can make progress tackling wicked problems with the seven steps.

Problem Definition

The MGI report sets out the dimensions of the problem as follows:

- Overweight and obese people are estimated to comprise 30% of the UK adult population, and the percentage continues to rise.
- The economic burden in the UK is estimated at $73 billion per annum in 2012, behind smoking at $90 billion.
- The direct medical costs of conditions related to being overweight or obese costs the UK Government $6 billion per annum.
- Healthcare costs rise with BMI levels (body mass index): Obese classes incur 58–86% higher medical costs than individuals with normal weight levels.

The MGI problem definition posited the UK government as the decision maker. Government agencies, clinicians, and researchers were consulted in the process. Few constraints were placed on solving the problem. Regulatory interventions, such as taxes on high-sugar drinks and public health programs, were considered. The main requirements were for them to be judged cost effective, to have impact, and to have an evidence basis to warrant the intervention. Healthcare payers were excluded in this report because of the NHS role in the UK as a universal care provider. The MGI study in 2014 proposed a goal of a 20% share of overweight and obese individuals to be brought to normal weight category within five years, a demanding target.

Cleaving the Problem

Chapter 3 gave examples of a number of ways to cleave societal problems. We can cleave the problem around incidence and severity, behavioral and clinical perspectives, even financial and non-financial considerations. MGI chose to cleave the problem around demand and supply, employing a cost curve, similar to the approach used for reducing CO_2 emissions in our earlier climate change example. The value of this cleaving perspective is that it provides a menu of opportunities in descending order of cost and size of impact.

Analysis

The MGI team categorized interventions in 18 groups, such as high-calorie food and drink availability, weight management pro-grams, portion control, and public health education. In all, they looked at 74 interventions. For each intervention, they estimated cost and impact in terms of dollars per disability-affected life years (DALY), a World Health Organization measure of disease impact. They selected 44 interventions deemed highly cost-effective, coupled with an evidence rating, that could achieve the 20% tar-get reduction in five years. The cost to the UK was estimated at $40 billion to implement the interventions. Exhibit 9.1 shows the MGI cost curve.

The cost curve shown helps policy makers in several ways, the most important being setting priorities. Typically, you will seek to imple-ment the low-cost, high-impact initiatives first, particularly those considered small wins, before tackling the more divisive and costly ones. On Exhibit 9.1 those are the widest bars toward the left-hand side. Over time, the ordering of initiatives will change on the cost curve as information is gathered on cost and impact, making it a dynamic tool for policy makers. And as we explain below on walk-ability, the cost-effectiveness can change for an intervention: For example, active transport gets easier to implement if higher prop-erty values reduce the net cost of redesign of cities for walking and cycling (via property tax funding).

We would like to have seen some interventions that had nega-tive cost, meaning it pays to do them, at the bottom of the cost curve, much as we saw with the carbon-abatement curve. The MGI analysis points to higher health costs of $750–$1,100 per annum for obese people compared to those in the normal weight range.

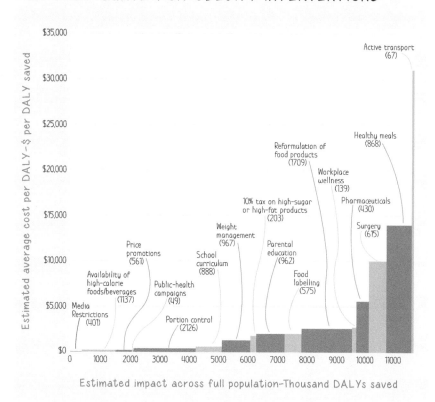

UK COST CURVE FOR OBESITY INTERVENTIONS

EXHIBIT 9.1

Where these costs are largely borne by a national health system, individual incentives are blunted in effecting savings. Nonetheless, individuals who can see a way to improve employment opportunities and extend longevity may choose to invest in weight loss and fitness programs without regulation. We return to the question of incentives shortly.

Synthesis and Call to Action

The MGI team expressed a guiding purpose to reverse the trend of obesity and reduce its personal and societal cost. In an arena with multiple players and interests, it was incisive in proposing interventions that were cost effective and, for the most, part had a strong evidence base. Having explored a range of choices in terms of cost and impact, the report set out a call to action to urge decision makers to act now on the portfolio of interventions, rather than waiting for an unlikely silver bullet solution. The MGI report emphasized government interventions over other types of action given their problem cleaving. Changing human behavior is really tricky, but we see a mix of rigor and pragmatism here that is consistent with the approach we have set out in the book, one that is useful for simple and wicked problems alike.

Brainstorming Further Ideas on Obesity

Throughout the book we have emphasized iterations between analysis and action. Wicked problems like obesity exemplify the need for iteration. When the next iteration of the MGI report comes along, we see an opportunity to include additional interventions, and particularly *behavioral interventions*. Here are five proposals that emerged from our brainstorming, analysis, and interviews with experts in the field. We have selected them because in problem solving we look for holistic approaches, incentives to change behavior, and high-leverage initiatives.

1. **Including income and education as policy variables in obesity**. In the United States, there is evidence reported in a recent Robert Wood Johnson Foundation analysis that adult obesity rates are "showing signs of leveling off." This better news is tempered by findings that "obesity rates are around 30% higher among adults without a college education and with incomes below $15,000 compared with other adults."[4] These findings are similar to ones that came out of the US city-based regression analysis in Chapter 6, where income and education, along with walkability and comfort, explained 82% of the differences in obesity for the population of 68 US cities. These findings argue for taking a holistic view and linking income, education, and prevention and treatment programs.

---

[4]*State of Obesity: Better Policies for a Healthier America*. Trust for America's Health and Robert Wood Johnson Foundation. August, 2017.

2. **Making more use of incentives for individual action**. For some time, life insurers have added loadings to policy costs related to obesity. Why wouldn't a health insurer be prepared to share savings of obesity costs with individuals? We are thinking of an incentive payment where half the savings are shared with individuals based on obesity reductions. The insurer could invite participants, who were deemed suitable for significant weight reduction, to enter an agreement with each person who brings BMI back to the acceptable range in a 12-month period and retains it for 12 months. Bundles of incentives could be tested in focus groups before launch of an incentive program. Employers could support this idea as well: Some Japanese employers provide vouchers and subsidies for public transport use, unlike American employers that typically provide parking spaces as an employee incentive. Many employers subsidize gym membership in both countries.

3. **Could social networks be a key to unwind obesity?** A large-scale study of obesity in the United States noted the increase in the obesity rate from 23 to 31% over a 32-year period. Their conclusion was dramatic: "Obesity may spread in social networks in a quantifiable and discernible pattern that depends on the nature of social ties."[5] Their findings were that if one person became obese the likelihood of a spouse becoming obese was 37% higher, 40% for siblings, and 57% for friends. They drew on this connectedness to argue that "medical and public health interventions might be more cost effective than initially supposed, since health improvements in one might spread to others." Could this insight lead to the great social unwinding project? And who better to involve than the UK Behavioral Insights Team, the so-called nudge unit. Where would they start? In the same way that one person becoming obese impacted others, one person as a spouse, friend, or sibling could take the lead and be supported by committing to regaining normal weight. We now know a lot more than we did a decade ago

---

[5]Nicholas A. Christakis and James H. Fowler, "The Spread of Obesity in a Large Social Network over 32 Years," *New England Journal of Medicine* 2007, no. 357 (2007): 370–379.

about social networks; tackling obesity with this knowledge seems a sensible avenue to explore.

4. **Supporting high-leverage programs such as reducing weight gain in pregnancy and early childhood**. The ramifications of excessive weight gain in pregnancy act like a chain reaction over three decades or more. For the 40% of pregnant women in the UK who enter pregnancy overweight or obese, there is a 33% increased risk of obesity in the child at birth and at six years,[6] 40% of overweight children continue to be overweight in adolescence, and 75–80% of obese adolescents will become obese adults.[7] The cumulative effects over a lifetime are huge. There is research under way to explore whether interventions for expectant mothers can reduce weight gain in the gestation period (6–20 weeks). If this can be demonstrated in randomized control trials, we have another especially high-leverage opportunity, and likely low-cost intervention.

Professor Louise Baur, a researcher who was a member of the WHO Commission on Early Childhood Obesity, cites a review of 17 studies where infants who experienced rapid weight gain from zero to two years were almost four times more likely to be overweight or obese later in life. She recommends specific strategies for providing nutrition advice to parents, promoting breastfeeding for the first 12 months, and having a monthly visit to a doctor to monitor weight gain.[8] There may be extraordinary leverage that can come from simple, straightforward actions to address the issue of child obesity and its knock-on effects.

5. **Walkability or Active Transport.** Cities like New York or Tokyo are good examples of walkable cities. We decided to look at walkability

---

[6]H. T. Tie, et al., "Risk of Childhood Overweight or Obesity Associated with Excessive Weight Gain During Pregnancy: A Meta-Analysis," *Archives of Gynecology and Obstetrics* 289, no. 2 (2014): 247–257.

[7]US data source provided by Professor Desiree Silva, the ORIGINS project at Joondalup Health Campus, Western Australia.

[8]Submission 10 to Senate Select Enquiry into the Obesity Epidemic in Australia, July 2018.

in 68 US cities: it is a statistically significant variable in explaining obesity differences. The relationship is that a 10% increase in walkability reduces obesity by 0.3%. For the UK, this would have impact similar to a 10% tax on high-sugar, high-fat products. While it is on the margin of highly cost-effective interventions in the MGI report, it is possible that if it included higher property tax levies it could improve benefit/cost ratios. For example, in the top 30 metro areas in the United States, "walkable urban places (walkUPs) rent at a 74% higher premium/sq. ft. over drivable suburban areas,"[9] suggesting that future property taxes could help fund the conversion to walkable cities. This isn't an impossible goal: The average Japanese citizen walks double the distance daily of their American counterpart.

Overweight and obese populations pose huge issues for policy-makers around the world. While there may be multiple causes—cultural, behavioral, socio-economic, and biological—this doesn't imply that the problem should be declared wicked and left to one side. We favor the reverse approach: setting ambitious targets and employing good problem solving approaches at the societal level with multiple intervention paths. Our look at obesity has made us more confident that we can find solutions than we were when our team first discussed this wicked problem. We don't claim the problem is solved. But this work shows a large number of promising avenues to fight obesity that have a strong evidence base, and reasonable costs relative to the economic burdens this epidemic imposes on society.

Overfishing: The Quintessential Wicked Problem

Environmental degradation is one of the most pervasive wicked problems. The famous article by Garrett Hardin, "The Tragedy of the Commons," written in 1968,[10] influenced many to reach the

---

[9]Walk Economy, *The Place Report* (2016), 7.
[10]Garrett Hardin, "The Tragedy of the Commons," *Science* (December 13, 1968).

view that so-called common-pool resources, such as public land, water, or fisheries, required either government intervention or private ownership to avoid overuse. Elinor Ostrom, winner of the Nobel Prize in economics, showed that there are solutions available to the problems of the commons, some of which are long-standing arrangements among resource users that have elements of community management via norms, and elements that mimic private ownership via certain kinds of harvest rights.[11] Let's look at an example of fisheries reform that employed clever problem solving to achieve much better outcomes.

Problem Definition

The fishery we want to highlight is the US West Coast Groundfish fishery off the coast of California, a portion of a vast fishery extending from the coast to 200 nautical miles between the US–Canadian border and the US–Mexico border. The fishery had been in decline for some time, from a catch valued at $110 million in 1987 to a catch of only $35 million in 2003. In 2001 a Federal judge ordered the Pacific Fishery Management Council (PFMC) to examine the impact of trawl fishing, in effect sweeping the bottom of the ocean, on marine habitats. The review confirmed trawling was having a substantial negative impact on habitat and species diversity. All of the players could assume that Federal regulation was on the way after this report—even though most government interventions on gear type and fishing access have had limited success in slowing resource decline. The California coastal fishery had all the classic elements of a common-resource problem: too much access and fishing capacity, no safe zones for fish reproduction, gear types that damaged productive seafloor habitats, declining populations of fish, and increasingly difficult economics for fishers.

---

[11]Elinor Ostrom, *Governing the Commons* (Cambridge University Press, 1990).

CONVENTIONAL SOLUTIONS TO OVERFISHING

| Problem aim | Strategy | Side effects |

Exhibit shows a diagram: **REDUCE NEGATIVE EFFECTS OF BOTTOM TRAWLING** branches to three strategies with side effects:

- **Trawl closure areas** → Shift trawling to new areas / Opposed by fishers affected
- **Reduce trawling effort** → Federal buyouts viewed as failing to reduce trawl effort
- **Modify gear design** → Higher costs / Regulatory burden on fishers already struggling

EXHIBIT 9.2

Conventional Solutions

While the problem was identified in the PFMC report, the solutions to reduce the negative effects of bottom trawling were difficult to implement. Three strategies had been adopted elsewhere with little success: trawl closure areas, trawl effort reduction via permit buybacks, and proposals to modify fishing gear to lower impact on species and by-catch. The typical consequences or outcomes of each strategy employed in a one-off way are shown in Exhibit 9.2.

Something had to change. Conventional top-down regulatory approaches had poor success and the economics of remaining fisheries participants were fragile and getting worse. Enter Chuck Cook and the Nature Conservancy (TNC). Chuck Cook, a veteran TNC staff member and now Senior Fisheries Advisor, was instrumental in much of the restructuring of the California fishery.[12]

---

[12]Oral communications, Chuck Cook and Charles Conn, August–October, 2017.

He and Charles worked together earlier on the conservation of Palmyra Atoll in the mid-Pacific. Chuck has deep experience in working with local communities, government, and partners to find common ground and find viable solutions to sustainable-catch issues. Chuck saw a potential solution path in applying an analogy from land-conservation easements and market transactions in the marine environment.

New Approach to Restructuring

A better solution emerged from TNC working closely with fishers in a process that started in 2004.[13] When Chuck met with the owners of 22 trawl permits, he expressed TNC's interest in purchasing trawl permits on the condition that they support the establishment of a marine protected zone prohibiting bottom trawling of 3.8 million acres. The discussions progressed between fishers and TNC, and in 2006 TNC bought over 50% of the permits for $7 million, making it the second largest holder of groundfish harvest rights on the West Coast. TNC then proceeded to lease the permits back to fishermen with conservation restrictions.

An additional obstacle had to be overcome to encourage fishers to use less-damaging gear than trawling in the form of hooks and traps. In Phase 2 of this project, led by long time TNC staffer Michael Bell, TNC entered into voluntary private agreements with fishermen that specified where fishing could take place, strict limits on catch by species and by-catch, and gear type restrictions by area. Cooperative fishing, as opposed to highly competitive fishing between individuals, became the norm in California's central coast, resulting in improving the economic and environmental performance of this fishery. In 2011 the National Marine Fisheries Service introduced a full catch share and individual transferable quota system. Catch shares allocate a total catch by species

---

[13]Mark Tercek and Jonathan Adams, *Nature's Fortune* (Island Press, 2015).

to each permit-holder, with limits on both the target and by-catch species harvested. This was the last critical element of the restructuring of the coastal groundfish fishery.

This innovative conservation fishing agreement has been likened to an easement on land, conferring limited property rights in the form of permits and quotas that can be bought and sold with conditions on use. These agreements were struck between the Pacific Fishery Management Council, fishermen, and TNC. They are based on principles relating to sustainable catch, the science of fish stocks, and a collaborative approach between conservationists, scientists, fishermen, and government. They incorporate many of the ingredients cited by Elinor Ostrom in her analysis of successful arrangements for managing common-pool resources (CPR).

Morro Bay Case Study

In response to these changes, a community quota fund (CQF) was established in Morro Bay, one of the California regional ports, as a local non-profit, with a board comprising the fishing community, the city of Morro Bay, scientists, and economists.[14] TNC has sold most of its permits and harvest rights to this body and others like it along California's central coast that hold them as community assets, leased out to individual fishers. The structure is shown in Exhibit 9.3.

The catch in Morro Bay, one of the four principal locations along California's central coast participating in the Pacific groundfish fishery, was valued at $10 million in 1995, but fell to $2 million in 2003, reflecting the loss of fish stocks. Following the new arrangements described above, the value recovered to $4 million in 2010 and $8.3 million in 2014. These improvements are partly due to recovery of fish numbers, but derive also from higher price per pound

---

[14]Morro Bay Commercial Fisheries. *2015 Economic Impact Report Working Waterfront Edition.*

COMMUNITY FISHERIES OWNERSHIP

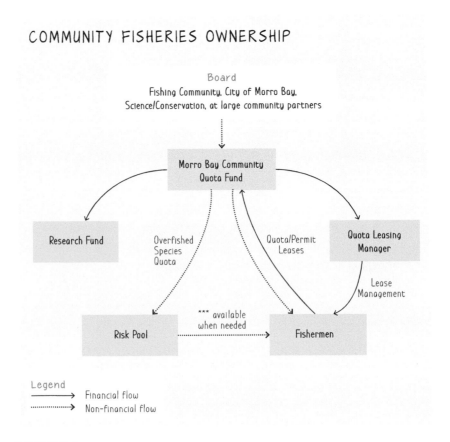

EXHIBIT 9.3

earned in quota fisheries, where catch volume is spread out over time and fishers can access higher value markets. Exhibit 9.4 shows a near-death experience for a fishery that a combination of regulation and a market solution via collective action has, so far, been able to address.

According to the Morro Bay 2015 Commercial Fisheries Economic Impact Report, "Morro Bay has successfully transitioned from a larger fleet reliant on trawl and large volumes of landings to a smaller fleet profile with a wide diversity of species and gear types. This is evidenced by the growth in earnings from a 25-year low in 2007.

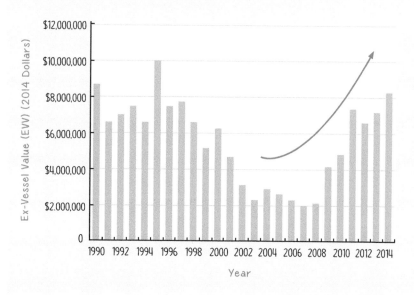

MORRO BAY CATCH VALUE
MORRO BAY, ALL SPECIES, EX-VESSEL VALUE

EXHIBIT 9.4

2015 is the strongest year in the last 20."[15] Beyond these economic measures is one of species diversity and the re-emergence of species, such as lingcod, factors that augur well to sustain the fishery into the future. The commercial fishing industry accounts for 195 jobs for fishermen, dockworkers, and seafood processing in Morro Bay. In addition there is tourism that attracts two million visitors each year, many of which come to Morro Bay to see a working port and to purchase or be served fresh seafood.

Overfishing may have been addressed at Morro Bay and other ports on the California coast, but it remains a huge issue around

[15]Morro Bay Commercial Fisheries. *2015 Economic Impact Report Working Waterfront Edition.*

the world. The examples of common-pool solutions and collective action provide encouragement that the problem doesn't have to be left in the too-hard basket. An innovative debt-for-nature swap in the Seychelles in 2016, again led by TNC and its NatureVest unit, has seen the creation of a marine-protected area (MPA) of 98.9 million acres, an area the size of Germany. What we see at work in California, the Seychelles, and other collective-action settings is problem definition, problem disaggregation, and analysis that lead to new solutions that work better than conventional regulatory interventions. Externalities, one of the defining characteristics of wicked problems, can be internalized and neutralized through the innovative mechanisms developed by systematic problem solving approaches.

Conclusion

We have explored several wicked problems and ways to develop innovative solutions. The solutions range from relaxing assumptions for what can be part of the solution, being prepared to revise incentives to internalize externalities, to cleaving problems differently to reveal new insights into interventions. These problems are more difficult, with more causes and difficult social issues to overcome. But they are just as amenable to systematic problem solving as the simpler problems of Chapter 1.

Are there other wicked problems where there are limitations to our problem solving approach? Some of the extreme dimensions of wicked problems present particular challenges, but we don't believe that makes them outside the scope of problem solving. Here are some examples:

- **Where the problem changes shape as a result of an intervention**. Social problems, such as addressing welfare payments, are often of this nature, where the intervention may lead to dependency and undermine positive behaviors. Theories of change, such as we used in Chapter 8, are needed to map feedback loops that may be negative and seek to get incentives right.

- **Where there is no such thing as a single right answer to the problem**. For example, determining whether nuclear power has a role in a country's energy mix: We accept that there may not be a right answer to a problem, given sharply conflicting opinions. If that is the case, we then explore trade-offs between reasonably right answers or in some cases least-bad outcomes. We are comfortable addressing these issues with more sophisticated versions of Charles's preference map for deciding where to live, or using game theory to achieve minmax solutions where you minimize the maximum loss involved.

- **Where values play an important role**. Gun control in the US is an issue where values play an important role in shaping the debate about the issue. Sometimes these look intractable. Nonetheless, common ground is most likely to emerge from good problem solving about the sources of accidental and homicide deaths from gun ownership, and the potential for addressing some of these causes with relatively simple interventions (mental health and criminal record background checks, waiting periods, closing sales loopholes). Death-penalty regulation may be a similar issue, where values are bridged when confronted with high error rates in death-penalty convictions. We have found that getting groups holding different values to participate in problem disaggregation and fact gathering, can create bridges to common ground.

- **Where the real problem is nested inside other, more apparent problems**. An example is homelessness, now an issue in many cities around the world. Few organizations addressing homelessness see shelter as the core issue, even though it has to be addressed. In addition to providing shelter, their efforts are directed at the underlying social, financial, and mental-health concerns and how they might be addressed. For example, a significant portion of women seeking shelter or refuge is related to domestic violence. The root cause of this mainly male behavior is complex to understand and address but is the key to long-term solutions. We are confident that the approach and tools we set out in the obesity case to arrive at cost-effective solutions are just as appropriate to addressing the issue of homelessness.

Our look at wicked problems gives us confidence that you can employ the seven-steps process to good effect and insight on even the most challenging problems. There is no reason to put problems in the too-hard basket. To be informed citizens and voters, we all need to be willing to put our problem solving creativity to work on these toughest societal problems.

Chapter 9 Takeaways

- Some problems are particularly difficult because they are part of complex systems, with multiple causes, many stakeholders, involve externalities, and require difficult behavioral change to affect—these have been labeled wicked problems in the policy literature over the past 40 years and include terrorism, climate change, homelessness, and obesity.
- While these problems *are* harder to solve, we believe the same seven-steps framework can unlock insights into solutions.
- Often the leverage on these most difficult problems comes from systems rather than partial solutions, from making externalities endogenous to the problem, and from novel ways of cleaving the problem.

Problems to Try on Your Own

- List all the problems you can think of that are complex systems with many actors and multiple causes.
- Build a tree for understanding the causes of homelessness; take one branch and see if you can think of ways to make the externalities internal to the problem.
- Build a tree for drivers of terrorism in Western countries; can you think of new ways to take this problem apart that uncover novel solution paths?

Becoming a Great Problem Solver

We started the book by outlining the need for creative problem solving capability in all walks of life. There was a time when problem solving was viewed as the domain of a few professions like science, engineering, and management consulting. With the accelerating changes of the twenty-first century, it is no longer a skill in limited domains but an expectation of individuals and teams across the business, non-profit, and government sectors. People are increasingly hired based on demonstrated analytic and thinking skills, evaluated for creative problem solving, and promoted for their ability to mobilize agile teams to rapidly address changing demands. This is the problem solving century.

We are convinced that good problem solvers are made not born. In the book we have taken a close look at what great problem solving entails. Our goal has been to help you become confident and creative problem solvers, to feel competent and empowered to employ these techniques for problems at any scale. The seven-step process we have outlined provides a way to take a business, personal, or societal problem you face and work it through to a solution. The 30 cases we have discussed cover the gamut of problems you are likely to encounter in your work and life. We hope no mystery remains about what is involved in great problem solving.

The seven-step bulletproof problem solving process doesn't require a degree in higher mathematics or logic. Great problem solving consists of good questions that become sharp hypotheses, a logical approach to framing and disaggregating issues, strict prioritization to save time, solid team processes to foster creativity and fight bias, smart analytics that start with heuristics and move to the right big guns, and finally a commitment to synthesize findings and turn them into a story that galvanizes action. We are confident that with practice and experience you will cleave problems in new and clever ways, learn to separate root causes from symptoms, and stay on the critical path of efficient problem solving. We have this confidence because over our careers we have seen others go from being bright graduates to impressive problem solvers in a short time.

There are some last words of encouragement and advice that we want to provide in this closing chapter. They are the watchwords of the seven-step process, what we feel so strongly about when we discuss this approach with our teams. There are 10 points in all to keep in mind. They are:

1. **Take the time up front to really understand your problem**. Often the initial problem that is posed isn't the right question. Take the time to probe the problem carefully with the decision makers involved before racing off to conduct analysis. Know the boundaries (it is often worth testing them to maximize creativity), the accuracy required, the time frame allotted, and any other forces acting on the problem. Be ready to revise your problem statement as you learn, refining it iteratively with one-day answers. Remember, the whole idea is to motivate action for change.

2. **Get started with nothing more than a problem statement**. You don't need to wait for giant data sets or fancy computer models. Get a large piece of paper and a pencil, or better yet a whiteboard, and begin sketching out a logic tree for your problem. When you dive into the data you can expect your thinking will evolve and move from a simple component structure to more sophisticated hypotheses. At this stage you are simply exploring what has to be true in order to support a hypothesis.

3. **Try several cuts at the tree**. We often write components or branches on sticky notes and move them around until they make sense in a logical grouping. You can think of this as solving the puzzle backward from the most tangible, known pieces you have. Try one or more cleaving frames to see which ones yield the most insight. Then lay out the main relationships that follow from the disaggregation you've selected, ideally in a mathematical fashion or one that exhausts possibilities.

4. **Use a team wherever you can**. Teams bring great advantages to problem solving via diversity in thinking and experiences that deepen the richness of creativity and reduce the chance of confirmation and other persistent bias. If you are on your own, make a team of colleagues, friends, family, and neighbors. We created virtual teams of knowledgeable people to test our thinking and hypotheses for our case examples, especially ones that involve deep-domain expertise. This made us much smarter than we are on our own, and it also makes it fun. Try techniques like team voting to overcome authority bias, red-team/blue-team competitions to be aware of other perspectives, and mock trials to advance the antithesis.

5. **Make the right investment in a good workplan**. A good workplan takes a little upfront time but will save so much wasted effort later. Prune your tree savagely by focusing on the big levers of impact that you can move. Be piercingly precise about what a particular output should look like, what hypothesis it questions, who will do it and by when. Use chunky plans that run only two to four weeks out so you don't over-run your initial thinking, and lean Gantt study plans to keep your work on track.

6. **Start your analysis with summary statistics, heuristics, and rules of thumb to get a feel for the data and the solution space**. Before you dive into giant data sets, machine learning, Monte Carlo simulations, or other big guns, we believe it is imperative to explore the data, learn its quality, understand the magnitudes and direction of key relationships, and assess whether you are trying to understand drivers to plan an intervention or predict a state of the world. Sophisticated analysis has its place, but it is our experience that one-day answers, supported by good logic and simple heuristics, are often sufficient to close the book on many problems, allowing you to move on to the more difficult ones.

7. **Don't be afraid to employ big analytic guns when required**. Sometimes a complex problem like bus routing across a major city, detecting disease in medical images, or optimizing production facilities for a global company, does require advanced analytics. Most of the tools you may have encountered in a statistics or operations research course are now more accessible with simple, powerful, and intuitive software packages. You also have the option of outsourcing your big-gun problems to eager teams of crowd-sourced machine learning practitioners who will analyze your data and make predictions for modest encouragement and occasional remuneration. When your objective involves other actors whose behavior will change when you make your moves, especially when played out over longer and more uncertain periods, it is time to invest some effort in game-theory models, risk-management actions, strategy staircases, and long-term theories of change.

8. **Put as much effort into synthesis and telling the story as doing the analysis**. It's natural to declare a problem solved when you have completed a powerful analysis that reveals great insight about a problem. But most of the problem solving you will ever do in business, non-profits, or politics involves *persuading someone to do something differently*. This is why the problem is rarely solved at the point of your Eureka moment. You'll have to be persuasive to convince powerful stakeholders to follow your plans. Remember, humans are visual learners and love storytelling above all else.

9. **Treat the seven-steps process like an accordion**. We have frequently referred to the seven steps as an iterative process. We have also sought to emphasize that you can compress or expand steps depending on the issue, so in some ways it is also like an accordion. Use one-day answers to motivate the team and decision maker to go to the level of analysis that the problem requires.

10. **Don't be intimidated by any problem you face**. If you invest the time in mastering the seven-steps process we are confident you will feel ready to tackle almost any personal, business, or societal problem that comes your way, even the wicked ones. This isn't hubris. It is simply saying that with a reasonable investment in systematic problem solving you will find insight into almost any problem of consequence. That is why bulletproof problem solving feels like a superpower when you get good at it.

We don't see the problems of our lives as individuals, workers, and citizens getting any easier. Most of our institutions haven't invested enough in creative problem solving to find clever solutions and bridge differences. Now we have that opportunity and we hope you'll do your part to contribute solutions to the challenges of our century.

Appendix: Blank Worksheets for You to Try

PROBLEM DEFINITION WORKSHEET:

Problem statement:

Decision maker(s)	Criteria/measures for successful effort

Key forces acting on decision makers	Time frame for resolution

Boundaries/constraints	Accuracy necessary

Problem Definition Worksheet

LEVERS THAT IMPACT RETURN ON INVESTED CAPITAL (ROIC)

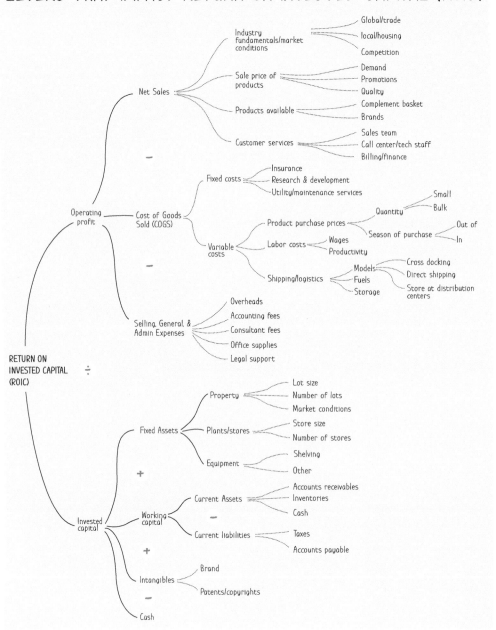

Levers That Impact ROIC (retail businesses; alter for your business levers)

PRIORITIZATION

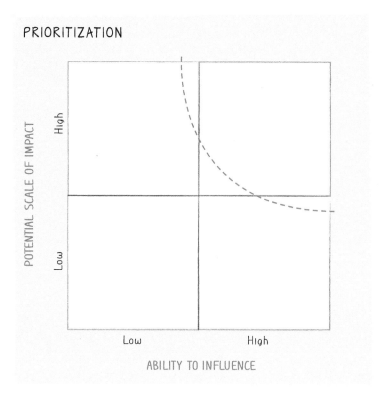

Prioritization Worksheet

WORKPLAN

Issue	Hypothesis	Analysis	Source	Responsibility +Timing	End product

Workplan Worksheet

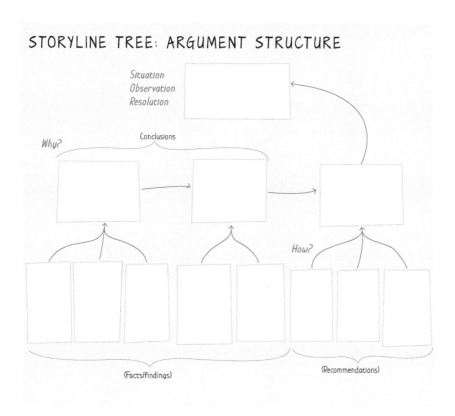

STORYLINE TREE: ARGUMENT STRUCTURE

Situation
Observation
Resolution

Why?   Conclusions

How?

(Facts/findings)   (Recommendations)

Storyline Tree Worksheet

About the Authors

Rob and Charles met at McKinsey & Company 25 years ago and formed a bond around doing the highest quality problem solving for their clients. After McKinsey, they continued to extend this problem solving methodology, developing approaches to societal scale problems, particularly around a shared interest in nature conservation. Both teach problem solving to graduate students, companies, and nonprofits worldwide.

Charles Conn

Charles recently completed his term as CEO of the Rhodes Trust, the organization that delivers the Rhodes Scholarships in Oxford. In this role Charles led a successful transformation effort to refresh the century-old organization's strategy and operations, including development of a problem solving training program for scholars. He sits or has sat on many company and nonprofit boards, including Patagonia, the Mandela Rhodes Foundation in South Africa, and Arcadia Foundation. Before this, Charles was senior advisor to the Gordon & Betty Moore Foundation, where his conservation projects included the wild salmon ecosystems initiative and the Palmyra atoll research station. Charles was a technology entrepreneur, and as founding CEO of Ticketmaster-Citysearch led the company through its IPO and acquisitions of Match.com, Evite, and other companies. He began his career at the Boston Consulting Group and was a Partner of McKinsey & Company. He is a graduate of Harvard and Boston Universities, and Oxford, where he was a Rhodes Scholar.

Rob McLean, AM

Rob is a Director Emeritus of McKinsey and Company. He led the Australian and New Zealand McKinsey practice for eight years and served on the firm's global Director's Committee. As Dean of the Australian Graduate School of Management (AGSM), Rob saw the growing need for stronger problem-solving capability for business leaders of the future. He is now an investor in mathematics education and data analytics software, alongside his philanthropic interests in conservation and social enterprise. He employs these techniques in his role as a Trustee of The Nature Conservancy in Australia and Asia to address water for wetlands, shellfish restoration, and improving human health from urban green spaces. He is a director of the Paul Ramsay Foundation, Australia's largest philanthropic foundation. He is a graduate of the University of New England in Australia and the Columbia University Graduate School of Business. He became a member of the Order of Australia in 2010 for his contributions to business, social welfare, and the environment.

Acknowledgments

We have benefited enormously from interacting with problem solving colleagues over 30 years in many different walks of life. Creative problem solving works best with critical friends, and we have had many. Our memories are imperfect, so we provide our apologies in advance for any we've accidentally omitted.

We will start with our colleagues at McKinsey, who have been formidable leaders in advancing problem solving approaches. These include our close colleagues David White, John Stuckey, and Mehrdad Baghai, but also Ron Farmer, David Balkin, Clem Doherty, Diane Grady, David Court, Nick Lovegrove, Andrew Nevin, David Ravech, Evan Thornley, Kate Harbin, Jeremy Liew, and Greg Reed (who co-authored the 1992 internal training document *7 Easy Steps to Bulletproof Problem Solving* with Charles). Rob would like to thank colleagues he learned so much from early in his career, including Sir Roderick Carnegie, Fred Hilmer, Don Watters, Robert Waterman, Ian Shepherd, and Charles Shaw. Special thanks to Rik Kirkland, who guided our book writing with a firm hand every step of the way, and to Dominic Barton, Charles's Rhodes classmate and now retired Managing Director of McKinsey.

We spent a wonderful summer with our Rhodes Scholar and Oxford graduate student research team, including Jess Glennie, analytic thinker and illustrator extraordinaire (Jess drew every exhibit in this book), Brody Foy, Bogdan Knezevic, Ashley Orr, William Rathje, Tim Rudner, and Evan Soltas. We also had help with particular case studies from JanaLee Cherneski, Linda Eggert, Nadiya Figueroa,

Max Harris, Michael Lamb, and Miles Unterreiner. Special thanks to Sir John Hood, Chair of the Rhodes Trust, for encouraging this work.

Charles would like also to thank his earlier colleagues at the Boston Consulting Group, including Steve Gunby, Gary Reiner, Steve Kaplan, and Thomas Layton, each a remarkably insightful problem solver. Thanks also to the founders and senior team at Patagonia, the boldest environmental and business problem solvers we know.

Both Rob and Charles had the good fortune to apply these problem solving techniques in environmental conservation work. We would like to thank colleagues and grantees of the Gordon & Betty Moore Foundation, including Aileen Lee, Ivan Thompson, Michael Webster, Pic Walker, Maureen Geesey, Heather Wright, Greg Knox, Greg Taylor, Bruce, Julia, and Aaron Hill, Mark Beere, Professor Jack Stanford, Jeff Vermillion, Spencer Beebe, and Guido Rahr. Special thanks also to those we have worked with on many complex projects at The Nature Conservancy, extraordinary problem solvers for the environment, including Chuck Cook, Nancy Mackinnon, Mark Tercek, Bill Ginn, Michael Looker, and Rich Gilmore.

The book benefited from the critical attention of many readers and advisors, including Professor Barry Nalebuff of Yale, Dan Lovallo of the University of Western Australia, David Lavin, Professor Stephen Roberts, Professor Sally Cripps of the University of Sydney, Ashok Alexander, Dr. Paul Scully Power, Jon Ireland, Nigel Poole, Cameron Conn, Dr. Timothy Ryback of the Institute for Historical Justice and Reconciliation, and two anonymous reviewers.

We had wonderful editorial help from Paula McLean, Rob's wife, an editor herself, who spent the summer at Oxford in the team room, reading drafts of all the chapters and making this a better book by constantly reminding us to explain our logic in more detail, write clean lines without business jargon, and tell good stories. Virginia Grant, Rob's daughter, also an editor, took on the task of editing the manuscript prior to submission. We thank her for fitting us into her busy schedule and improving the content substantially. We chose not to engage a literary agent but instead relied on the advice of

Margie Seale, former Managing Editor of a major publishing house in Australia.

Warm thanks to Bill Falloon from John Wiley & Sons, who believed in this book and its two first-time authors. Jayalakshmi Erkathil Thevarkandi, Michael Henton, and Richard Samson from the editorial team at Wiley were a pleasure to work with in getting the manuscript into print.

Camilla Borg and Paula McLean supported us through the long nights and weekends of research, writing, and editing. This book is dedicated to them.

Index

Page references followed by e indicate an Exhibit